# Stand Up AND Be Counted

## THE VOLUNTEER RESOURCE BOOK

Judy Knipe

**A FIRESIDE BOOK**
Published by Simon & Schuster
New York London Toronto Sydney Tokyo Singapore

FIRESIDE
Simon & Schuster Building
Rockefeller Center
1230 Avenue of the Americas
New York, New York 10020



DESIGNED BY BARBARA MARKS
Manufactured in the United States of America

10 9 8 7 6 5 4 3 2 1

Library of Congress Cataloging in Publication Data

Knipe, Judy.
Stand up and be counted : the volunteer resource book / Judy Knipe ; foreword by Richard F. Schubert.
p. cm.
"A Fireside book."
Includes bibliographical references and index.
1. Volunteerism—United States—Handbooks, manuals, etc.
I. Title.
HN90.V64K55 1992
302'.14—dc20 92-17350
CIP

ISBN: 0-671-74181-0

*For my family:*

*Tesse, Renata, and Ed*

# CONTENTS

In essence, volunteerism is a state of mind. It urges us to help resolve problems beyond the parameters of our daily lives. It propels us to act when we perceive a need. And it reminds us that, although our actions as volunteers are not always selfless, there is great reward in the accomplishment of a worthwhile task.

— Maria P. Smith, "Taking Volunteerism into the 21st Century: Some Conclusions from the American Red Cross VOLUNTEER 2000 STUDY," *The Journal of Volunteer Administration,* Fall, 1989

# ACKNOWLEDGMENTS

In the course of researching and writing this book, I spoke at length to hundreds of people in the volunteer sector—volunteer directors, volunteers for large and small groups, people for whom volunteerism is a profession—and their enthusiasm and conviction about their work and the benefits of volunteering were inspiring. I want to thank them all. For special generosity, for taking time to educate me, for willingness to share experiences and ideas, my deep gratitude to those mentioned here. Tucked into this list are the names of a sturdy band of friends and relatives—who really behaved pretty well, considering.

Ellen Ahlgren, founder of ABC Quilts; Linda Amster; Rosita Grant Arrastia of Planned Parenthood; Nancy Bambara, thanks for the leads; Jan Bayles of Chevron; Pat Bing for her information about community gardening in Tennessee and our discussion of grassroots community action groups; Pamela Bisbee Simonds of Dwight Hall at Yale; Jack Bode of the International Rescue Committee for his insights about disaster volunteers; Rich Bonlender, director of Minnesota Green; Laura Branca from the Ithaca, New York, Community Dispute Resolution Center; Toni Burbank, thanks for your good advice; Jill Charles, codirector of the Dorset Theatre Festival; Richard Cleveland, Chairman of the Vermont Quilt Festival; Jean Dargis of March of Dimes; Gerald Dash of Volunteers in Parole; Linda Doede of the Chicago Botanic Garden; Susan Ellis, author and president of Energize Associates; Sandy Epstein of the William Breman Jewish Home in Atlanta; John Ezell of Burr and Burton Seminary; Harriet Fagan, director of PACT Institute of Justice; Betty Fohrman, volunteer director of the Jewish Board of Family and Children's Services; Rosemarie Garipoli; Betty Gilbert for her very good suggestions; Janet Gilbert; James Gilbert; Martha Gilbert of the American Red Cross; Peggy Gilbert, thanks for the reading; Bruce Handley of The Nature Conservancy; Ray Hartley; Lois Hatch, formerly of RSVP; Martha Heilmann of Bennington County United Way; Judy Heinlein, director of AARP's Volunteer Talent Bank; Karen Heller of United Way; Nancy Hinton, former director of Behind-the-Scenes Volunteers at the Smithsonian Institution; Rebecca Hirsh; Lynda Hobson, who made order out of chaos; Cynthia Holley of Offender Aid and Restoration in Arlington; Thelma Honey for sharing her knowledge of horticultural therapy; Jane Janey of the Center for Volunteer Development in Virginia; Timmie Jensen of Refugee Voices; Beverly Jerman, director of volunteers at Hildene; Virginia Johnson of Offender Aid and Restoration;

Charles Kaiser; Michael Kaiser, director of Victim Services; Terry Keller of New York Botanical Garden and Bronx Green-Up; Marguerite Kelly for that lovely morning in your home; David Kidd, founder of American Free Tree; Sara Knight of the Vermont Quilt Festival; Joan Leavitt of VOCA; Ruth Lia of the Federated Garden Clubs of Vermont; Jenepher Lingelbach of Vermont Institute of Natural Science; Barbara Lohman of the Points of Light Foundation; Lela Love, a superb mediation trainer; Alan Luks; Margery Lutz, president of the Southern Vermont Art Center; Mary Rita Manley for her help with ELF; William Manley of the Dorset Historical Society; Barbara Marks for her wonderful design; Pam Marron; Richard Meislin; Bob Miller, thanks for the mail; Jackie Montgomery, thanks for Drew; Michael Mushett of United States Disabled Sports Teams; Jeff Myers of the American Community Gardening Association; Judy Nagy of United Cerebral Palsy Athletic Association; Mike Nawrath for all your help; Betsy Nolan for being my agent; Cynthia Parsons, creator of SerVermont, who shared so much with me about service learning education; Carolyn Partridge of From Vermont with Love; Connie Pirtle, director of volunteers at the American Symphony Orchestra League; Jerry Roberts of the Brooklyn Mediation Center; Reva Roorbach for her interest in and knowledge about horticultural therapy; Renata Rutledge; Ivan Scheier, founder of the Center for Creative Community; Al Scheps, for the best mozzarella; Bill Stout of Partners, Inc.; Karen Strand, for telling me about her experiences as a volunteer horticultural therapist; Carol Stuart of the Council of Better Business Bureaus; Josh Stulberg of Wayne State University for his patience and his brilliance as a mediation trainer; Dorothy Sullivan, director of RSVP in Bennington County, Vermont; Elenor Taylor of the Constitutional Rights Foundation; Carol Todd of Norwich University in Vermont for her advice and counsel; Annette Townley, executive director of National Association of Mediation in Education; Louise Townsend of *Quilters Newsletter;* Dick Traum, founder of the Achilles Track Club; Stan Turecki; Betty Tyler, director of Chicago Green; Helen Tyler; Terry Tyler; Michael Van Slyck, who helped me find my way through the thicket of mediation parlance; Mrs. Vass; Susan Walter of the American Red Cross; Richard Wertz of Prison Fellowship Ministries; Chris Whipple, mediation director of Victim Services; Danica Wilcox, for letting me into her life for a moment or two; Bill Winter, director of the International Association for Justice Voluntarism; Patricia Young of World Food Day; Edward Zlotkowski, who initiated community-service learning at Bentley College.

Thanks to Drew Montgomery, computer mavin supreme, for taking all those midnight phone calls, and to Ted Whittemore for the good morning walks.

Finally, to Sydny Weinberg Miner and to my editor, Kara Leverte—you're the tops!

# FOREWORD

All the information anyone could need to find one's path to volunteering opportunity and fulfillment is in Judy Knipe's lean, factual chapters.

Volunteering is the secret genius and strength of America. Almost alone among the world's peoples, we Americans believe in freely giving of our time, money, strength, skills,and vision to individuals in need and to projects in the community interest. Virtually every significant organization and institution in U. S. life has grown from volunteer roots. The idea and practice of neighbor helping neighbor is a fundamental value in American life.

Nearly 100 million Americans are volunteers today. You can get an unparalleled idea of the great variety of good things they do merely by scanning this book. What they do *for* all of us is beyond price: No public or private budget could pay, even at minimum-wage rates, for what volunteers do without any pay except the satisfaction they get from lives saved, lives turned around, pain diminished, hope restored, valuable people and projects made productive for the community.

But nearly 100 million volunteers aren't nearly enough. Particularly nowadays, when great numbers of Americans need the help of a friend, a mentor, a caring person in order to discover or rediscover hope, direction, and purpose in troubled lives; to get out of negative, self-defeating tracks onto positive, productive ones; to construct lives that go somewhere. The great need is for volunteers who have the courage and belief in self to knock at the door of other lives and become one-on-one people who are "there in time of need."

The need has never been greater for giving of oneself to help others. Judy Knipe's book will help you find where the rewards of caring await you.

RICHARD F. SCHUBERT
*President and CEO*
*Points of Light Foundation*

# Introduction

## Having a Wonderful Time . . .

It's true; I did have a wonderful time researching and writing this book, although I encountered a few surprises along the way.

I began with what I was confident would be a simple task: to give the experienced and the novice volunteer an idea of the scope of positions available. I was quite sure that from thousands of large, national charitable organizations and from hundreds of local grassroots groups that "employed" millions of volunteers, I'd be able to come up with a rich assortment of goodies. The organizations would group themselves automatically into neat categories with scarcely any overlap, and none of them would ever move or change phone numbers.

So it rocked me, just for a minute or two, when I discovered that there are *hundreds of thousands* of volunteer agencies, associations, centers, charities, coalitions, committees, councils, foundations, forums, institutes, leagues, projects, services, societies, clubs, and clinics out there, each with its own mission, goals, agenda, and mode of operation, and each with an individual approach to recruiting, training, and using volunteers. It was both thrilling and daunting to realize how much territory there was to be covered.

I confess, too, that I had rather a narrow view of what volunteers actually do, based very much on my friends' and my own experiences: Volunteers stuff envelopes, they read to sick children, they're docents, they set up computer programs for nonprofit organizations of their choice, they march and demonstrate, and they raise funds. They work in shelters, they organize local groups to protect their neighborhoods or their environment, they sit on school boards, they work for hospices, and they run thrift shops. Just the tip of the iceberg, I soon came to realize as, inevitably, in the course of researching one kind of volunteer activity, I would find myself veering off to pursue two others.

I've come to think of this book as an odyssey, a journey through America as reflected in the range of our voluntary activities, which are themselves a mirror image of Americans' concerns, convictions, conflicts, and passions. It's been an education.

Most enjoyable of all has been speaking to hundreds of people from all over the country who are involved with volunteerism. Almost without exception, they express dedication and enthusiasm. They are realistic about what has to be done and what can be accomplished. They shine with ingenuity, compassion, and straightforward good sense. They believe in their work and have strong feelings of achievement, of being able to make a difference even in the face of odds. They generously share information, make referrals, make phone calls, and send material.

I believe it is demeaning to exhort another person to volunteer, but it's my hope that this book stimulates you to think about the rich possibilities being offered and about the many ways there are for each of us to participate fully in our community and in our world.

PART ONE

# Becoming a Volunteer

When you see American volunteerism from the viewpoint of other countries, we look like a new phenomenon. The Russians were astonished that these [Achilles Track Club] people were doing it just for the joy of helping. From an international perspective, the U.S. is in first place in the concept of "the other," which means that after you take care of your own needs, you want to help other people.

— Dick Traum, founder of the Achilles Track Club

Volunteerism is deeply rooted in American history, kindled by religious conviction, strong social conscience, and the exigencies of life in the New World. Volunteers have been a continuing and crucial factor in recognizing the need for social change and then creating it. They have helped empower huge segments of the population, they have provided free goods and services to millions, and they have supported cultural institutions.

Now, after a decade of slumber, volunteerism is up and about. It's plastered on buses, bruited on pro bono TV announcements and feel-good network news stories, discussed in magazine articles and on front-page newspaper stories, seen in cable TV and newspaper classified ads. And it's not all hype.

Volunteers really are needed now more than ever to meet overwhelming needs, especially in social, health, and educational services. Cuts in government spending on the one hand and an increase in human misery on the other mean that voluntary agencies feel more pressure to step in. There's plenty to do.

If you've volunteered before and are looking for new experiences, or if you've decided to volunteer for the first time, this book will open the door to hundreds of organizations that can either provide or refer you to a wealth of opportunities and ideas for individual and group action.

## Taking Stock

Before you begin looking for volunteer work, take a personal inventory. Ask yourself about your motives for volunteering, your interests and the skills you can offer, your schedule, your predilections and personal habits, and your expectations.

### Motives

- Idealism
- Social activism
- Personal growth and change
- Acquiring work experience and professional skills
- Spiritual fulfillment

### Skills and Talents

- Professional training
- Work experience
- Fluency in languages other than English (even a passing acquaintance with a second language can be very helpful)
- Fields of special study in school
- Hobbies

### How Much Time?

- A long-term or short-term commitment?
- Full-time of part-time?
- How flexible is your schedule?

### Work Conditions

- Do you work well with others, or are you happier pursuing projects on your own?
- Can you take supervision, or do you chafe under it?
- Do you want to work for a large or a small organization?
- Do you enjoy working within the framework of a structured organization whose national programs are adapted at the local level, or do you prefer a looser structure or a more narrowly focused agenda?
- Do you want your responsibilities very clearly defined, or do you want flexibility in determining your activities?

### Expectations

- Do you need to see immediate results, or are you just as interested in working toward long-range goals? (It's possible to achieve both aims within the same program, of course.)
- Do you want recognition for your efforts?

## What's Out There

Everything! Within any field of volunteering, a multitude of organizations offer multiple ways to deal with the same or similar issues, and with considerable overlap in services. The volunteer community itself carries on a continuing discussion of the role private voluntary organizations should play: Should the voluntary sector take up the slack in social services that occurs when government funding has been withdrawn? What are the implications for organizations that are funded or connected in some other way with government?

All the more important, then, to volunteer for an organization whose aims you share. Begin by educating yourself about the issues in whatever field you have chosen. You don't have to write a position paper to know that you want to protect animals or help feed hungry people, but it's important to think about how you'd like to see it done. Then consider the very different means various organizations take to achieve their goals; find out which groups are in touch with and attempting to meet real needs. Get information about the policies, agendas, programs, and funding of any organization before you volunteer to work for it. Annual reports and other official literature will convey some of this information; speaking to people who have volunteered for the group will give you a sense of how policies are carried out at the local level. You also have to follow what your experience and instinct tell you about choosing a group.

Another criterion for judging an organization is the way it treats and honors volunteers. It's a sign of enlightened times that the idea of volunteer as well-meaning do-gooder has been replaced by volunteer as trainee, who can eventually perform the work of a professional. Volunteers with no previous experience are being instructed, sometimes over the course of months, to become volunteer leaders, mediators, mentors, and counselors. Some volunteers—ombudsmen, for example—must be accredited in order to practice, and their backgrounds are investigated. Trainees for such skilled and intensely involving work are usually asked to commit a minimum amount of time to volunteer work after their training.

Volunteer management is now an active profession, and volunteers are now taken very seriously indeed, especially by the organizations that use masses of them to deliver important services, raise funds, serve as advocates, and sit on committees and boards. Organizations using thousands of volunteers have developed guidelines for recruiting, training, supporting, and acknowledging the contributions of their skilled and dedicated volunteers. The March of Dimes publication *Basic Principles of Volunteer Development* contains "The Volunteer's 'Bill of Rights.'" They are:

- The right to be treated as a coworker with staff.
- The right to a suitable assignment.
- The right to know as much about the March of Dimes as possible.
- The right to receive training.
- The right to continuing education.
- The right to sound guidance and direction.
- The right to promotion and a variety of experiences.
- The right to be heard.
- The right to recognition.
- The right to a suitable place to work.

Equally, "The Volunteer's Responsibilities to the Organization," as posited by the March of Dimes, include punctuality, dependability, thoroughness, loyalty to the March of Dimes, its staff and programs, and pride in serving as a volunteer. Other groups may have less clearly enunciated volunteer policies. But in any organization, it is important that volunteers be recognized as critical to the work at hand. That appreciation can only foster the reciprocal respect of volunteers for the organization and increase the joy in their work.

## How to Use This Book

Part Two is a Directory of Nonprofit Organizations and Publications, which is intended as a jumping-off point for anyone interested in volunteering. Scan the categories for subjects that engage you, then check through the organizations in those sections. Let one group lead you to another. Clearinghouses in all categories are particularly helpful in referring people to agencies that meet specific criteria.

The principal consideration in selection is whether an organization provides or points the reader toward volunteer opportunities. The assignment of a primary category to each entry and the decision whether to cross-reference, and where, are quite arbitrary, since so many groups lend themselves to several categories; for that reason many of the entries *are* cross-referenced.

I tried to force the categories into natural "family" groupings, which would agreeably form themselves into a seamless sequence, but they resisted and wanted to go their own ways. So I took the coward's path and simply alphabetized them. Within categories there are often subcategories, and entries within subcategories are in alphabetical sequence.

Basic information for each organization includes name, name of program (if there is one), address, phone numbers (including TDD numbers for hearing-impaired callers), and where available, the title and/or name of the person to contact. Several organizations prefer written queries and their phone numbers have been withheld by request.

When I collected information about an organization's objectives, the causes to which it is dedicated—especially agencies that need volunteers to carry out their programs—these were some of the questions I asked:

- Are you national, regional, or local in coverage? How many chapters?
- What is your mission, and what role do volunteers play in achieving your goals?
- What is it volunteers actually do—trailblazing, computer programming, delivering food to the homebound?
- Are professional skills required? Physical skills?

- Is there on-the-job training? What kind?
- Is the work full-time or part-time? Long-term or short-term?
- Is there any commitment in terms of belief or life-style asked of volunteers?
- How do you recruit volunteers?
- How does a potential volunteer get more information?

My success rate was variable at prying loose this data from every organization, but readers will be able to use the information given here to find out more.

Part Three is concerned with starting and funding a new organization, whether a branch of an established group or an unaffiliated grassroots association.

In the back of the book, you'll find the addresses of regional ACTION offices, an Index of Directories, and the names and addreses of the almost 400 National Volunteer Centers.

# Resources

***By the People: A History of Americans as Volunteers,*** by Susan J. Ellis and Katherine H. Noyes. San Francisco: Jossey-Bass, Inc., 1990. Written by experienced authors and professionals in volunteerism, this is a chronicle of volunteering in the United States from 1607 to the 1990s and a companion volume to standard histories. *By the People* tells the story of America through the contributions of individual citizens and groups who helped to shape American society. Each historical chapter begins with a list of significant dates, then sketches in the major volunteer movements as they arose to meet public demands in areas such as business, employment, transportation, health, education, religious freedom, cultural access, justice, the military, and political and social action. Good will, generosity, and civic peace have not always characterized American history, and movements from vigilantism to the Ku Klux Klan to urban street gangs bear that out.

Chapters on recent trends include the professionalizing of volunteer leadership, the demanding training required of some volunteers and the new respect accorded them, the desire of volunteers to train themselves for new careers through volunteering, the infusion of older Americans into the volunteer force as a means of self-empowerment and of helping others, and the continuing discussion of volunteerism in terms of its aims and the fluid relationship between voluntary organizations and government. $24.95 plus $4.25 postage and handling. Order from Energize, Inc., 5450 Wissahickon Ave., Philadelphia, PA 19144, 1-800-395-9800.

***The Good Heart Book, a Guide to Volunteering,*** by David E. Driver, Chicago: Noble Press. 1989. This book is written for experienced volunteers and for those who are just starting out and is especially useful for people interested in human care and social services for the needy. Part I covers some of the reasons for volunteering, describes different kinds of volunteer work, poses questions to ask oneself before choosing a field and an organization, and suggests ways of improving performance and of maintaining the volunteer spirit. This section is an excellent primer for anyone choosing a new field of volunteerism, or even paid work. Part II is Driver's social service agenda, which encompasses problems faced by the homeless, abused women and children, the inner-city poor, at-risk teenagers, the elderly, adult illiterates, people with AIDS, and the disabled and shows how some of these problems can be remedied with the help of volunteers. Part III is a short directory of national volunteer organizations and also contains a listing of all the volunteer action centers (VACs) nationwide. Indexed. $18.95. Order through the National Volunteer Center catalog (NVC, page 37).

***Volunteer USA!,*** by Andrew Carroll with Christopher Miller. (See page 39.)

***Volunteerism: The Directory of Organizations, Training, Programs and Publications,*** 3rd edition, edited by Harriet Clyde Kipps. (See page 39.)

***Volunteers in Action,*** by Brian O'Connell and Ann Brown O'Connell, is a panoramic view of volunteer activity in almost every area of human endeavor. Intended as a source of information about the roles and impact of volunteers, the book is a testament to the good will, energy, and creativity of individuals and groups as they try to improve the lives of others. *Volunteers* begins with a brief discussion of the voluntary spirit that is ingrained in American life and ends with a section on future volunteers, or how the habit of volunteering can be inculcated in youth. The greater part of the book demonstrates the profound effects of voluntary action in seven broadly defined areas, which include the needy, religious volunteers, self-reliance groups, and others. Coauthor Brian O'Connell is the founding president of INDEPENDENT SECTOR, a Washington, DC–based coalition of almost 700 corporate, foundation, and national voluntary organizations involved with philanthropy and voluntary action. *Volunteers* ($29) was published by The Foundation Center (TFC, page 241) and can be ordered through their catalog, from the National Volunteer Center (NVC, page 37), or from INDEPENDENT SECTOR, 1828 L St., NW, Washington, DC 20036.

***You Can Make a Difference: Helping Others and Yourself Through Volunteering,*** by Marlene Wilson, an authority and trainer in volunteerism who has already written three books for professionals in the field, is intended for the general public, a book about the joys and responsibilities of volunteering. Wilson describes the many reasons people have for volunteering and then discusses some of the choices available, listing organizations and relevant publications. The book is studded with the personal stories of volunteers whom Wilson has met over the course of her career. Two appendixes list all the volunteer actions centers (VACs) in the United States and Canada and organizations for older people. Published by Volunteer Management Associates, 320 S. Cedar Brook Rd., Boulder, CO 80304, the book can be ordered through the National Volunteer Center catalog (NVC, page 37). $12.95.

PART TWO

# A Directory of Nonprofit Organizations and Publications

There are an estimated 500,000 nonprofit volunteer organizations in the United States, and you'll breathe a sigh of relief to learn that not all of them are listed here. Instead, this is a selected directory of national, regional, and local organizations chosen to illustrate the remarkable variety of interesting and worthwhile service opportunities available to potential volunteers in almost thirty spheres of activity, as well as publications that are themselves directories or idea resources for volunteers and groups.

Because the emphasis is on what you can do for whom, most of the groups listed in this section rely on volunteers themselves or will refer you to similar agencies that do use volunteers or will provide technical assistance to volunteer groups. For the same reason, major policy organizations that are run completely by staff are not included.

The directory begins with a bird's-eye view of charitable activities in the Northshire region of Bennington County in Vermont. Like communities all over the country, the Northshire is teeming with volunteers who help provide health and educational services, scholarships, cultural programs, and, for some of the region's population, the necessities of life. It is impossible to imagine how the community could survive without them.

A chapter on clearinghouses and umbrella groups, which provides an overview of volunteer opportunities, is followed by an alphabetical list of categories, from animals to veterans. There is apparent duplication in many fields—health care, trail work, museums, shelters for the homeless, and mentoring, for example—and for some of them, volunteers seem to be doing the same work over and over again. But it's a big country, and we absorb all of these services and ask for more every day. In fact, every volunteer job is unique, not just because each organization is singular in its perspective, intentions, and deeds, but because of what you can contribute and what you can learn.

Before you pick up the telephone or boot up the computer to write a letter, bear in mind that some organizations respond immediately and graciously, not to mention eagerly, to inquiries, while others are so large or so small or so discombobulated by personnel changes or a move to new offices that they may not respond without a second or even a third request. If you're truly interested in the group or in the information it can provide, patience and persistence will pay off.

## PORTRAIT OF A COMMUNITY: NORTHSHIRE VOLUNTEERS

One of the best ways you can start volunteering is to look around your own community. Once you do, you'll be astonished at the extent to which volunteers affect and improve almost every facet of life by providing services, time, experience, and, most of all, a strong sense of what it means to be a good neighbor.

The Northshire is the northern part of Bennington County, Vermont, a beautiful region in the foothills of the Green Mountains, with a few broad valleys that are, decreasingly, farmland. Major Northshire towns are Manchester (Village, Center, and Depot), Dorset (Dorset proper, South, and East), seven miles to the north, and Arlington (proper and East), twelve miles to the south. There are about 14,000 year-round residents in the entire Northshire plus second-home owners and tourists. Winter tourists come for nearby ski resorts such as Bromley and Stratton; summer and fall tourists have been coming since the nineteenth century to enjoy the scenery and now the shopping.

This sampling of volunteer activities in the Northshire serves as a microcosm of charitable activities going on in communities all over the country. It goes without saying that some people volunteer for more than one organization or cause, and that some people do not volunteer at all. (Note: Some of the sections that follow give a cross-referenced listing of organizations active in the Northshire community that are highlighted elsewhere in the book.)

### Civic Organizations

Dorset, East Dorset, Manchester, and Arlington have volunteer fire departments. Ladies' Auxiliaries for all these organizations raise money for the firemen's funds with bake sales, monthly breakfasts, and other events. Auxiliaries also provide food and coffee to fire fighters during a major fire or when the squads are fighting a fire in inclement weather.

Members of various town boards and commissions and school boards and committees are either elected or appointed. Except for the selectmen, school directors, town clerk, town treasurer, and town manager, almost everyone else serves without pay.

Dorset Sportsmen's Club maintains a millpond in town, stocks it with fish for the benefit of children aged fifteen and younger, and sponsors an annual fishing contest.

### Art, Culture, and History

Southern Vermont Art Center, which puts on art exhibits, concerts, and other cultural events in Manchester, uses about 100 volunteers every year. They serve on the board and as members of committees that make crucial decisions; they work as docents, flower arrangers, receptionists, gift shop staff, fund-raisers, organizers of special exhibits, and hostesses and caterers at exhibition openings. Volunteers are recruited mostly by networking.

Hildene, Robert Todd Lincoln's home, is entered in the National Register of Historic Places. Most of its 250 volunteers are docents who work on flexible schedules when the home is open from mid-May to October 31. Others coordinate special events, create decorations, and act as hostesses. Volunteers are recruited by word of mouth and receive their orientation in late April, before Hildene is open to the public. Every year, Hildene volunteers are publicly honored with an ad listing all of their names in one of the local newspapers.

The American Museum of Fly Fishing in Manchester is staffed with volunteers.

The Dorset Players is an all-volunteer community group of amateurs who act, design and build sets, make costumes, and serve as ushers, ticket takers, box office personnel, and press release writers. The Players' productions begin in October and run through May, after which the professionally run Dorset Theatre Festival takes over for the summer season. The Festival uses volunteer ushers and an occasional sewer or set builder who is prepared to work intensively during the preparation and rehearsals of a particular production.

Historical societies in Manchester, Dorset, and Arlington are volunteer-led and -run. The societies catalog and display artifacts from the past life of the towns, including photos, books, tools, and more, and they assist visitors interested in the town itself or perhaps in tracing family origins. Evening programs of community interest are held admission-free.

Libraries in each Northshire town operate largely with the help of volunteers, who serve on the board, catalog books, answer questions, stage fund-raising events, and arrange special exhibitions, lectures, and discussion groups.

## Education

Various community organizations in Manchester and Dorset provide about $33,000 annually in scholarship funds to local students.

Parent-Teacher Organizations (PTOs) work with all the schools in the area.

Local elementary and high schools have adopted programs that rely on the assistance of adult volunteers. The Dorset Elementary School can serve as an example. It has adopted Environmental Learning for the Future (ELF, pages 112–13), which is run by Dorset parents and other interested participants. The Dorset Aiders work on campaigns to bring in money for programs like ELF or for a dancer-in-residence to teach at the school for a week. The Aiders run an annual sale of donated and consigned ski gear, and most of the proceeds are used to enable needy children to participate in a Junior Instructive Ski Program (JISP, page 31). Individual Dorset parents with special skills work with teachers to put on special events for the kids—staging plays, baking gingerbread houses, teaching math in innovative ways, and so on.

## Student Volunteers

Student volunteer programs exist at several of the schools. In Manchester, Burr & Burton Seminary—a private boarding high school for students from a considerable distance away and the local high school for Manchester and outlying towns—was the first school in Vermont to establish a graduation requirement for community service: fifty hours of each student's own time over the course of four years, or twelve and a half hours each year. B&B receives calls from community groups and other nonprofit organizations requesting the services of student volunteers, who help set up and run school fairs, usher and occasionally work backstage at the Dorset Playhouse, work in the school cafeteria, volunteer in sports and recreation programs, and help with local environmental cleanups and recycling efforts. Whole homeroom classes become involved in Big Brother/Big Sister programs, and students volunteer to help individuals who are physically or financially unable to perform certain chores themselves: cutting and splitting wood, providing a specially cooked meal, or running errands, for example.

Student volunteers from other Northshire schools help nonprofit organizations and individuals with a wide range of activities from environmental projects to assisting elderly residents in fund-raising for worthy causes.

The Tutorial Center in Manchester uses staff and volunteers to tutor adults working toward a high school diploma.

**Literacy Volunteers of America (LVA, page 100)**

## Working with and for Children

Host families work with three organizations: ASSE (page 70), Nacel (page 71), and Academic Year in America.

Children's clubs include: Cub Scouts, Boy Scouts, Brownies, Junior Girl Scouts, and Girl Scouts, plus Bennington County 4-H Club. Many of the scouting units receive active support from local service and veterans clubs and from businesses in the community.

**Big Brothers/Big Sisters of America (BB/BSA, page 164)**

**Manchester Little League (page 216)**

**Starlight Foundation (SF, page 77)**

## Services for Low-Income People

Bennington-Rutland Opportunity Council (BROC) is an advocate for low-income people and provides direct service to clients, including homeless shelters and distribution of goods, such as those received from Coats for Kids.

**Manchester Community Food Cupboard (page 33)**

## Services for Older Persons

Southern Vermont Council on the Aging in Bennington advocates for the elderly and runs the county's Meals on Wheels program.

Senior Meals on Wheels (see Meals on Wheels, MOW, page 205) and a Senior Meals program provide midday meals for more than 9,000 people aged sixty and over.

Retired Senior Volunteers Program (RSVP, page 204), in Manchester Center, is the closest the Northshire comes to having a volunteer action center (VAC) (see National Volunteer Center, NVC, page 37). It's the only local agency actively recruiting among the entire population, of whatever age, and it serves as a clearinghouse for volunteers by working with local schools, Scout clubs, food distribution groups, churches, recycling projects, cultural organizations, and state agencies, and then matching opportunities with RSVP volunteers. The agency recruits by word of mouth and newspaper publicity.

**American Association of Retired Persons (AARP, page 203)**

## Service, Fraternal, and Veterans' Organizations

American Legion and Ladies' Auxiliary (page 231), Elks, Eagles, Knights of Columbus, Lions Club (page 115), Masons and an Eastern Star lodge, Moose (page 116), Rotary Club (page 116), and Veterans of Foreign Wars (VFW) and Ladies' Auxiliary (page 233) all make strong commitments of time and money to their own community projects, and they also work with other nonprofit organizations on joint projects.

## Health and Health-Related Organizations

American Red Cross (ARC, page 129), among other programs, runs blood drives and provides transportation for the elderly and the handicapped. Many of the churches and individual volunteers supply sandwiches and cookies for blood donors.

Manchester Rescue Squad and Arlington Rescue Squad are both wholly volunteer.

Dorset Nursing Association is staffed by professionals, but receives a lot of help from volunteers.

Manchester Health Services Thrift Shop is run by volunteers and accepts donation of clothing, toys, household items, and so on, for the benefit of the clinic.

Three Meadows Riders (part of North American Riding for the Handicapped Association, NARHA, page 211), which provides therapeutic riding for disabled people of all ages and abilities, uses thirty to forty volunteers every year.

Hospice (see National Hospice Organization, NHO, page 130) is active in the Northshire, providing twelve hours of training for its volunteers. Hospice raises some of its funds through an annual pie sale.

Volunteer families act as hosts for Special Olympics (page 212) athletes.

The March of Dimes Walkathon (page 128) is always a successful drive.

### American Cancer Society (ACS, page 134)

## Sports and Recreation

Junior Instructive Ski Program (JISP) is run by the Bromley Outing Club and Bromley Mountain and offers skiing to schoolchildren in grades 3–12 using volunteer ski instructors. Another Bromley Outing Club program, sponsored by an Arlington business, helps people who have social, physical, or mental disabilities learn to ski. The program is run by a certified instructor for the handicapped and relies heavily on volunteer ski instructors.

Manchester Recreation Department (MRD) offers residents of Manchester and Dorset facilities and programs for soccer, baseball, swimming, and other sports. MRD uses more than sixty volunteers a year to help out with almost all of the programs, including field maintenance, fund-raising, and preparing for and carrying out special events. Community businesses contribute money for MRD upkeep, and they make donations in kind, such as sand and soil for playing fields.

Mettowee Valley Youth Center, an outdoor recreation area for community use, was built with donated funds and materials and volunteer labor and is maintained the same way. The Center serves Dorset, Rupert, and Pawlet and provides various courts and other playing areas as well as a track and picnic area.

## Support Groups

There are support groups for cancer, diabetes, juvenile diabetes, abused women, heart disease, Alzheimer's, and breast cancer.

Alcoholics Anonymous is quite active in the Northshire. Its cofounder, Bill Wilson, was born and grew up in East Dorset, and his former family house, Wilson House, is a center for much of the organization's operations in the area.

## Environmental Groups

Garden clubs in Manchester and Arlington (each a chapter of National Council of State Garden Clubs, NCSGC, page 119) provide workshops, sponsor seminars and meetings to educate the public about energy issues, carry out environmental and conservation projects, contribute plantings in public places, carry out a garden therapy program at a local senior residence, decorate places of worship for holiday services, and give scholarships to college students working toward degrees in environmental studies or in farming and horticulture. Several fund-raisers are held every year to support these projects.

East Arlington Tree Project volunteers beautify the community and aid the environment with tree planting.

Merck Forest is a major environmental preserve in East Rupert, with trails, lectures, nature walks, and so on; almost all the work is carried out by volunteers and student interns.

Green Mountain Club raises money for various environmental causes by sponsoring hike-a-thons, potluck dinners, and other get-togethers.

Mettowee Valley Conservation Project, part of the Vermont Land Trust, by now has bought five of the historic farms in this fertile valley, preserving 3,000 acres as farmland. Fund-raising and other events are carried out with the help of volunteers.

Bennington County Humane Society in Shaftsbury (BCHS, page 40), just south of Arlington, has fifty volunteers working at any one time, half of them children.

## Other Services

Internal Revenue Service Volunteer Income Tax Assistors (VITA, page 87) set up free tax assistance sites in schools, churches, libraries, and other community centers.

United Way of Bennington County (see United Way of America, UWA, page 38) stages a major fund-raising event every year, and in turn helps support twelve nonprofit agencies that deliver services in the Northshire. UW also assists people looking for volunteer positions throughout the country.

## Individuals and Businesses

Many professionals—lawyers, doctors, nurses, therapists, plumbers, contractors, electricians, accountants, and a host of others—in the Northshire contribute their expertise to nonprofit organizations on a *pro bono publico* basis. The business community as a whole is supportive of a vast range of programs: They sponsor plays at the Dorset Playhouse, contribute food for fund-raising events, landscape public areas, sponsor free classical music concerts, and donate goods and supplies in kind. Some firms raise scholarship money to send needy youths to college or to get special training. Supermarkets place Community Food Shelf boxes in immediately visible locations so shoppers can donate food.

## Places of Worship

There are thirteen Christian churches and one synagogue in the three main Northshire towns, and each has volunteer programs that benefit the entire community as well as its own congregation. Fund-raisers (bake sales, rummage sales, and others) for specific causes—fixing a church steeple, for instance—are given space in the local newspapers, as are most charitable events. Places of worship collect clothing, toys, and household goods at any time a crisis arises, and at Christmas, churches are especially active.

The children's choir at the United Church of Dorset, about twenty-five local childen who rehearse after school, sing for special church occasions and make tapes of their folk and religious music. Tapes are sold to raise money for community projects and for the church.

The Interfaith Council of the Manchester Area is the coordinating body for joint charitable efforts, such as the Manchester Community Food Cupboard, whose activities are carried out successively by the synagogue and all the churches in Manchester.

## Holidays (Just a Few of Many Events)

An Easter egg hunt for local children is sponsored by Peltier's Market in Dorset and other businesses in the area.

Manchester VFW has an annual Halloween party for kids, with rides through town on fire engines, then cider and doughnuts served by the Ladies' Auxiliary.

Dorset Firemen's Auxiliary gives annual Halloween and Christmas parties for local kids.

Maelstrom Comics sponsors a Halloween open house in Arlington.

There are several major campaigns every fall to provide presents, clothing, and festive food for needy children and their families during the winter holidays. One is Coats for Kids, part of the holiday program run by the Interfaith Council's Christmas-Hanukkah Campaign, as is the "Adopt-a-Family" holiday project, which involves collecting donations of food and gifts for needy families.

Big Brothers/Big Sisters sponsors a Christmas party for children from economically disadvantaged and single-parent homes. Other Christmas parties are given by fraternal and service groups.

Kids' Christmas Workshop, a joint project of Mettowee Mill Nursery and Girl Scout Troop 450 in Dorset, teaches students aged three to ten to create handmade Christmas tree ornaments.

Various holiday efforts are sponsored and coordinated by organizations such as Arlington Nursing Service, Dorset Nursing Association, Catholic Women's Sodality, churches and Sunday schools, and groups of schoolchildren, who all help to collect and package food and toys.

Free concerts of Christmas carols and classical music associated with the holidays are given by choral societies and groups of carol singers.

A series of Christmas holiday programs for children is sponsored by Manchester Recreation Department and run by its summer volunteers, who are home from school during the holidays.

Manchester Rotary donates some of the profits from the sale of Christmas trees to the Community Food Cupboard.

Numerous appearances by Santa Claus can be counted on throughout the holiday season.

**From Vermont with Love: Toy, Mitten, and Clothes Project (page 144)**

## Getting the Word Out

Two weekly newspapers, *The Vermont NewsGuide* and *The Manchester Journal,* are published in Manchester. As part of their regular news coverage, both papers print notices of charitable programs and events based on information provided by the sponsoring church, organization, or individual. In fact, because these events engage so much of the Northshire community's energy and interest, they *are* news, and the items are published in plenty of time for potential volunteers to make plans to participate. Calendars of town meetings that are open to the public are also printed in the papers.

Fliers, posters, and other announcements are pasted in store windows, stacked on retail counters, and posted on bulletin boards at churches, schools, and supermarkets.

Galaxy Television, a local public-access cable channel, regularly places ads for volunteers in the community.

# Clearinghouses and Umbrella Groups

These organizations and publications will give you an overview of the tremendous range of ways in which people volunteer, and most of the groups either will refer you directly to an agency or send you information that will help you find one yourself. There are clearinghouses that are quite broad in scope, notably volunteer action centers (VACs) (see National Volunteer Center, NVC, page 37), Retired Senior Volunteer Program (RSVP, page 204), and the American Association of Retired Persons Volunteer Talent Bank (AARP/VTB, page 36), while others, such as Candlelighters Childhood Cancer Foundation (CCCF, page 134) and Citizen's Clearinghouse for Hazardous Wastes (CCHW, page 111), are focused on specific issues.

## ACCESS: Networking in the Public Interest

50 Beacon St.
Boston, MA 02108
1-617-720-5627, FAX 1-617-720-1318

ACCESS is a national clearinghouse of information about employment and internship opportunities in public and community service. Through its Non-Profit Organization Search, ACCESS provides job-seekers with tailored lists of such organizations. Listings of jobs, internships, and volunteer service at nonprofit and government agencies are published monthly in *Community Jobs* ($25 per individual for six months, $30 per individual for twelve months). Internships, many of which are unstipended, range from assisting the Better Government Association in Chicago in its investigation of waste, corruption, and inefficiency at all government levels to coordinating public relations for Women Express in Boston. Call or write to ACCESS for more information.

## ACTION

Office of Public Affairs
1100 Vermont Ave., NW
Washington, DC 20525
1-202-606-5108

ACTION is the federal government's parent agency for domestic volunteer service. ACTION's five programs enable almost 500,000 Americans from all walks of life to volunteer their services where they are needed: Student Community Service Program (SCSP, page 224); a community service program, Volunteers in Service to America (VISTA, page 88); and three programs for older Americans: Retired Senior Volunteer Program (RSVP, page 204), Foster Grandparent Program (FGP, page 204), and Senior Companion Program (SCP, page 205). For information about any of these programs, consult the pages above or get in touch with your regional ACTION office (page 35).

## American Association of Retired Persons

Volunteer Talent Bank (AARP/VTB)
601 E St., NW
Washington, DC 20049
1-202-434-2277

AARP's Volunteer Talent Bank is a clearinghouse that refers individuals who have registered with VTB as volunteers to work within AARP's own volunteer programs (page 203) or for other nonprofit organizations, such as American Red Cross (ARC, page 129), Peace Corps (page 190), Service Corps of Retired Executives (SCORE, page 65), The Nature Conservancy (TNC, page 105), and Student Conservation Association (SCA, page 106). VTB registrants do volunteer work as varied as the groups that use them. AARP members and nonmembers who are fifty or older can write to AARP/VTB to ask for information and a registration form.

**American Bar Association, Standing Committee on Dispute Resolution (ABA, page 155)**

**American Community Gardening Association (ACGA, page 122)**

**Candlelighters Childhood Cancer Foundation (CCCF, page 134)**

**Citizen's Clearinghouse for Hazardous Wastes (CCHW, page 111)**

**Conflict Resolution Center International, Inc. (CRC, page 159)**

**Family Service America (FSA, page 85)**

**International Association of Justice Volunteerism (IAJV, page 179)**

**CDC National AIDS Clearinghouse (page 132)**

**National Assembly of Local Arts Agencies (NALAA, page 51)**

**National Association for Mediation in Education (NAME, page 159)**

**National Citizen's Coalition for Nursing Home Reform (NCCNHR, page 206)**

**National Clearinghouse for Alcohol and Drug Information (NCADI, page 228)**

**National Coalition for Cancer Survivorship (NCCS, page 135)**

**National Federation of State High School Associations TARGET Program (TARGET, page 229)**

**National Institute for Dispute Resolution (NIDR, page 159)**

**National Organization for Victim Assistance (NOVA, page 91)**

**National Society to Prevent Blindness (NSPB, page 141)**

**National Student Campaign Against Hunger and Homelessness (NSCAHH, page 223)**

**One Plus One (PLUS, page 167)**

**People for the Ethical Treatment of Animals (PETA, page 48)**

## Points of Light Foundation (POLF)

736 Jackson Pl.
Washington, DC 20503
1-202-408-5162, FAX 1-202-408-5169

The Points of Light Foundation is an independent nonprofit umbrella organization whose mission is to stimulate people to make volunteerism central to their lives. The Foundation's particular focus is community service that addresses serious social issues, such as functional illiteracy, homelessness and hunger, drugs, teenage pregnancy, the crisis in health care delivery, and the AIDS epidemic. According to the Foundation, although 98 million Americans volunteer, only 5 to 7 per-

## FEATURED ORGANIZATION: THE NATIONAL VOLUNTEER CENTER (NVC)

736 Jackson Pl., NW
Washington, D.C. 20503
1-202-408-5162

In 1991 the National Volunteer Center (NVC), the national organization for almost 400 volunteer action centers (VACs) around the country, merged into the Points of Light Foundation and moved its offices to the Foundation's address. NVC provides technical assistance in setting up and running volunteer programs, sponsors a yearly conference, and helps corporations with employee volunteer programs. NVC has an extensive publications catalog featuring titles for volunteer managers and administrators as well as for individual volunteers.

A local or regional VAC is the first place to look for volunteer opportunities in your town or region. Each is an independent nonprofit organization whose primary functions include recruiting, referring, and placing volunteers in nonprofit organizations. VACs also run management assistance programs for local nonprofits, work with businesses to introduce volunteerism into company employee policy, and sponsor seminars to promote volunteerism in the community and in schools. About one third of VACs are wholly funded by United Way (UWA, page 38); others receive government and private funds as well. NVC can be reached or contacted at Points of Light Foundation. Check the Appendix for National Volunteer Centers (page 245).

cent of them put their energies into trying to ameliorate these problems. To promote community service, the Foundation has a national advertising campaign (created pro bono), with 800 numbers linking volunteers directly with local service opportunities. Business, educational, and civic organizations; unions; and religious groups participate with the Foundation to foster community volunteerism and to develop service programs.

**St. Vincent Pallotti Center for Apostolic Development, Inc. (page 201)**

**Share Our Strength, Prepared and Perishable Food Programs (SOS/PPFP, page 175)**

**TreePeople (page 109)**

**Volunteers in Prevention, Probation & Prisons (VIP, page 183)**

**Y-ME National Organization for Breast Cancer Information and Support (Y-ME, page 136)**

# Self-Help Clearinghouses

There are about twenty-five regional self-help clearinghouses in the country. Their services include referring individuals to local support groups, offering assistance to people who want to start a group, and publishing literature to help them do so. A list of regional clearinghouses can be ordered from either of the organizations listed on page 38.

## FEATURED ORGANIZATION: UNITED WAY OF AMERICA (UWA)

701 N. Fairfax St.
Alexandria, VA 22314
1-703-836-7100

UWA is an umbrella organization for over 2,100 autonomous United Ways nationwide, each one helping to meet community health and human-care needs. The national organization provides United Ways and other charitable groups with an extraordinary range of services that include training for administrators, personnel, and volunteer fund-raisers; liaison with other national charities; marketing support; and specially developed computer software and other technical assistance. UWA works with organized labor, large and small businesses, and other sectors of the community to create United Way programs that will involve employees in a full range of volunteer activities.

Apart from government, United Ways support the greatest variety of health and human services in the country. Each regional United Way is an independent community resource governed and largely operated by volunteers, whose functions include: fund-raising to meet local health care needs, assessment of current and future community needs, distribution of resources according to needs, recruiting and training volunteers, and management and technical assistance for community agencies. Some of the volunteer action centers (VACs) (see National Volunteer Center, NVC, page 37) are entirely sponsored and run by United Ways, Call your local United Way for information about volunteering.

### American Self-Help Clearinghouse (ASHC)

St. Clares—Riverside Medical Center
Denville, NJ 07834
1-201-625-7101
Contact: Edward Madara, Director

ASHC makes individual referrals to callers seeking information about national self-help groups and will send a list of all the regional local self-help clearinghouses. SHC publishes *The Self-Help Sourcebook,* with descriptions of over 600 national and model self-help groups covering a broad span of illnesses, addictions, and other stressful situations; general ideas and suggestions for starting a mutual aid group; information on computer support group networks; and other directories and toll-free helplines. The book is meant as a resource for people who want to form a group as well as for professionals. Contact ASHC to order the book and for referral to regional self-help clearinghouses.

### National Self-Help Clearinghouse (NSHC)

25 W. 43rd St., Room 620
New York, NY 10036
Contact: Frank Riessman

Support groups are a means for helping people through a range of life crises and adverse situations such as alcoholism, a chronic health condition, infertility, the death of a spouse or a child, mental illness, and the problems encountered by families of people with various illnesses. NSHC estimates that there are about 500,000 self-help groups nationwide. The NSHC data bank provides information about and referral to self-help groups and regional self-help clearinghouses, carries out research about the field, trains professionals to work with mutual aid groups, and publishes manuals (including *How to Organize a Self-Help Group*, $6), training materials, and a newsletter. For information about NSHC services, or for referral to a group or regional clearinghouse, write to NSHC.

# Resources

***Invest Yourself: The Catalogue of Volunteer Opportunities, A Guide to Action*** is published annually by the Commission on Voluntary Service and Action (CVSA), a coordinating council of over 200 nongovernmental voluntary service agencies nationwide. CVSA advocates social change, achieved by promoting individuals' participation in an independent volunteer movement made up of organizations that set their own goals and programs based on the needs of their constituencies. *Invest Yourself* is a directory of full-time volunteer opportunities offered by almost 200 independent groups, which range from very local grassroots secular and religious groups (Berkshire County Fuel Committee) to larger international organizations (Amigos de las Americas, AMIGOS, page 186). Each entry contains a general description of the organization's aims and activities, including the work performed by volunteers, the volunteer skills required, the areas where volunteers serve, and whom to contact. Interspersed with the entries are "stories from the field," written by volunteers in full-time service. Introductory text presents a clear case for a genuinely independent volunteer movement and also describes CVSA's position on potential dangers of government-sponsored volunteerism. Five indexes, including opportunities for volunteers under eighteen and an index to program locations. Send $8 to CVSA/Invest Yourself, P.O. Box 117-JK, New York, NY 10009.

***Volunteer USA!*** by Andrew Carroll with Christopher Miller. New York: Fawcett Columbine, 1991. This is a terrific book for anyone who wants to start volunteering, especially those interested in helping to provide social services and education; working to prevent AIDS; working with the homeless and hungry, children, the elderly, crime victims, the disabled, veterans, animals, or the environment. Carroll's first chapter describes how to use community resources, long-term volunteering, and socially responsible consumerism. Each succeeding chapter deals with a specific field of volunteerism in terms of why help is needed and what you can do, with many practical suggestions for reading and other activities, and gives a listing of national organizations that can provide information and volunteer opportunities. The environment chapter also lists products that are claimed to be nontoxic and environmentally safe. Well-indexed. $8.95.

***Volunteerism: The Directory of Organizations Training, Programs and Publications,*** 3rd edition, edited by Harriet Clyde Kipps. New Providence, NJ: R. R. Bowker, 1991. The title says it all. The listings in this 1,200-page book encompass every aspect of volunteerism, with comprehensive information on the broad range of resources for volunteer organizations and administrators and detailed listings of national organizations, local programs, and publications in fields from AIDS to welfare reform. Although the book is intended for volunteer managers, the Message to Volunteers section is a compact overview of what an individual should know before becoming a volunteer. This monumental achievement is available only in libraries.

# Working with and for Animals

For animal lovers, there are plenty of ways to work with beasts, both furry and otherwise:

- Work at a local humane society.
- Participate in bird counts.
- Provide pet therapy for people in health care and other facilities or for those who are homebound.
- Care for the pets of people with AIDS and other conditions.
- Raise puppies until they are ready for training as Seeing Eye dogs.
- Work at a children's zoo.
- Find an animal rights organization whose convictions match your own and work for it.

Some of these volunteer activities require special training and a long-term commitment; others take up less time and can be scheduled flexibly.

## Bennington County Humane Society (BCHS)

R.R. 1B, Box 262
Shaftsbury, VT 05262
1-802-375-2898
Contact: Administrative Assistant

BCHS's services are similar to those provided by humane societies and animal shelters nationwide. Some of the services are provided by volunteers, and at any one time BCHS has fifty volunteers, half of them children. Their duties include:

- Various administrative, office, and computer jobs.
- Pet visitation, which involves volunteer teams of pet owners and their animals who visit local nursing homes in order to share the benefits of human-companion animal bonding.
- Volunteer instruction for young children in preschools, teaching the kids about animals and pet care.
- Organizing special events.
- Leading tours of the shelter for groups of children or adults.
- Socializing with animals—the most popular volunteer job at the society. Socializers spend time with the animals at the shelter—playing, exercising, leash walking, training, touching, talking to, or grooming. Such attention helps companion animals become used to people and makes them more adoptable.

For information about volunteering at an animal shelter, look for a humane society in your area phone book.

## Cornell Laboratory of Ornithology (CLO)

Bird Population Studies
159 Sapsucker Woods Rd.
Ithaca, NY 14850
1-607-254-BIRD (1-607-254-2473)
Contact: Bird Population Studies, 1-607-254-2414

CLO has five ongoing bird population studies that rely on volunteer observers for their raw data. CLO works cooperatively with U.S. Fish and Wildlife Service (FWS, page 43) and the National Audubon Society (NAS, page 41) to organize the data, which is computerized and used for research. The results of that research are communicated to other researchers, wildlife managers, environmental policymakers, birders, conservationists, and the general public. CLO projects are conducted throughout the United States and Canada.

- Project Feederwatch: Observers monitor bird populations at backyard feeders during ten 2-day periods from November through March, recording peak numbers of each species on computer-readable forms. To volunteer you need not be an expert birder, but you must be able to identify birds that commonly visit your feeders and be willing to keep careful records. Participants receive the biannual newsletter *Feederwatch News,* which publishes the results of the survey.
- Breeding Bird Census (BBC), begun by NAS in 1937, and Winter Bird Population Study (WBPS), initiated in 1948: Both are conducted by volunteer observers. Results of these censuses are recorded annually in the *Journal of Field Ornithology.*
- The Christmas Bird Count database. (The count itself is organized by NAS, page 41, and local bird clubs.)
- The Nest Record Program: Information on species, location, habitat, and reproductive history of bird nests is collected, processed, and stored.
- The National Science Experiments are a series of short-term research questions that can be answered by a large-scale network of volunteers. The first three questions will focus on seed preferences of wintering birds, breeding biology of pigeons in cities, and breeding of tanagers in fragmented forests.

For information about any of these programs, contact Bird Population Studies at CLO.

## National Audubon Society (NAS)

Christmas Bird Count
950 Third Ave.
New York, NY 10022
1-212-832-3200, FAX 1-212-593-6254
Contact: Christmas Bird Count Editor

NAS is one of the best-known conservation associations in the country, with 500 chapters nationwide (although it is not the only organization to bear the name of the famous naturalist). Membership from individual chapters participate with other local agencies on environmental and wildlife projects, such as beach cleanups or working to protect a natural area.

The NAS Christmas Bird Count is an annual bird census taken by over 43,000 volunteers in all fifty states as well as in Canada, parts of Central and South America, Bermuda, the West Indies, and the Pacific Islands. Each bird count group, numbering between 1 and 300 observers, delineates a circle fifteen miles in diameter and then tries to cover as much of the circle as possible in a twenty-four-hour, single calendar day within two weeks of Christmas. Unusual or rare species are documented with photos or detailed descriptions. The counts are looked over by regional editors, then turned over to the Christmas Bird Count editor at *American Birds,* the highly respected NAS magazine, which publishes the counts region by region in a special fall issue.

For information about joining NAS, write to the headquarters in New York City. Membership is not necessary to participate in the Christmas Bird Count, but you must volunteer early in the fall. Write to the Christmas Bird Count editor for more information and an application.

**North American Riding for the Handicapped Association (NARHA, page 211)**

## FEATURED ORGANIZATION: DELTA SOCIETY (DS)

321 Burnett Ave. S., 3rd Fl.
Renton, WA 98055-2569
1-206-226-7357, FAX 1-206-235-1076

DS's mission is to improve human health and well-being by promoting mutually beneficial contacts with animals and nature, and it is a leading international resource center on the interactions of people, animals, and the environment, including human-animal bonding and animal-assisted therapy (AAT). There are seventeen DS chapters and networks nationwide, with a membership of over 2,600 people, among them pet owners, volunteers, therapists, educators, health professionals, and veterinarians.

DS funds studies and research on animal-human relationships, especially studies of the effects of animals on human health. There is evidence that animals can lower blood pressure, affect children's development, play a role in family life and with the elderly, help in prisoner rehabilitation, provide a means of reaching crack babies and autistic children, and enable people with disabilities to achieve independence and improve their physical condition.

DS is working to establish an interdisciplinary approach to animal-human relationships in order to educate health and social care professionals. To assist individuals and groups in establishing safe, effective animal companionship and therapy programs, DS provides guidelines for appropriate techniques, precautions, and evaluations and also offers practical help to potential pet owners and those who already own animals.

DS maintains a resource library in its Renton headquarters, and the organization is also compiling the only computerized program-profile database with information on people-pet programs and centers around the world. Using this database, the Renton office answers over 1,000 requests for help and information each month. The DS resource catalog is extensive and includes directories of animal-assistance training programs, hearing dog programs, and pet-loss resource persons; manuals, guidelines, and audiovisual material on topics such as therapeutic riding, the environment, and the health benefits of animals; scholarly publications and abstracts of DS's annual conference on human, animal, and environmental interactions; and resource packets with practical information about the effect of animals on various human populations.

DS's most recent national program is called Pet Partners Program (PPP), which assists individuals and organizations in training volunteer human-animal teams. The teams completing PPP's stringent requirements will be registered to visit nursing homes, schools, prisons, treatment centers, and other facilities to share their time with those in need. The minimum human age for registration is ten. Dogs, cats, birds, and other pets can be registered, and there are a number of options for registration. Becoming a Pet Partner requires intensive training and evaluation for you and your pet, but it is an enormously rewarding experience for the animals and all the humans involved. People registered as Pet Partners receive a newsletter, lowered fees, continuing education credits, inexpensive insurance, and other benefits. Existing AAT programs can participate in the PPP while maintaining their own names and logos.

For information about DS and volunteering at one of its affiliates, information about other AAT programs, or PPP, contact the Renton headquarters.

## Pacific Whale Foundation (PWF)

101 N. Kihei Rd., Suite 21
Kihei, Maui, HI 96753-8833
1-808-879-8860, FAX 1-808-879-2615
Continental U.S.: 1-800-WHALE-11
Contact: Research and Education Director

PWF is dedicated to saving the oceans through science and education, with special programs centered on marine mammals. Field research focuses on whale and dolphin populations in the Pacific Ocean. PWF's internship program gives dedicated interns the opportunity to work in the field alongside PWF's research staff, learning all aspects of field research. Two- and four-week internships are available in Hawaii and Australia throughout the year. For information, write to the program coordinator.

Pets Are Wonderful Support (PAWS, page 132)

Pets Are Wonderful Support/Los Angeles (PAWS/LA, page 132)

## U.S. Department of the Interior

Bureau of Land Management (BLM)
Adopt-A-Horse-Or-Burro Program
18th and C Sts., NW
Washington, DC 20240-0001
1-202-343-5717

Wild horses and burros, protected by law in public lands, have almost no natural predators to limit their population, which has steadily increased. In 1973, the BLM began the Adopt-A-Horse Program as a humane method for disposing of excess animals, and to date more than 65,000 animals have been placed in private foster homes that meet BLM standards. Providing a foster home for a wild horse or burro should not be undertaken lightly; for detailed information about the program, write to BLM.

## U.S. Department of the Interior

Fish and Wildlife Service (FWS)
Interior Bldg.
18th and C Sts., NW
Washington, DC 20240
1-202-208-5634

FWS has volunteer openings at national wildlife refuges and fish hatcheries, research stations, and regional offices. Volunteers are needed to take wildlife population censuses, work at habitat construction and maintenance, feed and look after animals, work with visitors, and do office work. Computer programmers, photographers, and audiovisual specialists can contribute valuable services. Write to the Washington office for a list of regional offices, and ask for a volunteer brochure.

## Brookfield Zoo

Children's Zoo
Brookfield, IL 60513
1-708-485-0263, Ext. 458
Contact: Gail Mikenas, Assistant Curator, Children's Zoo

Volunteers at the Children's Zoo work primarily with visitors. Among other duties, they supervise a walk-in farmyard, where visitors meet small farm animals, especially goats and calves, and they take a variety of small animals, such as ferrets and rabbits, for walks in the Children's Zoo to introduce the animals to visitors. Trained volunteers are allowed to bottle-feed baby goats and calves, and they also help in grooming demonstrations. Brookfield has a special populations program in which volunteers help take small animals to people who are unable to come to the zoo.

About forty volunteers a year work in the Children's Zoo. Volunteers must be at least eighteen, enjoy working with people of all ages, and must also be able to work outdoors in all types of weather. Applicants are screened by the volunteer coordinating staff and have interviews with the animal keepers as well. For information about volunteering for the Brookfield Children's Zoo, write to the assistant curator.

# Training Guide Dogs

## Guide Dog Foundation for the Blind, Inc. (GDF)

371 E. Jericho Tnpk.
Smithtown, NY 11787-2976
1-516-265-2121, FAX 1-516-361-5192
Outside New York: 1-800-548-4337
Contact: Puppy Walkers Supervisor

GDF furnishes guide dogs, free of charge, to qualified people who seek the independence, mobility, and companionship a guide dog provides. GDF breeds Labrador/golden retriever puppies for sound temperament, companionability, intelligence, and gentleness. At seven or eight weeks, a puppy is turned over to a volunteer puppy walker family with whom the dog spends a full year becoming socialized, housebroken, and accustomed to other family pets, and being exposed to as many outside activities as possible: trips to shopping centers, sporting events, restaurants; visiting friends in city and suburban areas; train rides—anywhere a sighted person can go. A GDF puppy supervisor visits regularly to monitor the dog's progress and guide the family. At the end of the year, the family returns the dog to GDF for the next stages of training and graduation. As part of puppy walker training, GDF has a monthly half-day session called Camp Guide Dog, at which walker families and puppies review discipline and obedience, work on stairs, practice walking the puppies on leashes, and try to correct any problems. Local GDF programs are in part supported by the area's veterinarians, who volunteer their care to one or more guide dog puppies a year. GDF has programs in New York, Virginia, Iowa, and Maryland and needs about 120 puppy walker families a year. For information about becoming a puppy walker, contact the Smithtown office.

## Guiding Eyes for the Blind, Inc. (GEB)

Foster Puppy Program
Route 164
Patterson, NY 12563
1-914-878-3330
Contact: Jane Russenberger, Breeding Program Director

GEB breeds and trains guide dogs and instructs visually handicapped people in ways that increase their mobility through guide-dog use. At approximately ten weeks after birth, guide-dog puppies are placed with volunteer puppy raisers who provide a loving environment for about fourteen months. These volunteers train and socialize the young dogs in a variety of ways, as outlined in the "Puppy Raisers Manual." GEB area coordinators stay in close touch with puppy raisers, offering support and helping to solve problems. A volunteer puppy raiser must be an individual or family willing to spend considerable time each day with the puppy (usually about two hours), taking it for walks and teaching it good manners. When the training period is over, the now mature dog is returned to GEB for approximately three months of formal guide-dog training alone, followed by a month of training with one of the blind students. Puppy raisers can attend graduation ceremonies where they again meet their dog and the blind student to whom the dog has been assigned.

GEB has puppy-raising regions in Maine, Massachusetts, Connecticut, Rhode Island, Vermont, New York, Virginia, and North Carolina, and needs at least 400 puppy raisers a year.

# Animal Rights Organizations

The organizations listed here run the gamut from mainstream to militant. Each in its own way advocates more compassionate treatment of animals, whether they are house pets, farm animals, or creatures of the wilderness. Although animals are the focus of these groups, their aims, policies, and activities very often overlap with positions and initiatives undertaken by environmental organizations (pages 102–114) with similar goals.

## American Humane Association (AHA)

P.O. Box 1266
Denver, CO 80201
1-303-792-9900

AHA was founded in 1877 and is the oldest national animal rights organization in the United States. Among its activities are advocacy on animal welfare issues; education and training programs for agencies and individuals involved in animal safety, animal control, and animal cruelty investigations; certification of animal services that meet AHA's standards of excellence; emergency animal relief; and information and referral services about animal care and welfare issues. AHA also has a large number of publications for professionals in the field and for individual pet owners. *The Advocate,* AHA's quarterly magazine for members, has current information on animal welfare issues.

## The Hearing Dog Resource Center (HDRC)

321 Burnett Ave. So., 3rd Fl.
Renton, WA 98055-2569
1-800-869-6898 (Voice/TDD)

HDRC, a joint venture of American Humane Association (AHA, page 45) and Delta Society (DS, page 42), promotes and educates society about the importance of hearing dogs.

## Animal Protection Institute (API)

2831 Fruitridge Rd.
P.O. Box 22505
Sacramento, CA 95822
1-916-731-5521, FAX 1-916-731-4467

API is a nonprofit organization with 150,000 members active in stopping and preventing the abuse of animals of all kinds—pets at home, farm and ranch animals, and those in the wild. Members receive the quarterly magazine *Mainstream,* filled with information on current problems and campaigns for solving them. API members volunteer by the thousands for various task forces: Over 7,000 people volunteer for the API Emergency Force; others work on more specialized campaigns. Act Force is API's outreach to local communities. Write to API for information about membership and volunteer opportunities in your area.

## Animal Rights Mobilization (ARM!)

P.O. Box 6989
Denver, CO 80206
1-303-388-7120
ARM! Hotline: 1-800-CALL-ARM (1-800-225-5276)

ARM! is a grassroots national organization committed to helping create a popular mass movement that will end the use of animals as food, fur, game, and subjects of laboratory testing, as well as the deliberate breeding of animals for profit. ARM! has a network of over ninety affiliated local groups across the country for which it acts as a coordinating body and information and resource center. ARM! also provides support services, information, and networking opportunities to nonaffiliated grassroots animal groups. Individuals or groups interested in animal rights issues can call the Information and Research

Center at the 800 number, which is a clearinghouse for animal rights information. The organization provides listings and information on local groups and their campaigns, and its speakers bureau can send experienced activists to participate in and support local groups' events. For information, call or write to ARM!

## Farm Animal Reform Movement (FARM)

P.O. Box 30654
Bethesda, MD 20824
1-301-530-1737

FARM was formed in 1981 to expose the impact of intensive animal agriculture on animal welfare, consumer health, and environmental quality. FARM's educational programs and campaigns are undertaken by a national network of several hundred local groups and individual activists across the country. Two of FARM's programs are the Great American Meatout and World Farm Animals Day, observances that are held in over 1000 cities and include festivals, exhibits, picketing, candlelight vigils, mock funeral processions, and similar activities. Other programs are a campaign to ban veal, an industry watch, training seminars for experienced activists, legislative initiatives, and an education module for schools. There is work for interns and volunteers in the Bethesda office. Write to FARM for the location of animal activist groups in your area and for information about FARM.

## Friends of Animals (FOA)

National Headquarters
P.O. Box 1244
Norwalk, CT 06856
1-203-866-5223, FAX 1-203-853-9102
1-800-321-PETS (1-800-321-7387)

FOA is a United States-based international nonprofit organization working for the advancement of animal protection and to reduce and eliminate the suffering inflicted by humans upon animals. FOA is involved in public education as well as changing laws that foster animal abuse, enacting new legislation to prevent cruelty, and ensuring proper enforcement and administration of those laws. Members of FOA are encouraged to work in their own communities as volunteer activists by voicing their positions on issues to their legislators through letter-writing and phone calls, distributing literature, getting involved with public education programs, encouraging landowners to post their property to prevent sport hunting, and attending demonstrations. FOA programs and activities include:

- A nationwide spay/neuter program with 1,300 participating veterinarians.
- An anti-fur campaign, launched every fall in New York City with a blitz of provocative messages on telephone kiosks, billboards, and the "Fur Free Friday" demonstration.
- Prevention of hunting, trapping, and all other activities by special interest groups on national wildlife refuges and public lands. FOA conducts these campaigns in the courts, in the media, and on the public grounds themselves, using FOA activists.
- Protection of marine mammals and animals in the wild.
- An antivivisection campaign and an investigation of the dog and cat theft trade.

FOA also needs volunteers from across the country to supply the national office with news clippings on animal-related issues. Members receive periodic updates on these issues and news of the organization's activities through *Act'ionLine*, FOA's bimonthly magazine, and other reports. For information, call the national headquarters at the 800 number.

## In Defense of Animals (IDA)

816 W. Francisco Blvd.
San Rafael, CA 94901
1-415-453-9984
Animal Abuse Hotline: 1-415-453-9994

With over 50,000 members, IDA is one of the country's principal organizations dedicated to defending the rights, welfare, and habitat of animals. IDA conducts national campaigns in a broad range of areas: World Laboratory Animal Liberation Week, a national boycott of Proctor & Gamble, a campaign against military abuse of animals, anti-fur demonstrations and the Fur Amnesty donor drive; *March for Animals*, lobbying to stop the slaughter of seals, halting animal research generally and also targeting specific laboratories and other research venues.

Grassroots activism is a central part of IDA's operations. The Contact Network is a data base of people across the country who wish to be actively involved in IDA's national events. These experienced volunteers are also on file for referral for assistance in local cases of animal abuse. IDA uses volunteers working from their own communities for letter writing, coordinating local campaigns with support from the national headquarters, and distributing literature, which IDA provides free. Volunteers—many of them filling court-ordered Community Service hours—work in IDA's three Bay Area chapter groups. IDA also has three regional coordinators, who run campaigns in their areas and who always need volunteers. Members receive IDA's biannual magazine and notices of current activities. For information about volunteering or membership, contact the San Rafael headquarters.

## Sea Shepherd Conservation Society (SSCS)

1314 2nd St.
Santa Monica, CA 90401
1-213-394-3198, FAX 1-213-394-0360
Contact: Peter Wallerstein, Director

SSCS is an activist ocean-policing organization whose mandate is to see that international treaties for the conservation of ocean animals—whales, dolphins, seals, and others—are enforced. SSCS ocean patrols have all-volunteer crews trained by on-board experience. The patrols investigate and document illegal slaughter of marine animals by nations, corporations, and individual entrepreneurs. Then, if necessary, SSCS will take steps to enforce the law. SSCS is a nonprofit membership organization. The quarterly newsletter, "Sea Shepherd Log," has articles about the most recent SSCS actions, suggested boycotts, and stories about marine ecology offenders. For information about volunteering as a crew member, write to the Santa Monica office. For other information, write to Sea Shepherd, P.O. Box 7000-S, Redondo Beach, CA 90277.

# Resources

### ANIMAL RIGHTS PUBLICATIONS

***The Animal Rights Handbook: Everyday Ways to Save Animal Lives,*** by Living Planet Press. Venice, CA: Living Planet Press, 1990. This handbook is filled with animal rights information, from fur ranching to product testing to factory farming to shopping with a conscience to vegetarianism, with many useful suggestions for acting on your principles. The last chapter is a directory of publications, organizations, personal care companies (which may or may not use animals for product-safety testing), and cruelty-free products. $4.95.

*Save the Animals! 101 Easy Things You Can Do,* by Ingrid Newkirk. New York: Warner Books, 1990. Ingrid Newkirk is one of the founders and the national director of People for the Ethical Treatment of Animals (PETA, page 48), one of the country's leading animal rights organizations. Her book is a practical guide to actions you can take to help prevent the abuse of

## FEATURED ORGANIZATION: PEOPLE FOR THE ETHICAL TREATMENT OF ANIMALS (PETA)

P.O. Box 42516
Washington, DC 20015-0516
1-301-770-PETA (1-301-770-7382)
Action Line: 1-301-770-8980
In Los Angeles: Last Chance for Animals Hotline: 1-213-271-1409
Contact: Volunteer Coordinator

PETA is one of the leading national organizations working to establish and defend the rights of all animals. Its basic principle is that no animal should be eaten, worn, experimented on, or used for entertainment. Since its founding in 1980, PETA has heightened public consciousness about animal suffering, with special focus on three areas: factory farms, laboratories, and the fur trade. Through public education, research and undercover investigations, legislation, special events, direct action, and assistance in grassroots organizing, PETA has successfully documented and forced the cessation of cruel treatment of animals in laboratories, slaughterhouses, and animal acts.

Instead of forming chapters, PETA has created a National Activist Network, a computerized listing of animal rights groups and individuals committed to promoting the cause of animal rights. PETA is a clearinghouse for information on animal rights issues, and provides technical assistance to people starting community action groups. Animal Rights 101, PETA's traveling eight-hour seminar, is given in cities across the country, and participants attend lectures, see videos, and recieve guidance on starting an organization. *Becoming an Activist: PETA's Guide to Animal Rights Organizing* (free to seminar participants; otherwise $5 postpaid), by Sue Brebner and Debbi Baer, is a valuable, clearly written manual that can be applied, with changes in focus, to forming other activist groups.

PETA produces books, leaflets, and brochures with information about all aspects of animal mistreatment: animal experiments, fur, pet shops and puppy mills, cosmetics testing, zoos and aquariums, and others, and has available for sale or rental videos on some of those subjects. PETA also sells campaign leaflets targeted at rodeos, circuses, and zoos, among others, which can be photocopied and used for leafleting outside stores and at events. Members ($15 a year) receive periodic action alerts and updates as well as the four-color quarterly newsletter, *PETA News,* which reports on current campaigns and investigations and is packed with tips and suggestions for individual and group actions. Call PETA's Action Line for up-to-date information about specific issues, or contact the volunteer coordinator in the Washington office for a starter kit with information on how to create an animal rights activist group in your own community.

animals, including political action, and contributions of money and time. Each chapter poses a specific problem and offers a number of cogent solutions, including the names of organizations and publications that can provide further information. There are chapters on buying pets, education about animal issues, humane treatment of all sorts of pets, companies that use animals for research (and how to reach them), animal performers, and more. The last chapter is a list of the leading animal rights organizations. $4.95.

# Volunteering for the Arts

Even if you don't sing like Pavarotti, write plays as well as Wasserstein, or paint like Matisse, you can still contribute to the cultural life of your community or your nation by helping to stage a gala fundraiser for the local opera company, working on the crew of a regional theater that's putting on a Wasserstein play, running a photography workshop for kids living in shelters, or being a docent at a nearby museum. In lean times, funding for the cultural organizations is the first item cut from the budget, and volunteers are needed now more than ever.

Almost any cultural institution in your area is likely to rely on volunteers for many services. Start with your local museums and libraries; try the yellow pages of the phone book for that hidden-treasure organization. To find organizations further afield, call your nearest arts council (check your local white pages under state offices, and see below). Volunteers who are themselves artists can contribute immeasurably to worthy causes by offering their skills and time.

## Museums and Related Institutions

Although volunteerism is almost unknown in European museums, it is the mainstay of those in the United States, which receive very little government funding. Because as Americans we belive that art should be accessible to everyone (and the earlier in life the better), museums and other cultural institutions have developed outreach programs to diverse populations—schoolchildren, the elderly, people with disabilities, and tour groups with special interests, among them. Trained volunteers are especially useful in carrying out these programs.

### American Association for Museum Volunteers (AAMV)

1225 Eye St., NW, Suite 200
Washington, DC 20005
1-202-289-1818
Contact: Cynthia Pinkston, (Home) 1-703-356-0369

There are over 350,000 museum volunteers working full- or part-time in many capacities in all of the nation's museums. AAMV, an affiliate of American Association of Museums (AAM, page 51), is a membership organization for museum volunteers and staff that promotes professional levels of service by volunteers and recognition of volunteers' contributions. AAMV publishes a newsletter for members and provides a forum for exchange of ideas by offering regional and national conferences for museum staff and volunteers. Members can use AAMV as a clearinghouse for information about various museum volunteer programs. For more information, write to the Washington address.

## American Association of Museums (AAM)

1225 Eye St., NW, Suite 200
Washington, DC 20005
1-202-289-1818, FAX 1-202-289-6578

AAM is a national organization representing all museums (about 2,700 institutions) and museum professionals (8,500 individuals). For people interested in museum volunteer work, AAM's catalog of publications for professionals includes several books that you might be unable to find elsewhere: *A Directory of Museum Volunteer Programs* (pages 61–2), *The Good Guide* (page 62), and *The Official Museum Directory*, which provides detailed information on more than 700 institutions in eighty-five categories of museums and exhibition centers nationwide. *The Official Directory* is available only in libraries. Write to AAM for a free publications catalog.

## National Archives and Records Administration (NARA)

8th St. and Pennsylvania Ave., NW
Washington, DC 20408
1-202-501-5205, FAX 1-202-501-5005
Contact: Patricia Eames, Office of Public Programs

The National Archives is dedicated to preserving and making available for reference and research the permanently valuable records of the U. S. government. Archives holdings date back to the eighteenth century and contain literally billions of textual, cartographic, and photographic documents, as well as films and video and sound recordings. Among NARA's most important documents are: the Declaration of Independence, the Constitution, and the Bill of Rights. NARA operates fourteen records centers, eleven regional archives, and eight presidential libraries in fifteen states. Volunteers are needed for four categories of service:

- Docents, who receive an intensive eleven-week training program, introduce small groups to the records and activities at the National Archives, develop and conduct school projects for visiting classes, and conduct outreach programs for community groups. Docents work primarily in the District of Columbia Archives and in the presidential libraries.
- Information desk aides, who work in Washington, welcome visitors, and answer questions about the Archives and other Washington areas of interest.
- Volunteer staff aides and curatorial assistants, who work mainly in Washington.
- Genealogical staff aids, who themselves should have some experience doing family histories, work with new genealogical researchers using the Archives in Washington and at regional branches, lead genealogical workshops, and provide assistance on projects preparing records for use.

Except for docents, volunteers receive a two-day orientation and then on-the-job training. For more information about volunteering, contact the Office of Public Programs.

## National Assembly of Local Arts Agencies (NALAA)

927 15th St., NW, 12th Floor
Washington, DC 20005
1-202-371-2830, FAX 1-202-371-0424

Local nonprofit arts agencies nationwide are the organizations that determine the cultural life of the community, providing some of the funding and other assistance for arts organizations in the region. NALAA is the national organization for about 3,800 local arts agencies. Of that total, 1,000 have professional staff and volunteers, with the remaining 2,800 agencies run completely by volunteers. Contact NALAA for the location of the nearest local arts agency.

## National Trust for Historic Preservation

1785 Massachusetts Ave., NW
Washington, DC 20036
1-202-673-4000
Contact: Office of Human Resources and Volunteer Services

The National Trust was chartered by Congress in 1949. Its mission is to foster an appreciation of the diverse character and meaning of American cultural heritage and to preserve and revitalize the livability of our communities by leading the nation in saving America's historic environments. At present about 4,000 volunteers work for the National Trust, primarily at seventeen house museums located in sites throughout the nation. Their responsibilities include guiding tours, supporting special events, lecturing, publicity, marketing, fund-raising, craft production, education, curatorial support, and other necessary functions. For more information, write to the Office of Human Resources and Volunteer Services and ask for a copy of "Museum Property Volunteers," which clearly explains the opportunities, benefits, privileges, and responsibilities of volunteers.

## Smithsonian Institution

1000 Jefferson Dr., SW
Washington, DC 20560
1-202-357-2700 (daily), TDD 1-202-357-1729
Contact: Smithsonian Information

The Smithsonian, queen of institutions, is the world's largest museum complex, with fifteen museums, most of them in the District of Columbia. Smithsonian volunteer programs are extensive and use the skills and energy of over 5,000 people every year.

- Docent programs are operated through each museum. Volunteer docents provide group learning experiences in the form of museum tours. There are tours for schoolchildren, general "highlight" tours of popular and significant museum exhibits, and special-interest tours, which provide an in-depth look at a particular collection or exhibit. Some docent programs have outreach components that visit schools, nursing homes, and other organizations.
- For Smithsonian information programs, volunteers learn how to respond to visitors' questions about the Institution, its exhibitions, activities, services, and programs at both museum visitor information desks and in the central telephone office.
- Behind-the-Scenes volunteers assist Smithsonian staff in their ongoing work. Projects include the full spectrum of Institution operations, from administrative activities to science technology, social and cultural history assignments, library, aviation, and archival projects, and translation assistance. Volunteers do work as varied as piecing together ancient pottery, reorganizing a million pinned mosquitos, researching the original architectural drawings for the Smithsonian museums, cataloguing posters in different fields, cataloguing thousands of photographs that relate to American culture, answering museum mail, transcribing oral history tapes of famous Americans, and foreign language translation of written material.
- Special support programs using volunteer assistance are available at the National Museum of Natural History, the National Zoological Park, and the Smithsonian Resident Associate Program.
- Seasonal programs, one for summer opportunities for students sixteen and older, the other the annual Festival of American Folklife, use hundreds of volunteers every year.

For information about volunteer opportunities, contact the Smithsonian and request the booklet "Opportunities for Volunteer Service."

## PORTRAIT OF A SPECIAL VOLUNTEER

*I'm happy to say that Renata Rutledge is my aunt. She came to the United States from Austria in 1939, a refugee from Nazi-occupied Europe. Her father's Italian citizenship helped in allowing her family to leave. Once here, however, that Italian passport simply meant the family were enemy aliens during wartime. Enter Renata, teen volunteer:*

I wanted to contribute to the war effort, but it was very hard for an "enemy alien" like me to get permission to volunteer, even though my father worked for the U.S. government at Voice of America. First I tried to volunteer as a nurse's aide, but they wouldn't have me—possibly they thought I'd sabotage the X-ray machines. Finally I saw an article, "Farm for Freedom," in *The New York Times* about how the manpower shortage was affecting farmers who needed summer volunteers to weed and harvest crops. So, with a group of girls from Chapin and Brierly, I spent two summers working on farms in upstate New York.

After I graduated from Parsons I got a job in Waterbury, Connecticut, and at the same time I worked at a local hospital as a nurse's aide for a year, mostly reading to children. Then I moved back to New York City and volunteered at the Metropolitan Museum Costume Institute, doing costume repairs. And after I married and had my daughter, I just did a little political work.

Then there was the divorce, and I married Ed [author's uncle] and we moved to Croton. Because all the kids were in school, I became president of the PTA and really raised a lot of money —enough to have the Metropolitan Opera Guild perform at Croton High School. About 1960–61 I taught a kids' art class at home for a year because budget cuts had forced the school to go on half-sessions. Then when Headstart began, I taught another kids' art class once a week in Ossining.

Sometime in 1963 or 1964, I was one of a group in Croton who organized a Shakespeare Festival, which in fact ran for about twenty-five years. Being a fashion designer, I designed costumes for some of the productions—*The Tempest, A Winter's Tale*—and worked at the festival until [our] kids got out of school around 1968. At the same time, around 1965, I took a course in draft counseling from the Society of Friends, and I became a counselor for about a year and a half, working with an organization of lawyers against the war, going to draft board hearings with the young men who were about to be drafted.

About two years after that, I got involved in teaching arts and crafts once a week at the Westchester penitentiary in Valhalla. The program had so few supplies that I had to persuade my neighbors who worked in advertising to contribute things that their agencies were throwing out—paper, boards, pencils, leftover paint, brushes, things like that. I also brought in fruit, doughnuts, and other foods—to draw and then eat. Finally there was a big exhibit in Albany of art from all the prisons. I still have two of the paintings they gave me: a self-portrait of a prisoner in his cell—he was my prize pupil—and a portrait of a prisoner's girlfriend.

In 1966 and 1967 I was in charge of fund-raising for CRIA [Committee to Rescue Italian Art, which was formed after the 1966 floods in Florence] in northern Westchester County.

Sometime in 1974 I met a counselor for the Senior Citizens Club of Chinatown, and when I found that the residents never got out of the city, I thought it might be a nice thing for the Croton senior citizens club to invite them up here. They agreed, and through publicity and word of mouth,

*continued*

*continued*
we got the Lions Club to pay for a bus to and from New York City. The Chinatown club came up in the middle of July; it was a gorgeous day, and we had persuaded Cortlandt Manor House [a local landmark] to invite everyone to the grounds. It was a huge success; there was a story in *The New York Times,* and I had hopes that we could start a movement something like the Fresh Air Fund, but for seniors. We had one more picnic the next year, and the people from Chinatown brought Chinese food for everyone and then entertained their hosts with tai chi and Chinese music. Then Ed and I moved to Washington, and the idea fizzled.

In Washington I became an almost full-time volunteer for the Smithsonian and the Institute for Museum Services [IMS]. I'd already taken a course in bookbinding and repair, and for a while I worked in the rare book laboratory at the Smithsonian, mostly cleaning the books—oiling and cleaning the leather bindings in the Dibner Library of Science and Technology, many of them incunabula [books printed before 1501].

After two years I decided to use my language skills, and I did all the foreign correspondence for the museum reference center—part of the Smithsonian. Finally, between volunteer stints, the Smithsonian offered me a few paying jobs working for the Smithsonian Traveling Exhibition Service.

And in the late seventies, I did a lot of research and became an instant expert on museum security for IMS. IMS sent me to speak at various conferences on security—as a volunteer—and eventually I wrote the first chapter of a book called *Museum and Library Security,* for which they did pay me.

Since the eighties, I've done more work for the Smithsonian. I wrote an article about volunteering in European museums (it's nonexistent) for *The Torch* [Smithsonian's publication for volunteers]. In 1984–85 Smithsonian Libraries asked me to represent them, on a volunteer basis, as editor of English terms for an international dictionary for museums called *Dictionarium Museologicum,* with about 2,500 terms in twenty languages. With a team of German, French, and Italian museum experts, we supplied English terms for the book and suggested others that weren't in it already—for instance, terms connected with volunteers, like *docent.* Once a year I went to a one-week editorial session in Hungary, attended by other museum people from twenty different countries, most of them from what was then the Eastern bloc. I was the only American, and they treated me with some hostility. But there were fascinating arguments about the terms and exactly what they meant. When the book came out, it did well in Europe, but not here.

Fairly recently at the Smithsonian, I edited and retranslated from the French three volumes of the history of zoos—a marvelous book, but no takers. I also suggested that Smithsonian publications produce a public service booklet of guidelines on book collecting and conservation, with a bibliography. Ellen Wells and I wrote it with John Hyltoft, and the third edition is now available on request at Smithsonian Libraries.

The Smithsonian has a fantastic volunteer staff: scholars, people of extraordinary skills, especially the older ones, many of them as knowledgeable as some of the staff. There's a volunteer computer group, artists, biologists. One of their book lab volunteers trained at the best bookbinding schools in France.

Now that we're back in Croton, I've become a member of the committee for exhibitions at the library gallery, and the first thing we did was a Mozart Bicentennial exhibit, which was taken by the Croton school system and is now circulating in the schools. I'll see what else comes along. There's always lots to be done.

## FEATURED ORGANIZATION: MUSEUM OF SCIENCE, BOSTON (MOS)

Science Park
Boston, MA 02114-1099
1-617-589-0380
Contact: Office of Volunteer Services

MOS uses more than 800 volunteers ranging in age from as young as fourteen to well into senior citizen-hood in a wide range of programs. Here are some of the jobs they do:

- Explain computers to visitors in the Computer Discovery Space.
- Help young children and their families learn hands-on science.
- Interpret science exhibits to visitors.
- Lead informal guided tours of the museum for groups of inner-city children.
- Work with visitors in the Human Body Discovery Space.
- Answer visitors' questions at the Information Desk.
- Become library aides.
- Catalog museum collections with the staff.
- Assist in the Live Animal Center.
- Help out as Birthday Party Partners for kids aged five to ten.
- And there's a lot more!

MOS uses the American Association for the Advancement of Science (AAAS) Science-By-Mail program (page 96), which pairs four- to nine-year-old children with volunteer scientists to solve science challenges presented by the museum. The scientist pen pals can work from home, but sometimes come to the museum to work with children's groups. For more information about all the museum volunteer opportunities, contact the Office of Volunteer Services.

# Quilting

Quilting is an art that can be pursued individually and/or collectively, and it engages the energy and talents of thousands of men and women nationwide. There are about 3,000 state and local quilt guilds, and regional quilt collaboratives as well. Some guilds work in cooperation with state quilt heritage projects, which document and exhibit the quilts of a particular state; once the research and exhibitions have been completed, some of the projects continue to be active in expanding the audience for quilts and in offering workshops and seminars for quilters of all skill levels. For instance, the Kentucky State Heritage Quilt Guild, which began in 1981 and became a model for other states, continues to exhibit new and historic quilts. Contact your local state arts council to find out more about your state's heritage quilt guild.

Other quilt guild members work together for the benefit of local community agencies and for national charities as well. They donate quilts to be used in police cars or in a nearby Ronald McDonald House (RMH, page 74), they raffle off quilts for the benefit of a local hospital or nursing home, and they work for projects such as ABC

Quilts (opposite). In small communities, an easy way to find the nearest quilt guild is to ask at a local store where fabrics are sold.

### The NAMES Project AIDS Memorial Quilt

2362 Market St.
San Francisco, CA 94114
1-914-863-5511
Workshop: 1-914-863-1966

The NAMES Project, an international Quilt memorial for those who have died of AIDS, is meant as a positive, creative symbol of remembrance and hope. The Quilt began in San Francisco in 1987; today over 15,000 Quilt panels, each measuring 3 by 6 feet, have been hand sewn, displayed, and seen by more than 2 million visitors in many countries overseas and in all fifty states. Panels are made in homes and workshops all over the world by friends, family, and lovers of those remembered, then sent to San Francisco where they are stitched together in blocks of eight and organized for showings. Donations collected at every display are disbursed to hundreds of AIDS service organizations nationwide. The NAMES Project is operated almost entirely by volunteers. Here's some of the work you can do: make a Quilt panel, host a Quilt display, hold a quilting bee, assist with the ongoing display and preservation of the Quilt. There are thirty-two U.S. NAMES Project chapters across the country. Contact the office for information. If you're interested in starting a new chapter, call the chapter coordinator at the same number.

### The Vermont Quilt Festival (VQF)

Box 349
Northfield, VT 05663
1-802-485-7092
Contact: Volunteer Coordinator

VQF is an annual three-day event that takes place in mid-July and is attended by visitors from all over the United States and other countries as well. The festival includes showings of historic New England quilts, a judged exhibit of over 160 new quilts, classes, lectures, workshops, suppliers' exhibits, and evaluations of quilts made before 1960. What started in 1977 as a one-day show attended by about 700 people now draws up to 8,000 visitors a year.

VQF is volunteer-run: Ten board members serve 200 or more hours over the course of a year working on the contest and workshop committees, providing publicity, and doing promotion and paperwork. Up to 450 people volunteer from one to twenty hours during the actual festival and the days leading up to it. The whole town of Northfield works to make the event a success, including Norwich University, where much of the festival is held and whose dorms are used as accommodations for visitors. Many volunteers are local; others are festival visitors from as far away as Brazil who either just want to help out or want to receive priority credit toward festival classes or lectures the following year. Individuals or groups that wish to volunteer for VQF can contact the volunteer coordinator.

## The Performing Arts

There are thousands of performing arts organizations throughout the United States, and almost all of them offer opportunities for volunteers. Depending on the performing company, and on your own experience, talents, and commitment, there is always something to do.

For purposes of volunteering, there are two types of theaters: community theaters and professional theaters. Community theaters are entirely volunteer, with the occasional exception of a hired director or designer. The actors, crew, set designers and builders, costumers, and lighting

## FEATURED ORGANIZATION: ABC QUILTS (ABCQ)

P.O. Box 107
Weatherford, OK 73096
1-405-772-2229
Contact: Susan Lucky, Executive Director

Ellen Ahlgren of Northwood, New Hampshire, had already been a teacher, a mother, and a certified grief counselor, working with hospice and cancer patients. Ahlgren is also a quilter, and one day as she was finishing her twentieth quilt for her family, she wondered about who would receive the next one. Then she read about the plight of AIDS babies living in hospitals, and she thought: Why not make quilts for these children? That's how ABCQ was born. From a small group of people in New Hampshire, ABCQ has become an international network of quilters and other volunteers, and by now it has collected and distributed over 35,000 handmade quilts as gifts to at-risk small children who are born with the HIV/AIDS virus or addicted to drugs, or who are orphaned or abandoned and living in hospitals and called "boarder babies." The message put on every quilt is "Love and comfort to you," then each quilt maker signs his or her first name and state.

Publicity, including local newspaper stories, an article in *Newsweek*, an appearance on *Good Morning America*, items in *Quilter's Newsletter, Modern Maturity*, and many other publications plus word of mouth and the ABCQ flier have been the means of finding volunteers. Individual quilters, quilting guilds, and schools and youth organizations, churches, extension groups, and 4-H have picked up the project. Ahlgren says that children working on the quilts ask many questions about how a baby could get AIDS, and as they learn, they become even more interested in the work. One year she and her husband visited a junior high school in Vermont where the seventh- and eighth-grade classes had made several beautiful, creative quilts. Teams of students designed quilts on graph paper, enlarged the designs, transferred them, and figured out how to fit the pieces together. Kids who weren't actually working on quilts went to the library and wrote reports on AIDS. Then quilters and researchers met and exchanged information with other seventh- and eighth-grade classes. This same school has now made ABCQ one of its yearly projects. According to Ahlgren, boys in the fifth and sixth grades are more interested in the process than girls because they love the mechanics of working on a sewing machine.

By now ABCQ has eleven Zone Coordinators and about 200 Area and Co-area Coordinators in forty-eight states. ABCQ also works with a network of children's hospitals, foster care agencies, homes where children are HIV positive, and day-care facilities for children with HIV, by filling the quilt needs of one facility completely and then moving on to the next one. Since each child takes home his or her own quilt, the quilts are open-ended gifts, and hospitals can call for more if they're needed. For information about getting started, get in touch with Susan Lucky, who will refer you to your local coordinator.

people, to say nothing of ushers, ticket sellers, fund-raisers, and people who furnish promotional artwork and press releases, are all volunteers. Such groups are often membership clubs, with dues and regular meetings, and they are as much social as they are cultural. Community theater group members are generally expected to work backstage as well as onstage, and some even require members to work on a crew in order to be eligible for auditions.

Volunteering at a professional theater depends to some extent on the commitment you're willing to make. Most volunteers work as ushers; others do fund-raising or put on special events. Major events sometimes require eight or nine months to plan and carry through, and the best volunteers for such work are members of the community who know which businesses and people will contribute money, goods in kind, and time. If you really have a strong artistic bent and are serious about wanting to learn scene painting or to sew costumes or to work at some other crew function, there is often work to be found at nonprofit theaters. But that kind of work involves intense schedules that must be rigorously adhered to, since plays are put on very quickly and volunteers generally must commit their time for at least one entire production.

Contact your state arts council to find out about performing arts projects in the state or read local newspapers, posters, and fliers. If you are a student, ask your drama department to advise you.

## Friends of A.C.T. (FRIENDS)

450 Geary St.
San Francisco, CA 94102
Friends: 1-415-749-2301
A.C.T.: 1-415-771-2200
Contact: Volunteer Coordinator

Friends of A.C.T. is the volunteer organization affiliated with the American Conservatory Theatre, a repertory theater founded in 1964 that offers contemporary and classic works. Members of Friends work behind the scenes in a variety of activities that help in many phases of A.C.T.'s operation. Among other functions, volunteers organize and host events; serve as ushers; run the library; assist in educational outreach to Bay Area schools; work in the office; help in play reading, and assisting at rehearsals. For information about becoming a Friend of A.C.T., get in touch with the volunteer coordinator.

A.C.T. itself offers full-time internships in stage managing, design, props, sound, lighting, costume crew, and management. Call or write to A.C.T. for information.

Hospital Audiences, Inc. (HAI, page 127)

## Playhouse on the Square

51 S. Cooper
Memphis, TN 38104
1-901-725-0776
Contact: Executive Director

The Playhouse, the only professional theater in Memphis, is a nonprofit company that describes itself as "dedicated to ensemble company work for resident company and interns." From August through the following June, the Playhouse, which has two stages, puts on about seventeen productions including contemporary and classic plays, musicals, and children's theater. Internships—ten to twelve a year—are available in acting, technical crew, and costuming and are split into two sessions: fall/winter and winter/spring. For information, contact the executive director.

## The Volunteer Council of the American Symphony Orchestra League

777 14th St., NW, Suite 500
Washington, DC 20005
1-202-628-0099, FAX 1-202-783-7228
Contact: Director of Volunteer Services

The League is a national service and education organization for all of North America's symphony orchestras, providing technical consultation and information about orchestra management, volunteer fundraising and leadership, and community outreach.

The Volunteer Council was founded to guide the League's development of programs for orchestra volunteers, whose expertise and leadership strengthen and improve symphony orchestras of any size. The Council's direct services to orchestra volunteers include sessions specifically for volunteers at the League's annual national conference, one-day seminars for volunteers to strengthen their skills, a quarterly newsletter, "Recorder," the Volunteer Consulting Program, a national arts advocacy network for orchestra volunteers, and *The Gold Book* (page 59).

Nationwide, there are close to 500 symphony orchestra volunteer associations, whose many services include organizing special fund-raising events and creating education programs, like bringing children to concerts or taking the musicians to the kids in school. Other volunteers do office work, help with visiting-artist hospitality and transportation, and feed musicians at rehearsals for guest artists. For instance, when there is a heavy concert schedule and many regular rehearsals for the New York Philharmonic, their volunteer association organizes rehearsal potluck meals, with volunteers from a special committee to feed musicians, bringing what amounts to covered-dish dinners. If you are interested in becoming an orchestra volunteer, contact the League's director of volunteer services, who can direct you to the orchestra nearest you.

**FEATURED PUBLICATION**

The Volunteer Council's annual *Gold Book* is a directory of over 900 successful volunteer projects from the preceding year—galas like San Francisco's Black and White Ball (a black-tie block party attended by 15,000 people), more modest dinner/dances, decorators' show houses, picnics, auto shows, auctions, cooking demonstrations, special concerts, education programs that include poster contests, concert previews, concerts for children, and various scholarships, and lots of other programs designed to enrich the local community through contact with its orchestra. *The Gold Book* is distributed free to each league member volunteer association as a source of ideas for effective programming and for revitalizing current projects. However, the book is also a gold mine of creative projects, especially for fund-raising, that can be adapted to different kinds of cultural and even noncultural organizations. For a copy, send $41 to the League's director of volunteer services.

# Other Organizations

## American Institute of Architects (AIA)

1735 New York Ave., NW
Washington, DC 20006
1-202-626-7300
Contact: Sheri Daniel, AIA, ext. 7360;
Charles Zucker (CAI), ext. 7532

AIA is the national organization for professional architects, with about 300 local and state chapters across the country and 55,000 members. AIA has several national programs that require the pro bono services of its members.

- Regional/Urban Design Assistance Teams (R/UDAT) is a service launched to help communities requesting assistance with urban design issues such as land use, growth management, traffic, and urban decay, among others. R/UDAT multidisciplinary teams consist of six to eight professionals who are tops in their fields. To date, R/UDAT has used volunteers from twenty-three disciplines: architects, urban planners, landscape architects, sociologists, preservationists, economists, political scientists, lawyers, and many others. Each team is formed to meet the specific needs of the project, and members must commit to spending two or three months on it (although not full-time). No one on the team can have any ties to or stake in the community. The team is assisted by local architects and architecture students. Local team members are also volunteers: elected officials, business people, providers of various social services, other special-interest groups, and ordinary citizens. After the local team completes an extensive months-long preparation, the R/UDAT team makes a four-day visit to the community, reviews and evaluates the materials, listens to the community voices, and, after what has been described as a brainstorming blitz, prepares a report that is delivered at a community meeting. R/UDAT teams are recruited through professional networking and a data base of people who have served on earlier teams. For more information, get in touch with the Director of Regional and Urban Design, and ask for "The R/UDAT Handbook: A Step-by-Step Guide to the R/UDAT Process."

- Community Assistance Initiative (CAI) is a national extension of R/UDAT, a program to apply the process to specific housing problems using the same techniques. For information, contact the Director of CAI.
- Disaster Response is a national leadership training program, which prepares architects to participate in community evaluation, planning, and execution of projects to renovate or rebuild after a disaster has occurred. AIA members interested in disaster response can get in touch with their local chapters.

## American Library Association (ALA)

50 E. Huron St.
Chicago, IL 60611
1-312-944-6780, FAX 1-312-440-9374
1-800-545-2433

ALA is the oldest and largest library association in the world, with 50,000 members representing all kinds of libraries. Its programs relate to every type of activity related to libraries: legislation, intellectual freedom, publishing, accreditation, library outreach, personnel, and more. More than 5,000 of its members work as volunteers on the ALA's boards and committees. Almost all libraries—public, private, and school—use volunteers in a broad range of positions: clerical, fund-raising, and many other functions. Call your local library to find out what volunteer work is available. If your interests are focused rather than general, ask the head librarian for a list of libraries in the fields you want to work in.

## Archaeological Institute of America (AIA)

675 Commonwealth Ave.
Boston, MA 02215-1401
1-617-353-9361, FAX 1-617-353-6550

AIA is the oldest archaeological organization in North America, with eighty-eight local U.S. chapters and 11,000 members from the scholarly community and the interested general public as well. AIA offers members information about latest finds, lectures, field trips, and archaeological tours led by prominent scholars. AIA publishes *Archaeology*, a richly illustrated bimonthly magazine written by professionals for the general public. In two issues each year, the magazine offers travel guides with listings of archaeological excavation sites where volunteers (who must pay their own travel and living expenses) can come to volunteer for a week or longer. Descriptions of each site and its history are colorful and evocative. "Travel Guide to the Old World" appears in the March/April issue, and "Travel Guide to the

New World" is in the May/June issue. A one-year subscription to *Archaeology* costs $20. AIA also publishes the yearly *Archaeological Fieldwork Opportunities Bulletin* ($10.50 for members, $12.50 for nonmembers plus shipping), with straightforward entries for ongoing excavations, listing the positions open, costs, dates, deadlines for application, and other pertinent information, including bibliographies for some of the sites. For information about AIA or to get a publications catalog, call or write to the Boston headquarters.

### Shooting Back Education and Media Center (SBEMC)

1901 18th St., NW
Washington, DC 20009
1-202-232-5169
Contact: Program Coordinator

*or*

1517 E. Franklin
Minneapolis, MN 55404
612-871-8772
Contact: Program Coordinator

SBEMC was founded in 1989 by photojournalist Jim Hubbard to provide weekly photography workshops for homeless and at-risk children living in the Washington, DC, and Minneapolis metropolitan areas. The workshops, which are given on-site at shelters, youth centers, and schools have expanded to include writing and other media. They offer young people an alternative to the drugs, crime, and violence of their surroundings and give them a chance to learn a medium of self-expression, build self-esteem and develop a sense of accomplishment. Volunteer photographers, writers, and artists, work regularly with the young people and may act as mentors to those who show a strong interest in the medium. An exhibit of 150 works from the project has become a touring show. Plans are under way for increasing the number of sites in which the program is given and for bringing Shooting Back into the public schools. For information about volunteering, contact the program coordinator.

### Smithsonian Research Expeditions (SRE)

490 L'Enfant Plaza, SW, Suite 4210
Washington, DC 20560
1-202-287-3210, FAX 1-202-287-3244
Contact: Charlene James-Duguid, Program Director

SRE offers volunteers, who pay their own expenses and make a contribution to the expedition, the opportunity to work alongside Smithsonian scientists and curators and personally experience what it's like to do hands-on research. The expeditions, which last from one to two weeks, fall into three kinds of projects: environment/natural history, social science/art, and working inside a museum. Projects are extremely diverse, ranging from the study of an active volcano in Costa Rica to observation of the annual Native American Crow Fair in Billings, Montana, to researching the activities of desert tortoises in the Mohave Desert. Each year over 200 volunteers participate in SRE. For more information, ask SRE to send a free expeditions catalog, which describes the purpose and setting for each project and explains volunteers' responsibilities and costs.

## Resources

*A Directory of Museum Volunteer Programs,* edited by Marian Nielsen. Washington, D.C.: American Association for Museum Volunteers (AAMV, page 50), 1988. This book is the result of a nationwide survey of more than 700 museums with volunteer programs. Although it by no means lists all the museusms or cultural centers in the United States, the book does contain information about volunteer programs in some of the most interesting cultural institutions in the country. Among the categories covered: anthropology; art; botanical gardens and arboretums; children's museums; historical museums and historic houses; industrial and transportation museums; living history, maritime, and natural history museums; science centers; and zoos and aquariums. Some of the institutions are very large and use hundreds and even thousands of volunteers; others are considerably smaller and use fewer than 100. Volunteers function as docents (by far the largest group), office and administrative workers, curatorial assistants, and museum shop assistants, and assist in fund-raising, research, maintaining collections, and animal care. It is unlikely that you will find this book at your local bookseller's; however, it's worth checking with a nearby university library to see if they have it. Otherwise, order the book through the American Association of Museums catalog (AAM, page 51). $11.50 (members), $12.50 (nonmembers).

*The Good Guide: A Sourcebook for Interpreters, Docents, and Tour Guides,* by Alison L. Grinder and E. Sue McCoy. Scottsdale, AZ: Ironwood Publishing, 1985. This book is a practical resource for tour guides and others who instruct the public in various museums and for environmental organizations. Some of the topics discussed are the different kinds of visitors and special groups, how to impart learning to groups on tours, various means of interpreting collections, and other information important for guides. The book can be ordered from American Association of Museums (AAM, page 51).

## THE PERFORMING ARTS

*The Gold Book,* an annual publication of the Volunteer Council of the American Symphony Orchestra League (ASOL). (See box, page 59.)

*Regional Theatre Directory,* compiled and edited by Jill Charles. Dorset, VT: Theatre Directories, annual. The *Directory* is a national guide to employment in regional and dinner theaters for Equity and non-Equity performers as well as designers, technicians, and management. Internship opportunities for students are also included. Although intended for professionals in the performing arts, this guide offers specific information on hiring and casting procedures at over 400 theaters nationwide, including information on internship opportunities for students and young professionals. Internships are available at theaters as varied as Mabou Mines in New York and A.D. Players in Houston, Texas. Five appendixes, an index of companies, and another of "specialty" companies make the book even more useful. Two companies listed in the directory, Friends of A.C.T. and Playhouse on the Square, are described on page 58.

*Summer Theatre Directory,* compiled and edited by Jill Charles. Dorset, VT: Theatre Directories, annual. For theater professionals and students seeking summer employment, this directory provides vital statistics on 385 summer theaters, Shakespeare festivals, theme parks, and outdoor dramas in the United States and Canada, with a full profile of each company, including opportunities for interns and apprenticeships.

Look for this and the preceding directory in theater and drama bookstores, in public libraries, or in the libraries of colleges and universities with strong drama departments. The books can also be ordered through trade bookstores, or write to Theatre Directories, P.O. Box 519, Dorset, VT 05251.

# Volunteers for Business and Corporate Volunteerism

## Volunteers for Business and Nonprofit Organizations

Individuals with business and administrative experience have invaluable skills to offer newly formed or struggling businesses and nonprofit groups in their communities. Organizations like Service Corps of Retired Executives (SCORE, page 65) and American Woman's Economic Development Corporation (AWED, page 64) are especially useful to inexperienced entrepreneurs, while National Executive Service Corps (NESC, page 65) provides services only to nonprofit agencies. But if you don't necessarily want to join a group, ask a volunteer action center, (VAC) (see National Volunteer Center, NVC, page 37) or the local United Way (UWA, page 38) which nonprofits can use your talents. Because of their expertise in management, business volunteers are usually welcome as board members of charitable organizations. As they do at Bentley College (page 220), business school students can set up projects to help social service groups and shelters that need help organizing and running an organization.

### Accountants for the Public Interest (API)

1012 14th St., NW, Suite 906
Washington, DC 20005
1-202-347-1668, FAX 1-202-347-1663

API is the only national nonprofit accounting organization solely dedicated to encouraging accountants to volunteer their time and expertise to help nonprofit groups, small businesses, and individuals who cannot afford those services. Nineteen local API affiliates recruit volunteer accountants, screen requests for help, and match the two. Beneficiaries of these services range from other *pro bono publico* organizations to people who are taught to be self-sufficient in day-to-day financial affairs to cultural groups. API volunteer accountants receive a manual on nonprofit accounting and an API directory listing more than 260 volunteer accounting programs state by state nationwide. For information, contact the national headquarters in Washington.

## American Woman's Economic Development Corporation (AWED)

641 Lexington Ave., 9th Floor
New York, NY 10022
1-800-222-AWED (1-800-222-2933)
New York Office: 1-212-688-1900,
FAX 1-212-688-2718

AWED is a membership organization helping women entrepreneurs achieve their business goals. AWED programs include in-house, one-to-one business counseling services, which are set up by appointment, and training programs designed for entrepreneurs at different stages in their business careers. Counselors and trainers are experienced business persons who volunteer to provide practical information about organizing and operating all levels of business, from how to structure a business to marketing strategies for increased sales and profits to developing a business plan to managing personnel—whatever it takes to help these women succeed. Most volunteers own their own businesses or are professionals who service entrepreneurs. Often, a woman who has been trained by AWED will return to become a volunteer counselor or trainer herself. Most volunteers are recruited through word of mouth. AWED is located in three cities: the national headquarters in New York and offices in Los Angeles and Washington, DC. Call the 800 number for information about volunteering.

## Arts and Business Council, Inc.

Business Volunteers for the Arts/USA (BVA)
25 W. 45th St., Suite 707
New York, NY 10036
1-212-819-9361
Contact: Martin Cominsky, Director, BVA/USA

The BVA program operates in 30 cities primarily to recruit, and train, and place business executives to be management consultants on a *pro bono publico* basis with nonprofit arts organizations. BVA offers consultation in such areas as marketing and communications, financial management, fund-raising, personnel administration, and planning. Volunteers are required to attend an orientation before they are matched with organizations. Other components of BVA involve special events task forces and the development of Business Advisory Committees.

"A Businessperson's Guide to Volunteering in the Arts" enumerates the myriad functions performed by volunteers for different arts groups and lists other national organizations. Contact the BVA/USA director if you are interested in becoming a BVA volunteer, in establishing an affiliate in your community, or in receiving copies of the "Businessperson's Guide."

**Bentley College, Bentley Service Learning Project (BSLP, page 220)**

**Citizens Democracy Corps (CDC, page 186)**

**Constitutional Rights Foundation (CRF, page 152)**

**Council of Better Business Bureaus (CBBB, page 158)**

## International Executive Service Corps (IESC)

8 Stamford Forum, P.O. Box 10005
Stamford, CT 06904-2005
1-203-967-6000
Contact: Vice President, Recruiting

The IESC was founded as a private, nonprofit organization in 1965 to help introduce modern business practices and to develop private enterprise in developing nations and emerging democracies. Since then, IESC volunteer advisers have been sent to over ninety nations to work as consultants on more than 13,000 projects ranging from a poultry breeding and hatchery farm in Indonesia to a lingerie factory in Costa Rica to a glass manufacturer in the Philippines. Enterprises of almost every size and description are assisted, from small private businesses to companies employing several thousand, and each pays a small fee. Volunteers are recruited from the ranks of retired U.S. executives and technical advisers, then matched with overseas clients who need specific assistance. For information about becoming an IESC volunteer, get in touch with the vice president for recruiting.

**Junior Achievement, Inc. (JA, page 164)**

**Kiwanis International (KI, page 151)**

### National Executive Service Corps (NESC)

257 Park Ave. S.
New York, NY 10010
1-212-529-6660
Contact: Vice President, Human Resources

NESC, which follows the same overall concept as International Executive Services Corps (IESC, page 64), provides management counseling assistance to other domestic nonprofit organizations by using retired men and women with substantial corporate and professional experience as volunteer counselors. NESC consults in a variety of problem areas facing nonprofit agencies in the fields of social services, education, the arts, religion, and health care. NESC has also developed educational programs for schools, bringing retired executives into classrooms, some as volunteers or to be certified as teachers, others to be management consultants or executive mentors. NESC, which operates in the metropolitan New York area, Connecticut, and northern New Jersey, serves clients as diverse as Actor's Fund of America, Federation of Protestant Welfare Agencies, Brooklyn Technical High School, The Chamber Music Society of Lincoln Center, and Drugs Don't Work. NESC has affiliates in twenty-three states and Washington, DC. For more information, contact the vice president for human resources.

### Service Corps of Retired Executives Association (SCORE®)

409 Third St., SW, Suite 5900
Washington, DC 20024-3212
1-202-205-6762
Contact: Mark Sewell, Director of Communications

SCORE, which is partially funded by the U.S. Small Business Administration, is dedicated to helping small businesses in the United States prosper. Since it was founded in 1964, SCORE has offered free counseling and training to over 2.5 million people. A dedicated corps of 13,000 executive and professional volunteers—some retired, some still at work—serve as counselors, workshop organizers and instructors, publicity persons, speakers, and administrators. SCORE operates at 380 chapter locations and 380 branch locations and recruits volunteers at the local level, often through networking. If you are interested in becoming a SCORE volunteer, call the communications director.

## Corporate Volunteerism and For-Profit Organizations

Corporationwide volunteerism is becoming more widespread, encouraged by conscientious business policymakers, many of whom serve as board members of nonprofit organizations, and by company employees and ex-employees who are eager to serve the community. Corporate volunteerism takes a number of forms, depending on the means and convictions of the company. Nonprofits like National Volunteer Center (NVC, page 37),

## FEATURED ORGANIZATION: CORPORATE ANGEL NETWORK (CAN)

Westchester County Airport, Bldg. One
White Plains, NY 10604
1-914-328-1313
Contact: Jay Weinberg or Pat Blum

Corporate Angel Network, also known as, CAN, is the brainchild of Jay Weinberg and his friend, Pat Blum. These two recovered cancer patients came up with a way to transport ambulatory cancer patients to or from cancer treatment centers around the country. CAN patients use the empty seats on corporate aircraft that are headed in the right direction on the right date. Because the jets are on scheduled business flights, there is no cost to either the patient or the corporation. Weinberg and Blum arranged their first CAN in late 1981. Since then, they have flown more than 4,500 flights through the cooperation and generosity of over 500 participating corporations. There are now about 7,500 flights a year in and out of every state. In large cities, CAN arranges for ground transportation, if required, and will also line up a complimentary hotel room if needed to take advantage of a CAN flight.

Except for a paid staff of three, CAN is an all-volunteer organization, with fifty volunteers who operate the telephones, computers, and faxes, talk to corporations and patients, and coordinate flights. Volunteers all receive training, and they continue learning on the job. According to Weinberg, CAN volunteers love working with people, love talking, and love getting results in a few days. Weinberg, a volunteer himself, asks volunteers to give a full day (nine in the morning to four in the afternoon) at least one day a week. For information, contact Jay Weinberg or Pat Blum.

United Way of America (UWA, page 38), American Red Cross (ARC, page 129), March of Dimes Birth Defects Foundation (page 128); other environmental, health, education, and social service groups; and organizations that specialize in volunteer management and training all work closely with large and small businesses to establish suitable programs.

### The Body Shop

45 Horsehill Rd.
Cedar Knolls, NJ 07927-2003
1-201-984-9200, FAX 1-201-984-8437
Contact: Communications Office

The Body Shop makes naturally based skin-care and hair products and sells them in over 700 Body Shops worldwide. The company's products reflect its environmental and community concerns: The cosmetics are based on natural ingredients, they are not animal tested, and they are manufactured and packaged as much as possible with recyclable materials. The Body Shop's "Once Is Not Enough" campaign encourages customers to use a refill service and to return empty containers and packaging for recycling.

Because The Body Shop believes that community projects are inseparable from its day-to-day operation, within three months of opening, each affiliate is required to make a one-year commitment to a local community project, and all employees are allowed to work on it four hours a month on company time. The company has created what it calls the "Local Action Workbook," a step-by-step guide for Body Shop managers and projects coordinators to use as they set up community projects. It has practical suggestions about major areas of focus, tells how to set up a community project, and then lists an "A–Z Network for Local Action," with names and addresses of organizations and some of the work that can be done for them. The workbook closes with brief descriptions of some of the ongoing projects run by different affiliates. Here are a few of them: delivering food to homebound AIDS patients, providing an evening shelter for kids aged thirteen to seventeen, working with pet therapy for elderly or disabled people, writing letters for Amnesty International, and teaching inner-city children about animals at a children's zoo. There are presently seventy-eight Body Shops in the United States. For more information, get in touch with the Communications Office.

## Chevron Corp.

Chevron Retirees
1401 Eye St., NW, Suite 1200
Washington, DC 20005
1-202-408-5800
Retirees: 1-800-888-2701

Thousands of Chevron's current and retired employees are actively involved with serving their communities in diverse ways: working for the environment, including habitat restoration; educating, tutoring, and mentoring youth, with a special emphasis on science education in elementary schools; fund-raising for local and national organizations that benefit the community; and working closely with organizations such as Junior Achievement (JA, page 164), The Nature Conservancy (TNC, page 105), American Red Cross (ARC, page 129), and others. During the course of a year, a typical Chevron division works on about fifty local projects and with many organizations, which range from schools to Meals on Wheels (MOW, page 205) to regional theaters, museums, and zoos. If you are working for a Chevron division, contact your officer volunteer coordinator; if you are a retiree, you will know where to find the Chevron division nearest you.

## Esprit

900 Minnesota St.
San Francisco, CA 94107
1-415-648-6900
Contact: Eco Desk

Esprit sells the clothing it designs and manufactures in fifteen stores across the United States and in thirty-two nations worldwide. The Eco Desk is responsible for coordinating the company's employee volunteers—who are called the Esprit Corps (EC)—encouraging them to find creative ways of getting involved to help others, and assisting in the development of ideas. EC promotes long-term continuous volunteer involvement, granting employees up to ten hours paid leave each month to work for the community organization of their choice, provided they donate an equal amount of their own personal time. EC volunteers work on suicide crisis hotlines, counsel homeless youth, organize fund-raising events, deliver meals to homebound AIDS patients, tutor refugees, and much more. Esprit also supports employees' projects with financial and in-kind donations, especially for organizations that involve and educate both the public and Esprit employees. The Eco Desk regularly organizes group volunteer projects that may be completed in one day: On Earth Day, Esprit donates over 3,600 work hours planting trees, cleaning up beaches, and assisting in habitat restoration. Other short-term activities include holiday workshops in schools, renovation of low-income housing, and staff support at fund-raisers. Esprit strongly encourages active deskside recycling in its own offices as well.

## Telephone Pioneers of America (TPA)

930 15th St., Room 1249
Denver, CO 80202
1-303-571-9270
Contact: Sue Saunders, District Manager

With 104 chapters and a membership of over 800,000 active and retired employees of the telecommunications industry in the United States and Canada, TPA is one of the largest industry-related volunteer groups dedicated to serving others. TPA members include active employees with fifteen years of service with sponsor companies, such as AT&T or Pacific Bell, retired Pioneers, Future Pioneers, and Pioneer spouses. TPA members contribute more than 30 million hours annually to their communities and raise more than $10 million annually to fund various projects. Here are a few projects:

- Retrofitting parks and other public areas for disabled access.
- Planting over 1 million trees and seedlings as well as work in cooperation with local schools.
- Habitat restoration for The Nature Conservancy (TNC, page 105).
- A variety of other environmental projects, including helping with recycling, adopting a highway, cleaning hiking trails, planting trees, constructing a new Little League (LL, page 216) baseball field, building raised garden plots for residents in nursing and retiree homes and other sites.
- Projects for the visually impaired, including the repair of "talking books," the invention of "beeping" sports equipment, which allows visually impaired people to participate in nearly every sport. Beep softball teams are sponsored by over fifty-five chapters.
- Work at the Smithsonian Institution (page 52) in the Information Age exhibit at the National Museum of American History, and work at other museums as well.
- Many community activities at the local chapter level, including more than half a million teddy bears (Hug-a-Bears) supplied to police, fire, and rescue squads for children in traumatic situations.

For more information, contact Sue Saunders.

# Working with and for Children

Organizations in almost every category in this book attempt to answer children's needs. And since children have all the needs that adults have, and more, several chapters in addition to this one are devoted almost entirely to serving children: Education (page 95), Student Volunteers (page 219), and Mentoring (page 162). Many community organizations (page 85), especially those concerned with improving family life, have programs that bear directly on children.

Inquire at your local volunteer action center (VAC), (see National Volunteer Center, NVC, page 37), schools, garden clubs, service clubs, social service agencies, churches, and recreation department for programs that provide opportunities to work directly with children or on their behalf.

## Volunteer Host Families and Cultural Exchange Organizations

Each year thousands of foreign exchange students come to the United States to study, improve their English, and experience the country firsthand. Two kinds of volunteers contribute tremendously to the success of these visits: regional or area coordinators and volunteer host families.

It is the coordinator who is instrumental in recruiting and helping evaluate host families, making the matchup between individual student and host family, and orienting them all to their new lives together. Coordinators make transportation arrangments for the students, work closely with the schools, and monitor the progress of the visit, offering assistance whenever necessary. Most organizations pay coordinators a minimal stipend for each student, which ordinarily covers travel costs and other out-of-pocket expenses.

Volunteer host families are the hub of any student foreign exchange program. Host families spend a lot of time with their student visitors, and both are profoundly affected by the experience. Requirements for host families vary with the organization, but a family unit is usually two people living under the same roof: They can be retired or single or families with or without children. Families are very carefully evaluated, and among the qualities coordinators look for are commitment to the program and open-mindedness and flexibility, particularly when dealing with teenagers. Host families are entirely volunteer, and they provide more than just room and board—they welcome the students into their homes and share with them the warmth and intimacy of their family lives.

There are perhaps ten nonprofit organizations that specialize in arranging for foreign high school students to come to study in the United

States and for American students to study abroad. We list five here, beginning with the oldest.

## American Field Service (AFS)

AFS Intercultural Programs
313 E. 43rd St.
New York, NY 10017
1-212-949-4242, FAX 1-212-949-9379
1-800-AFS-INFO (1-800-257-4636)

AFS is a volunteer community-based organization, with 2,000 local U.S. chapters and over 100,000 volunteers worldwide. AFS arranges for over 3,200 foreign high school students to come to the United States to live with host families, study, and participate in community life for a year, a semester, or a summer. AFS performs the same role for American students studying abroad.

Volunteers are trained to recruit and screen student applications and host families. At the local level volunteers are needed to serve as coordinators, host families, fund-raisers, public relations people, and drivers for transporting students to and from the airport. Contact the New York office for the chapter nearest you or call the 800 number.

## American Institute for Foreign Study (AIFS)

Homestay in America, East
25 Bay State Rd.
Boston, MA 02215
1-617-267-0058, 1-617-267-0190
1-800-262-0475

AIFS places about 1,800 foreign teenage students a year with American host families for a minimum of five months. Homestays are usually located in suburban areas close enough to a major metropolitan center for the students to visit. AIFS also has several short-term programs, which last from one week to two months, and programs designed for individuals or groups interested in a particular area of the United States or in a special field of study. For information about becoming a volunteer area coordinator or host family, call the 800 number.

## American Scandinavian Student Exchange (ASSE)

ASSE International Student Exchange Programs
228 N. Coast Hwy.
Laguna Beach, CA 92651
1-714-494-4100, FAX 1-714-497-8704
1-800-333-3802
Contact: Executive Director

ASSE started in Sweden and has expanded to encompass all the European countries and Australia, New Zealand, and Japan. The organization brings high school students, fifteen to eighteen years old, to the United States to live with host families and attend local schools for a full school year. Volunteer area representatives and host families are always needed. Area representatives are reimbursed for expenses for each student, and most of them are involved with four or five students each year, although some place up to ten students. Call the 800 number for information.

## Fresh Air Fund (FAF)

1040 Sixth Ave.
New York, NY 10018
1-800-367-0003, 1-212-221-0900

As it has been doing since 1877, the Fresh Air Fund provides free vacations for underprivileged New York City children:

- The Friendly Town program enables more than 7,200 children to visit the homes of volunteer host families in over 315 rural and suburban communities from Virginia to Maine and Canada. Most of the children, boys and girls from six to sixteen, are black and Hispanic, and many live in single-parent homes. FAF children are enrolled by participating social service organizations. Thousands of volunteers are needed to make the program work: It is supervised by local networks of FAF volunteer committee members who recruit and screen new hosts and renew the commitment of participating families. The program works so well that over 60 percent of the children are invited back by the same families year after year.

- Four FAF summer camps in upstate New York give kids the chance to have free two-week camping experiences. One of the camps is for disabled children. There are also weekend camping programs for homeless children and their families and for the families of physically and emotionally disabled children.
- Career Awareness Camp, attended by twelve- to fifteen-year-old youngsters, is intended to help kids understand how school and work are related and how to make choices that will enhance their career opportunities.

Aside from host families, about 400 volunteers implement all of FAF's camp programs and work in the New York City headquarters as well, where volunteers do fund-raising and publicity work, put on special events, provide outreach to children, and function as general office support. For information, call the 800 number.

### Nacel Cultural Exchanges

3460 Washington Dr. #109
St. Paul, MN 55122
1-800-622-3553
Contact: Rebecca Lueck

Nacel has the largest homestay summer program in the United States, annually placing over 6,900 teenagers from France, Germany, and Spain in American homes for one-month stays and also sending U.S. teenagers overseas. The program has forty-seven paid state coordinators. Local volunteers across each state help locate host families to open their homes and daily lives, and also find families who want to send their own kids abroad. Local volunteers speak about Nacel at community group meetings, service clubs, and churches, give orientation sessions for teenagers and host families, and visit the families from time to time during the youths' stay. For information about the nearest affiliate, call or write to the St. Paul office.

# Children's Clubs

They're fun, they're learning experiences, they challenge the mind and body, they build character, promote self-discipline, and teach the value of being a good neighbor, they inspire community service and compassion, and they train kids to work together for a common goal. Children's clubs cut across all racial, religious, and economic barriers, and they reach out to diverse groups of kids with diverse needs. Many lifelong volunteers get their first community service experience as club members, and they often return to the organizations as volunteer leaders.

A person who volunteers to work with children's club must believe in the ideals of the organization and have the temperament for spending lots of time with groups of children. Volunteer leaders, who have the most contact with the kids, receive intense training that enables them to cope with everything from finding local club sponsors to starting a club to health and safety to planning club programs to understanding something about child development.

**ASPIRA Association, Inc. (page 79)**

## Boy Scouts of America (BSA)

1325 W. Walnut Hill Lane
P.O. Box 152079
Irving, TX 75015-2079
1-214-580-2000

BSA is now over eighty years old and still growing, with over 4.3 million young members aged five to eighteen, and over 1.2 million adult members, who are volunteer Scout leaders. BSA is committed to instill in each Scout the values of self-reliance, integrity, courage, and thriftiness and to inspire its membership to take an active role in protecting the weak, needy, and destitute. Famous for its community public service projects, since 1987 BSA has addressed what it regards as the five "unacceptables"—hunger, illiteracy, drug abuse, child abuse, and teenage unemployment—by mounting an annual national food drive, and providing career counseling, literacy training, and education for both youth members and leaders. Volunteer leaders, either men or women, meet weekly with troop members to help them with rank advancement, choose community service projects, make suggestions for fund-raising, follow through on projects, and, of course, take the Scouts out for camping and field trips. For more information on Scouting in your community, consult the phone book for the Scout troop nearest you.

## Boys & Girls Clubs of America (B&GCA)

771 First Ave.
New York, NY 10017
1-212-351-5900
Contact: Public Relations Director

Boys & Girls Clubs of America is the parent organization for more than 600 local Clubs, with 1,340 facilities nationwide serving more than 1.7 million girls and boys aged six to eighteen. B&GCA's primary mission is to offer children, particularly those from disadvantaged circumstances, opportunities for personal growth and achievement. One national program addresses problems such as drug and alcohol use and premature sexual activity; another provides career counseling and guidance by adult mentors, with field trips, workshops, and aptitude tests. Targeted Outreach helps recruit delinquent or at-risk youth into the Clubs. Keystone Clubs are teen groups within the Clubs that help develop leadership through community service. Still another program involves young people in the visual and performing arts. Volunteers with specific talents are needed to assist professional staff at every Club as tutors, mentors, fund-raisers, and coaches, and to serve in many other functions. Check your local phone book for a listing or call or write to the national headquarters for the location of a Club near you.

## Camp Fire Boys and Girls (CFBG)

4601 Madison Ave.
Kansas City, MO 64112-1278
1-816-756-1950
Contact: Communications Department

CFBG is a national coed youth organization with a current membership of about 600,000 children and 83,000 adult volunteers helping kids from kindergarten through high school develop self-reliance and self-confidence, learn to solve problems, and take personal and social responsibility. Many CFBG programs are initiated at the local level; others are part of the national agenda. CFBG has four basic divisions: self-reliance courses, which include a unique training program for teenagers to provide short-term care for developmentally disabled children; school-age child-care groups, which meet every day after school; a youth leadership program, which trains adolescents for community responsibility and decision making; and finally the Camp Fire Clubs, which have a wide variety of projects and activities. CFBG is looking for volunteers with a broad range of experience and skills, including budget and finance, committee work, facilities maintenance, child development, and public speaking. Check the local phone directory for the council in your area or call or write to the national office for information.

### Girl Scouts of the U.S.A. (GSUSA)

830 Third Ave.
New York, NY 10022
1-212-940-7500

GSUSA is the largest voluntary organization for girls in the world, with more than 2.5 million girl members aged five through seventeen and over 800,000 adult volunteers. GSUSA's mission is to help girls develop to their full potential and grow into competent, resourceful women. To meet the needs of as many young women as possible, the organization has devised innovative ways of reaching out to girls who might otherwise be unable to participate in Scouting. Girl Scouting in the School Day, a supplement to classroom curricula, is offered to girls who cannot participate outside of school. For example, troops have been set up in shelters for the homeless in California, New York, Washington, DC, and Philadelphia, in public housing in Savannah, and for teenage mothers in Bloomington, Illinois. To volunteer for GSUSA, look in your local phone book for the nearest council, or contact the national headquarters in New York City.

### Girls, Inc. (GIRLS)

30 E. 33rd St.
New York, NY 10016
1-212-689-3700, FAX 1-212-683-1253

In 1990 Girls Clubs of America became Girls, Inc. (see Boys and Girls Clubs of America, B&GCA, page 72). With over 200 affiliates nationwide serving over 350,000 girls and young women aged six to eighteen, the organization believes that girls still have needs that are separate and distinct from those of boys. Through its advocacy, research, and programs, Girls, Inc., is dedicated to helping girls from at-risk communities overcome gender barriers and discrimination, enabling them to become successful independent citizens. Its programs include preventing teenage pregnancy, building family communications skills, helping girls learn assertiveness, education and career planning, deterring drug and substance abuse, and teen health. Although many of the programs are staffed by paid professionals, volunteer support is important. Volunteers, all from the affiliates' local communities, serve as board members, work as fund-raisers, provide assistance for the professional staff (some are professionals themselves), donate goods and services, and run various technical projects. Contact the New York office for information about the affiliate nearest you.

**Kiwanis International, (KI) Key Club International, and Circle K International (page 115)**

**Optimist International (page 82)**

## Working with and for Sick Children

Contact the volunteer departments of hospitals in your area to offer your time and skills to children, call the local volunteer action center (VAC) (see National Volunteer Center, NVC, page 37) about other organizations helping sick kids, check service clubs in the area for special programs, and find out about projects sponsored by churches and synagogues.

**ABC Quilts (ABCQ, page 57)**

**Candlelighters Childhood Cancer Foundation (CCCF, page 134)**

## Clara Barton Camp for Girls with Diabetes, Inc. (CBC)

P.O. Box 356, 68 Clara Barton Rd.
North Oxford, MA 01537-0356
1-508-987-2056
Contact: Camp Director

For girls aged six to sixteen who face the daily challenge of living with diabetes, CBC's summer camp program offers a chance to enjoy outdoor activities, learn about their diabetes, and share their feelings with friends. Summer camp begins in mid-June and ends in mid-August, with four two-week sessions and one week of precamp training. The camp itself is run by paid staff, but volunteers are needed for a number of jobs, including those of a volunteer physician or nurse in residence and two or three other professionals—diabetes educators, social workers, registered dieticians, and psychologists. Volunteers also are important for CBC's Family Weekend programs, which are offered during fall, winter, and spring and held in affiliation with the American Diabetes Association (ADA). Weekends are age-specific and offer the families a chance to share the girls' camping experiences. Weekends are planned and run by a volunteer coordinator who is trained and assisted by ADA, and each weekend requires five or more general staff volunteers in addition to the professionals listed above, to assist with games, discussions, meals, and children's activities. These volunteers are usually young adults who either have diabetes or have worked with youth who have diabetes. For information, contact the camp director.

International Child Health Foundation (ICHF, page 128)

## Mail for Tots (MFT)

P.O. Box 8699
Boston, MA 02114
1-617-242-3538
Contact: Edmund G. Burns, President

MFT is a nonprofit organization dedicated to boosting the moral of seriously ill children and adults by asking volunteers to send them cheerful, friendly mail. Newsletters and updated, numbered lists of names and addresses, with descriptions of the patients' medical circumstances, are sent out regularly to donors and nondonors. For information, call or write to MFT, enclosing a stamped, self-addressed envelope.

## Ronald McDonald House (RMH)

500 N. Michigan Ave.,Suite 200
Chicago, IL 60611
1-312-836-7104
Contact: Director of Ronald McDonald House Program

Ronald McDonald Houses offer families of sick children a "home away from home," where they and their children (if they are outpatients) can stay when treatment is given far from home. There are about 150 Ronald McDonald Houses in the United States and Canada, each created by a group of local citizens. The houses are run independently, and each is staffed largely by volunteers whose main objective is to make the families' stay as pleasant as possible, for instance by visiting with the families and their children, serving refreshments, helping the families do errands, making holiday celebrations, or babysitting children when the parents are out. Volunteers are carefully interviewed and checked. They must have upbeat personalities and be able to get along with both children and anxious parents. For information about volunteering, check the phone directory for Ronald McDonald House, or write to the Chicago office for the address of the one nearest you.

## FEATURED ORGANIZATION: SKIP OF NEW YORK, INC. (SKIP)

990 2nd Ave., 3rd Fl.
New York, NY 10022
1-212-421-9160
Contact: Executive Director

SKIP's ("Sick Kids (need) Involved People") primary goal is to help people, especially the families of chronically sick and disabled children, to secure and maintain quality home care. To achieve this, SKIP treats the families as equal partners by providing them with information, support, and critical feedback as they prepare to bring their children home from the hospital: SKIP then continues the assistance throughout the home care period, all without charge.

SKIP's services to the family include:

- Working with the family and health care professionals to achieve the best possible home care plan.
- Helping the family work through the maze of information about support services to obtain coverage for home care and all available financial entitlements.
- Coordinating the training of family members.
- Providing emotional support and advocacy, and continuing help in solving problems as they arise.

SKIP has twenty-four state chapters, each autonomous and all of them staffed almost entirely by volunteers who serve in the most varied ways, depending on the size of the chapter and its particular needs:

- Health and social service professionals who donate their skills to the organization and sometimes assist individual families.
- Lawyers and other people with organizational experience who can assist with setting up SKIP chapters.
- People who offer business support, providing in-kind gifts such as office materials, printing services, office space for holding meetings.
- Individuals who have or develop expertise in helping families with complex and extraordinary health care needs, acting as troubleshooters, making referrals, providing leadership and advocacy skills on behalf of families by working with local and state groups to develop action initiatives.
- People who can provide guidance in finding and applying for special grants and foundation programs.
- Volunteers who lend families a helping hand—baby-sitting or running errands or providing transportation assistance.
- Office workers.
- Fund-raisers.
- Translators of foriegn material into English and other languages.

For more information about SKIP or for the location of the the chapter nearest you, contact the national headquarters.

### United Hospital Fund of New York (UHF, page 130)

Bedtime Story Project
55 Fifth Ave.
New York, NY 10003
1-212-645-2500
Contact: Director of Voluntary Initiatives

The Bedtime Story Project brings together books, donated by twenty publishers, and over 100 volunteer storytellers who read to children in the pediatrics departments of twenty New York City hospitals. The program is designed to ease a child's adjustment to a hospital stay and provide a learning experience. Children are also able to take home a book with them. The UHF Task Force on the Needs of Hospitalized Children, which coordinates the project, solicits books twice a year and oversees book distribution to the hospitals. A training session for volunteer coordinators was conducted by the New York Public Library children's services division and provided tips on reading to children. This "train the trainer" approach is helpful for new volunteers, who are recruited by each hospital. Since reading to children is one of the most popular volunteer activities, there are often more volunteer applicants than there are hospitalized children. Some volunteers are encouraged to participate in other volunteer opportunities, which include reading to elderly patients. UHF is always in need of additional books, especially those written for teenagers (who don't need readers) and books in foreign languages. For information about volunteering time or donating new children's books, contact the director of voluntary initiatives.

## Granting Wishes

*Wish Fulfillment Organizations,* a free publication of Candlelighters Childhood Cancer Foundation (CCCF, page 134), is a directory (updated periodically) of more than twenty-five wish-granting organizations. Here are the names and addresses of a few more:

### Brass Ring Society, Inc.

National Headquarters
314 S. Main St.
Ottawa, KS 66067-2332
1-800-666-WISH (1-800-666-9474)

### Famous Fone Friends

9109 Sawyer St.
Los Angeles, CA 90035
1-213-204-5684

Provides telephone links for sick children and athletes or entertainers.

### Grant a Wish Foundation

c/o Brian Morrison
P.O. Box 21211
Baltimore, MD 21228
1-800-933-5470, 1-301-242-1549

For cancer patients and their families.

### Make-a-Wish Foundation of America

National Office
2600 N. Central Ave., Suite 936
Phoenix, AZ 85004
1-800-722-WISH

Make-a-Wish grants the special wishes of children up to the age of eighteen who have life-threatening illnesses. With seventy-three chapters operating in forty-five states, Make-a-Wish annually grants about 3,500 wishes, which are limited only by the children's imaginations. In every case, the child's family takes part in the wish so that children and families can share joyful memories. Many of the wishes involve meeting celebrities, traveling to some specific place—

a theme park, perhaps—doing a particular kind of work, or receiving a special gift.

When a wish is to be fulfilled, the appropriate chapter puts together a team to work out details and make it happen, relying on gifts, donations, and the services of many volunteers, including some celebrities. Fund-raising, working on special events, public relations, interviewing the children and their families, making phone calls, arranging transportation, and working with the children and their families to see that everything goes as smoothly as possible are some of the volunteers' functions. Call the 800 number for more information.

### Starlight Foundation (SF)

12233 W. Olympic Blvd., #322
Los Angeles, CA 90064
1-800-274-7827

SF is an international organization dedicated to brightening the lives of seriously ill children from four to eighteen years of age. SF's eleven chapters (seven in the United States, the others in Canada, the U. K., and Australia) help critically, chronically, and terminally ill children by granting special wishes and providing entertainment and recreation activities for pediatric patients who are hospitalized. Although each chapter is managed by a paid administrator, SF is largely sustained by volunteers, including its board of trustees, many of whom are celebrities in enter tainment, sports, and business. Volunteers work on children's committees, do fund-raising, train other volunteers, and implement the children's wishes in cooperation with families, doctors, and social workers. They also organize puppet shows, holiday parties, toy delivery, and clown and character visits for young patients in over fifty hospitals. About 1,000 active volunteers in the United States and abroad help grant the wishes of over 1,500 children a year and provide entertainment for many more. Write to the address shown to learn more about SF's volunteer opportunities.

### Sunshine Foundation

P.O. Box 255 (5400 State Rd., 547 N.)
Loughman, FL 33858
1-813-424-4188

# Child Abuse Organizations

According to the National Committee for Prevention of Child Abuse (NCPCA, page 78),over 1 million American children suffer from child abuse every year. The hotlines and organizations in this section will refer you to local organizations helping abused children and working to prevent further abuse. Some agencies rigorously screen and train volunteers who want to work directly with children.

## HOTLINES

**National Child Abuse Hotline: 1-800-4-A-CHILD (1-800-423-4453) Provides referrals for reporting child abuse, counseling, and shelters for runaway children. See Childhelp USA, page 78.**

**National Council on Child Abuse and Family Violence: 1-800-222-2000 Makes referrals for people who want information or counseling and publishes literature on domestic violence and child and elder abuse.**

**Parents Anonymous Hotline: 1-800-421-0353 (outside California); in California: 1-800-352-0386 See Parents Anonymous, page 78.**

## Childhelp USA

National Headquarters
6463 Independence Ave.
Woodland Hills, CA 91367
1-818-347-7280, FAX 1-818-593-3257
Childhelp/Foresters National Child Abuse Hotline 1-800-4-A-Child (1-800-423-4453)
Contact: Phyllis Sindleman

Childhelp is the nation's largest nonprofit organization working to combat child abuse through treatment, prevention, and research. Childhelp runs the Childhelp/Foresters national child abuse hotline, which is answered by a trained professional staff that handles over 200,000 calls every year, over half of them crisis calls from children, troubled parents, and adult survivors of abuse. It provides informaton on reporting and preventing child abuse and has the ability to refer callers to over 60,000 agencies nationwide. Childhelp offers evaluation and educational services for families, conducts research on the psychological and sociological impact of child abuse, and provides public education through the media and public service announcements. The Village of Childhelp, in Beaumont, California (near Palm Springs), a residential treatment center for severely abused and neglected children, and two group homes in Orange County, California, need volunteers to work with the children. Volunteers are carefully screened, fingerprinted, and trained to work with this special population. For information, contact the national headquarters.

## Parents Anonymous (PA)

520 S. Lafayette Park Pl., Suite 316
Los Angeles, CA 90057
1-213-388-6685
Hotline: 1-800-421-0353

PA is a national organization committed to the treatment and prevention of child abuse through peer-led self-help groups (called chapters) for parents, and groups for children. Over 1,200 chapters across the country serve more than 30,000 families yearly. Chapter members are highly motivated parents experiencing difficulty in parenting, and each parent group is led by a volunteer parent-group leader assisted by a vol-

## FEATURED ORGANIZATION: NATIONAL COMMITTEE FOR PREVENTION OF CHILD ABUSE (NCPCA)

332 S. Michigan Ave., Suite 1600
Chicago, IL 60604-4357
1-312-663-3520
Contact: Training and Technical Assistance

NCPCA is a national, volunteer-based organization dedicated to the prevention of child abuse in all of its forms. NCPCA approaches prevention through advocacy, public awareness, education, research, and the dedication of volunteers, thousands of whom are working with NCPCA's sixty-seven chapters to implement abuse-prevention programs. NCPCA will also refer volunteers to other community, state, and national groups with similar aims. The organization believes that everyone, regardless of skills and experience, has some way of helping. Write to NCPCA for "Think You Know Something about Child Abuse?" a brochure in question-and-answer format, and "It Shouldn't Hurt to Be a Child," which has more information about child abuse and NCPCA. Call the Training and Technical Assistance Office for the location of the NCPCA chapter in your area.

unteer professional. PA has programs for children, teen parents, minority populations, grandparents, and adults who were sexually abused as children. Almost 11,000 volunteers assist a small paid professional staff in delivering PA's free and confidential services. For information about volunteering or forming a new chapter, call the 800 number.

# Other Organizations

### American Red Cross

The Name of the Game Is Caring (TNGIC)
Washington, DC 20006
1-202-737-8300
Contact: Your local Red Cross chapter or Youth Associate, Programs and Services

TNGIC is an eight-session training course that prepares young volunteers to work with children, teenagers, the elderly, the disabled, the ill, or the convalescing in a variety of settings. The course encourages young people in grades 7–12 to learn leadership skills and enhance their sensitivity to the needs of others. TNGIC is taught to groups of youngsters by Scout leaders, local Red Cross volunteers, or volunteer-trained schoolteachers in schools. Once the youth are trained, they may serve in a number of local volunteer activities, and work often in hospitals, nursing homes, daycare centers, and Red Cross disaster shelters. For information about TNGIC or other Red Cross programs for youth, contact your local chapter or youth associate at the Washington headquarters.

### ASPIRA Association, Inc.

National Office
1112 16th St., NW, Suite 340
Washington, DC 20036
1-202-835-3600

ASPIRA, which takes its name from the Spanish verb *aspirar,* "to aspire to something greater," is a national organization with headquarters in Washington, DC, and offices in Connecticut; Florida; Illinois; New Jersey; New York; Pennsylvania; and Puerto Rico. ASPIRA's mission is to increase the welfare of the Hispanic community by working with Puerto Rican and Latino youth (called *Aspirantes*) to develop their potential for intellectual and political leadership. ASPIRA Clubs are the heart of the organization—Hispanic student clubs in over 100 high schools. ASPIRA works with 17,000 youth and 5,000 parents a year in a variety of programs geared toward dropout prevention, leadership development, community service and career exploration. Volunteers from the Hispanic community and other communities are needed for most local programs. Volunteer mentors make very important contributions to several of these programs, especially to the clubs and for *Aspirantes* who are part of the leadership training program.

### Athletes & Entertainers for Kids (AEFK)

P.O. Box 191, Bldg. B
Carson, CA 90248-0191
1-213-768-8493, FAX 1-213-768-8307
1-800-933-KIDS (1-800-933-5437)
Contact: Director of Volunteer Services

AEFK is a nonprofit community-based service dedicated to improving children's lives through education, hospital programs, and special events. Athletes and entertainers help deliver AEFK's programs to children, and they, along with a lot of noncelebrity volunteers, act as role models for the kids. Located in southern California, AEFK serves the region by offering public and private schools, community youth groups, and other agencies educational programs that address immediate problems such as school dropouts, substance abuse, AIDS, and teen pregnancy, and other issues such as self-esteem. AEFK educators, celebrities, and health professionals present the information and lead workshops and discussions groups. AEFK's community services provide monthly motivational events and outings to over 260 youth organizations and agencies. Carefully planned entertainment and activities are delivered monthly at hospitals serving low-income families and youth at risk. Special events include miniature golf tournaments, Halloween masquerade balls for kids, and more. AEFK uses about 500 community volunteers a year. They are recruited through public service announcements, volunteer fairs, and corporations with employee volunteer programs. It goes without saying, being an athlete or an entertainer is *not* one of the requirements. Call the director of volunteer services at the 800 number for information.

Brookfield Zoo, Children's Zoo (page 43)

## Children's Aid Society (CAS)

105 E. 22 St.
New York, NY 10010
1-212-949-4800

CAS was founded in 1853 to care for New York City's orphaned and poor children, and today it is one of the country's largest child welfare agencies in the country, serving more than 100,000 children and their families every year with the assistance of a large professional staff and hundreds of volunteers. CAS offers a comprehensive response to children's and family needs in adoption and foster care; visual and performing arts projects; community centers providing health, recreational, and educational programs; education and counseling for the prevention of substance abuse and teenage pregnancy; nutrition; a wide range of health services; transitional housing for homeless families; job counseling; and youth mediation. CAS needs tutors for junior and senior high school students and fund-raisers, and more.

## For Love of Children (FLOC)

1711 14th St., NW
Washington, DC 20009
1-202-462-8686
Contact: Volunteer Coordinator

FLOC has been serving at-risk children and their families in the District of Columbia since 1965. FLOC's programs are volunteer intensive:

- The Learning Center, an alternative school for students aged twelve to twenty with emotional and behavioral difficulties, needs tutors and mentors.
- The Foster Home Program, which provides trained, caring foster families for abused and special-needs children and family reunification services, uses volunteers to help with transporting the children, assist with special activities, and act as mentors and tutors.
- Hope and a Home, transitional housing and family support services, recruits tutors, mentors, and support people to help families learn basic housekeeping, budgeting, and other fundamental family skills. Volunteers also help with renovations.
- The Outdoor Education Center, which offers wilderness expeditions and adventure-challenge camping for inner-city youth, needs mentors to visit regularly with the campers after they return home to reinforce the gains made at camp.
- Community Adventure, a therapeutic group home for adolescent boys, needs male tutors.

FLOC also needs professionals who will act as career counselors, people with business and entrepreneurial skills to mentor kids and help them set up their own projects, and fund-raisers. FLOC also welcomes donations of goods ranging from playpens, toy chests, and computers to paint and rollers for renovations, tools, and pool tables. Call FLOC for information about volunteering or the donations wish list.

HOSTS Corp. (HOSTS, page 163)

## Joint Action in Community Service (JACS)

P.O. Box 1700
Washington, DC 20013

JACS is an outgrowth of Job Corps, the federal program that provides disadvantaged youth aged sixteen to twenty-one from urban ghettos and depressed rural areas with educational and vocational training. JACS, a national nonprofit organization, was founded by a coalition of religious leaders who sought a means of meeting the needs of Job Corps graduates. JACS volunteers offer counseling services, encouragement in finding and keeping jobs, and help in locating medical services, legal assistance, housing, and additional training. There are over 5,000 JACS volunteers nationwide from every part of the community—concerned unaffiliated individuals, members of national and local nonprofit groups, corporations, students at colleges and universities, labor union members, homemakers, plant workers. Volunteers are recruited and trained by staff in the ten JACS regional offices. Write for JACS's information brochure and flier as well as a list of regional offices, each of which can be reached by an 800 number.

Junior Achievement, Inc. (JA, page 164)

## La Leche League International

9616 Minneapolis Ave.
P.O. Box 1209
Franklin Park, IL 60131-8209
1-800-LALECHE (1-800-525-3243),
1-708-455-7730

La Leche was founded to give information and encouragment, mainly through personal help, to all mothers who want to breast-feed their babies. The organization's mission is to support breast-feeding worldwide through education, mother-to-mother help, and a network of 8,000 volunteer group leaders in forty-eight countries. The group leaders hold monthly meetings to help mothers learn to breast-feed and to promote a better understanding of breast-feeding, parenting, childbirth, and related subjects. La Leche is almost completely volunteer-run, with about 6,500 group leaders—trained and accredited by La Leche—in the United States alone. Leaders must fulfill a number of specific requirements, among them having breast-fed a baby for about a year, and support La Leche's purpose and philosophy. For information, call either phone number.

MENTOR (page 165)

## National Court Appointed Special Advocate Association (CASA)

2722 Eastlake Ave. E, Suite 220
Seattle, WA 98102
1-206-328-8588, FAX 1-206-323-8137
Contact: Communications Department

"Speak up for a child" is the motto of the award-winning CASA concept. CASA volunteers are Court Appointed Special Advocates for abused and negelected children who have been removed from their homes and placed in foster care or institutions. A CASA worker is a trained community volunteer who is appointed by a judge to act as a child's advocate by helping the child to understand what is happening in court, researching the facts of the case for the judge, speaking for the child in the courtroom, and following the case through to its end. Because volunteers work very closely with children, they are expected to be mature, responsible adults who are willing to commit ten to fifteen hours a month working for CASA. The CASA volunteer training course averages about twenty hours.

There are over 485 CASA programs nationwide, operating under different names. For the location of the CASA program nearest you, or for information about forming a new program, contact the national office.

**One Plus One (PLUS, page 167)**

**One To One (1 to 1, page 166)**

## Optimist International

4494 Lindell Blvd.
St. Louis, MO 63108
1-314-371-6000

Optimist Clubs are service organizations whose focus is youth. A membership of 175,000 business and professional men and women conducts over 50,000 service projects a year. Each of Optimist's 4,300 clubs has projects created to meet the needs of the local community, and the clubs can also choose from among Optimist International's official programs, such as the 700 Optimist youth clubs that perform community service; Just Say No, a drug prevention program; Help Them Hear; a golf tournament and other sports competitions; an essay contest; Respect for Law Week; and others. Check the local phone book or contact the St. Louis office for a club near you.

**Partners, Inc. (page 166)**

## The Pearl S. Buck Foundation (PSBF)

P.O. Box 181
Green Hills Farm
Perkasie, PA 18944-0181
1-215-249-0100, 1-800-220-BUCK
(1–800–220–2825)
Contact: Director of Communications

PSBF helps poverty-stricken Amerasian (half-American, half-Asian) and other displaced children who are either abandoned or neglected in Southeast Asia. The primary means of help is the sponsorship of individual children by single persons or couples, religious groups, schools, organizations, and businesses. Although most of the Amerasian children remain in Asia, a number of them immigrate to the United States, where they are placed with volunteer foster families who provide a loving, stable environment under permanent guardianship arrangement. Foster families are legally and financially responsible for youth under twenty-one or for five years, whichever is longer. PSBF assists with some of the expenses of bringing the children to the United States. PSBF also needs volunteer families to provide temporary homes for Amerasian youth.

Members of the Pearl S. Buck Volunteer Association work at the foundation's headquarters as docents conducting guided tours of Pearl S. Buck House. Other volunteers organize fund-raising and information meetings across the United States to familiarize people with the plight of needy children.

For information about volunteering, call the 800 number or get in touch with the director of communications.

**Project Concern International (PCI, page 191)**

**Rotary International (page 116)**

## Unitarian Universalist Service Committee (UUSC)

130 Prospect St.
Cambridge, MA 02139
1-617-868-6600, FAX 1-617-868-7102
Contact: Citizen Action Department

UUSC, a nonsectarian membership organization (page 201), contributes money, educational and office equipment, facilities, and the skills of individual volunteers to groups and programs active in meeting the needs of children from low-income families. UUSC has also initiated its own programs in numerous communities. UUSC's booklet, *Promise the Children: A Guide for Uni-*

*tarian Universalist Congregations to Focus on the Rights and Needs of Children in the United States,* $3, gives specific instructions for forming and running a local children's committee to address problems of health, poverty, and education. The booklet also lists local UUSC congregations and other groups with such programs already in place. For a copy of the booklet and more information about UUCS children's programs, write to the address above.

## U.S. Department of Agriculture

National 4-H Council (4-H)
Cooperative Extension Service, 4-H Youth Development (4-H)
Washington, DC 20250-0900

4-H is the Cooperative Extension System's nonformal educational program combining the cooperative efforts of youth, volunteer leaders, state land grant universities, and all levels of government. The goal of 4-H is to stimulate young people to develop life skills: competency, the ability to cope with stress, and the desire to help others.

4-H Clubs recruit their youth membership through the schools and at the same time reach out to parents, many of whom become volunteer leaders. There are currently over 660,000 adult volunteer leaders serving about 5 million young people nine to nineteen years old. 4-H programs are conducted in over 3,000 U.S. counties and are designed for youth in urban, rural, suburban, and small-town areas. Projects range from agriculture and science programs to nutrition, diet, and health projects to drug abuse prevention, a teen apprenticeship program, and many others. For information about 4-H and about volunteering, contact your local county extension agent.

## Variety Clubs International (VCI)

1560 Broadway
New York, NY 10036
1-212-704-9872, FAX 1-212-704-9875

VCI is an international membership club founded in Pittsburgh in 1923 by eleven men involved in the theater and performing arts. VCI has thirty-five chapters (called "tents") nationwide and fifty-five worldwide, and each operates autonomously within its own community to serve underprivileged and seriously ill children. Chapters do fund-raising for local children's charities and for specific VCI programs like the Sunshine Coaches, vans designed specially for disabled children, which VCI buys and gives to medical facilities and residences for sick children. Members also spend time with children. Variety At Work (VAW) volunteers take sick kids to special events such as a trip to the circus or a ball game or to a VCI-sponsored Christmas party; they also help disabled children with rehabilitative and educational projects, giving personal attention in large and small ways. For more information and the location of the VCI nearest you, write to the New York headquarters.

## Youth Development International (YDI)

P.O. Box 178408
San Diego, CA 92177-8408
1-619-292-5683, FAX 1-619-277-1365
Youth Crisis Hotline: 1-800-HIT-HOME
Contact: Robert N. Botsford

YDI is a Christian nonprofit organization that ministers to the needs of youth in trouble. The Youth Crisis Hotline receives over 25,000 calls a month, which it routes to fifty outposts across the country, where trained crisis volunteers, some of them teenagers themselves, respond to pleas for help in dealing with many kinds of problems, among them drugs, pregnancy, sexual abuse, beatings, and broken homes. Volunteers refer kids to shelters and other facilities that can offer sleeping accommodations, food, clothing, and guidance. Free transportation is provided to the shelters or to their homes. YDI sponsors other programs carried out largely through volunteers. The National Wilderness Expedition provides kids with one-week camping trips led by experienced volunteer campers, fishermen, and outdoors people. Holiday Outreach needs volunteers to gift wrap Christmas packages for children in juvenile halls in major urban areas. There are volunteer opportunities for graphic artists, writers, public relations people, and corporations to sponsor YDI projects in their communities. If you are interested in volunteering or want to start a hotline center in your town, call or write to YDI.

# Resources

*How to Save the Children,* by Amy Hatkoff and Karen Kelly Klopp. New York: Fireside Books, 1992. This book has everything you want to know about helping children—proposing hundreds of ways to make a difference as an individual or as part of a group. The book focuses on four main areas: providing the basics such as food, health, clothing, and housing; offering friendship and activities in one-to-one relationships; creating opportunities for children to achieve their full potential in education and jobs; and advocacy. Although many of the suggestions apply only to children, quite a few others could be used just as well to address problems faced by the needy and other special populations living at a disadvantage in the United States. The directory of clearinghouses and national organizations is indispensable.

## WORKING WITH AND FOR SICK CHILDREN

*Camps and Vacation Retreats for Children with Cancer and Their Families* is a state-by-state directory of camps for young patients (primarily those with cancer) and their siblings and parents. Many of the camps are free. Each entry includes information on the ages of the campers, length of stay, and other pertinent data. There are volunteer opportunities at most of the camps. Send $1 with your request to Candlelighters Childhood Cancer Foundation (CCCF, page 134).

# Community Service

There are thousands of charitable groups working to improve the quality of community life. Some of them are national organizations with chapters throughout the country; others are groups that spring up in response to specific local problems.

Family issues are a major concern of many community agencies, and there's a lot of organizational overlap with children's, educational, holiday, religious, service, and veterans' groups as well as with organizations serving the needy. To see what's available in your region, begin with the nearest volunteer action center (VAC) (see National Volunteer Center, NVC, page 37), then try Retired Seniors Volunteer Program (RSVP, page 204) and United Way (page 38), all of which will help match you with volunteer opportunities.

## The Association of Junior Leagues International, Inc. (AJLI)

660 First Ave.
New York, NY 10016
1-212-683-1515

Although AJLI has long been known for its promotion of volunteerism and community improvement, its members have also been perceived as do-gooders, women in hats and white gloves who graciously minister to the welfare of the needy. This Lady Bountiful image is far removed from today's reality in which each of the 277 national and international Junior Leagues (JL) actively reaches out to a diverse membership whose racial, religious, and cultural backgrounds reflect the community it serves.

Volunteer training programs are the hallmark of the JL and the core of its effectiveness. Committees within each JL identify local problems and, in collaboration with government or private nonprofit organizations, initiate projects to meet those needs, which are primarily related to children and youth, education, women's issues, health, community and cultural affairs, and a growing concern for the environment.

Membership is required for involvement in any JL project. To become a member, contact your local JL (usually located in a large town or city) or ask the New York office to direct you.

## Family Service America (FSA)

11700 W. Lake Park Dr., Park Pl.
Milwaukee, WI 53224
Contact: 1-800-221-2681

FSA has a network of 290 member agencies in the United States and Canada, all working to strengthen family life. With a total professional staff of 11,000, who are supported by over 10,000 volunteers, each agency assists individuals and families to solve problems associated with marital difficulties, parent-child tensions, drug and alcohol dependency, teenage pregnancy, child abuse, family violence, and other problems. All member agencies have family counseling, but programs vary widely with the community's needs and resources. FSA's national office provides technical support for member agencies to develop initiatives, serves as a clearinghouse on family issues, publishes research reports, and sets national programs. All full members of FSA are accredited to assure that their programs meet standards for quality. For information about the FSA agency nearest you, call the 800 number.

**La Leche League International** **(LA LECHE, page 81)**

## National Council of Jewish Women (NCJW)

53 W. 23rd St.
New York, NY 10010
1-212-645-4048, FAX 1-212-645-7466
Contact: Naomi Fatt, Director of Program Services

NCJW is a volunteer organization, which, in the spirit of Judaism, is dedicated to improving the well-being of children, the elderly, and families of all races, religions, and economic backgrounds. Help is provided by volunteers who work in multifaceted, coordinated programs of education, advocacy, and service. NCJW initiatives and programs are focused on women and children, and they involve such issues as family day care (the care of a small group of children in the provider's home), the participation of businesses in helping to meet the child-care needs of their employees, pro-choice education and advocacy, and training and support for educationally and economically disadvantaged families. NCJW has 100,000 members and 200 local affiliate Sections in 500 locations nationwide. Members are encouraged to become actively involved in implementing programs, which are often undertaken in participation with other community groups. Volunteer work involves field research to investigate community needs; publication of reports based on that research; advocacy at the local, state, and national levels; education; direct service to clients; and much more. NCJW also sponsors a number of educational programs in Israel. For information about the organization, get in touch with the New York office.

## New York Cares (NYC)

140 E. 58th St.
New York, NY 10022
1-212-753-6670
Contact: Executive Director

NYC is a nonprofit membership organization leading young, working New Yorkers in volunteer, hands-on, team projects that help people in need. In partnership with a wide variety of nonprofit social service organizations and programs throughout the city—American Red Cross (ARC, page 129), Fresh Air Fund (FAF, page 70), nursing homes, tutorial programs, shelters, soup kitchens, AIDS programs, Special Olympics (page 212), and many others—NYC creates and manages over 150 volunteer team projects each month. Projects are designed to accommodate a variety of volunteer schedules: one-day projects that meet immediate problems or seasonal community needs, monthly team projects, and individual assignments for volunteers able to maintain a regular weekly commitment. NYC also develops customized corporate programs for teams of employees from companies interested in providing community service. Projects are run by veteran volunteers who put together the teams. About 3,000 active volunteers work on the projects on weekends and before and after work on weekdays. NYC's annual coat drive collects as many as 31,000 coats during a twelve-day period, then sorts and delivers them to organizations for local distribution. Other programs include soliciting commercial and business surplus, such as computers and office furniture and supplies, and distributing them to other nonprofit organizations. Recruitment for NYC is mostly through word of mouth or as a result of media stories. Similar organizations have been set up in other cities with technical assistance from NYC.

## Planned Parenthood Federation of America (PP)

810 Seventh Ave.
New York, NY 10036
1-212-541-7800
Contact: Volunteer Coordinator

PP believes that all people, regardless of age or income, have the fundamental right to make their own personal and private decisions about childbearing, and it is committed to making that right a reality for everyone by assuring the availability of family planning informaton and services, nationally and internationally. There are about 175 PP affiliates and 900 clinics nationwide, each complying with PP's standards, but each autonomous in terms of the services offered and use of volunteers. PP has a full range of family planning services that include contraception and prevention and treatment of sexually transmitted diseases; early pregnancy detection; services for adolescents; abortion; and sexuality education programs for professional training, patient education, and comunity education programs. Depending on the size and needs of a PP chapter, volunteer opportunities include: public speaking about PP's services; escorting clients in PP clinics; public advocacy—from letter writing to voter registration; working in thrift shops; fund-raising; mentoring; and a host of other functions. PP volunteers come from diverse backgrounds, and each is interviewed before receiving formal training. Check your local phone directory for the PP chapter nearest you, or call the New York office.

**SerVermont (page 221)**

**Thomas Jefferson Forum (TJF, page 222)**

## Travelers Aid International (TAI)

1001 Connecticut Ave., NW, Suite 504
Washington, DC 20036
1-202-659-9468

There are chapters of TAI nationwide, most of them in cities, located near bus depots, train stations, and airports. Every chapter offers information and other services to travelers, including community programs for lost and runaway children. Volunteers serve in various capacities: doing office work, counseling, and giving referrals. Call your local TAI for information.

## U.S. Department of the Treasury

Internal Revenue Service, IRS Volunteers (IRS)
Contact: Taxpayer Education Coordinator

The IRS has several community programs to assist people with their taxes. At the core of these programs are thousands of volunteers, some recruited individually and some through local groups such as American Association of Retired Persons (AARP, page 203), which has 28,000 Tax-Aide volunteers who work with over 1 million people nationwide. All volunteers are trained by the IRS before they begin to help the public. Among the programs are:

- Volunteer Income Tax Assistance (VITA) to help elderly (over sixty and homebound), disabled, or non-English-speaking taxpayers with basic tax returns.
- Free tax counseling for the homebound elderly over sixty—some of it from volunteers who are themselves retired.
- Tax education lectures and seminars tailored to specific groups, such as farmers, retirees, and others.
- Small business tax education in the form of workshops, seminars, and other courses for people just starting a business.

## FEATURED ORGANIZATION: JEWISH BOARD OF FAMILY AND CHILDREN'S SERVICES (JBFCS)

120 W. 57th St.
New York, NY 10019
1-212-582-9100
Contact: Division of Volunteer Services, ext. 248

JBFCS helps more than 45,000 New Yorkers from all the city's ethnic and religious populations with a diverse network of services that are offered in 102 sites in the city's five boroughs and two neighboring counties. Over 1,000 volunteers help a staff of about 1,400 social workers, psychiatrists, psychologists, teachers, and child-care workers deliver JBFCS services, which include: counseling, mentoring, community services for various population groups (the homeless, emotionally disturbed teenagers, Russian immigrant adolescents), educational therapy and bereavement consultation, and help with myriad other programs.

Here are some of the ways in which volunteers work: helping people with AIDS by talking with them, caring about them, and doing chores such as shopping or answering mail; being a Big Brother or a Big Sister (BB/BSA, page 164), or participating in Compeer (page 137); working on the JBFCS camp program; soliciting toy companies for free gifts for all children in agency programs; answering a hotline for battered women; providing help to families involved in court matters; working as arbitrators or mediators at the Jewish Conciliation Board of America; screening phone calls for a quick, friendly response for information and referrals; and working with children on special assignments ranging from child-care assistance to being a play group assistant. Special training is required for many volunteer assignments. For information about volunteering, contact the Division of Volunteer Services and ask them to send you "Volunteer Services," a full description of all volunteer opportunities, including the time commitment for each.

- Teaching or helping to teach tax basics to high school students.
- Practitioner education.

Consult the U.S. Government listings in your local phone book for the number of the IRS district office nearest you and call for the brochure, "A Rainbow of Opportunities."

### Volunteers in Service to America (VISTA)

ACTION
1100 Vermont Ave., NW
Washington, DC 20525
1-800-424-8867

VISTA is the ACTION (page 35) volunteer program for men and women eighteen years of age or older who commit themselves, full-time for a year, to assisting low-income people to achieve self-sufficiency. More than half of VISTA's volunteers serve in agencies devoted to promoting good health and to alleviating and preventing unemployment, hunger, homelessness, alcohol and drug abuse, and illiteracy. To be a VISTA volunteer, you must be a U.S. citizen or permanent resident, and ready to live and work among the poor in urban or rural areas or on Indian reservations. VISTA volunteers very often serve as community mobilizers, raising money and enthusiasm for a project. Projects usually originate when a local agency develops an idea involving the use of VISTA volunteers and submits a proposal to VISTA. When the proposal is approved, volunteers are recruited locally either through the sponsoring organization or through one of VISTA's nine regional offices. Volunteers are given a basic subsistence allowance for living expenses and a small monthly stipend paid at the end of service. For more information on becoming a VISTA volunteer, contact your regional office.

## Women in Community Service, Inc. (WICS)

1900 N. Beauregard St., Suite 103
Alexandria, VA 22311
1-703-671-0500, FAX 1-703-671-4489
1-800-442-WICS (1-800-442-9427)
Contact: Communications specialist

WICS is a private nonprofit corporation incorporated in 1964 and sponsored by a coalition of five major national groups: American G. I. Forum Women, Church Women United, National Council of Jewish Women (NCJW, page 86), National Council of Catholic Women, and National Council of Negro Women (NCNW, page 171). This coalition represents a combined membership of approximately 27 million people. WICS is dedicated to the empowerment of women struggling to break the cycle of poverty, and the organization also provides supplementary services that enhance the outcome of training and education of disadvantaged youth for the job market. WICS is a primary contractor for the U.S. Department of Labor/Job Corps. Its programs services are carried out by a staff of 150 and about 5,000 volunteers. For more information, call the WICS communications specialist.

## YMCA of the USA

101 N. Wacker Dr.
Chicago, IL 60606
1-312-269-1185, FAX 1-312-977-9063

YMCA is part of a worldwide movement that puts Christian principles into practice through programs that promote good health, strong families, youth leadership, community development, and international understanding. As a community service organization, YMCA serves all people, with a focus on children and families, through a variety of programs. These include health and fitness, sports, day camps, swimming, child care, CPR training, lifeguard training, smoking cessation, stress management, exercises for those with disabilities, and corporate health enhancement programs. The environment, family nights, job training for young people, substance abuse prevention, and teen leadership are among the areas addressed by local Ys responding to needs within the community. There are over 2,000 Ys nationwide, run by almost 65,000 volunteer policymakers on Y boards and committees, and about 320,000 volunteer program leaders plus many occasional volunteers. The staff-to-volunteer ratio overall is about one staff person to fifty volunteers. For information about volunteering, check your local phone book for the Y nearest you.

## YWCA of the USA

726 Broadway
New York, NY 10003
1-212-614-2700, FAX 1-212-677-9716
Contact: Susan Einarson, Communications, 212-614-2846

YWCA has a twofold mission: to empower women and girls by giving them opportunities to grow and succeed in all areas of life, and to eliminate racism. These goals are accomplished by activities that center on education and personal development for women and girls in a very broad range of programs. People who join the Y and participate in its programs are encouraged to volunteer their time and skills. As one means of empowering women, the Y gives them the opportunity to make decisions about how the programs they use are run, and many women using a Y service, such as the child-care program offered in about half the Ys or the services for battered women, are invited to be part of the advisory group developing guidelines for the program. There are more than 400 Y community and student associations operating in 4,000 locations nationwide. Each Y is autonomous and designs programs, activities, and services tailored for its community's interests and needs. Most services rely heavily on the efforts of volunteers. Check the phone book for the nearest Y or call the national headquarters for information.

# Assisting Victims

Victim assistance programs and organizations are on the increase as victims begin to insist on their rights. Victim assistance takes many forms: counseling, mediation (page 160), working at shelters for battered women and children, advocacy, pro bono legal and medical aid, fundraising, research, horticultural therapy, and support groups, to name a few. National Organization for Victim Assistance (NOVA, see box, opposite) and National Victim Center (NVC, page 90) can refer you to the nearest agencies, as will a volunteer action center (VAC) (see National Volunteer Center, NVC page 37) or United Way (UWA, page 38).

## National Victim Center (NVC)

309 W. 7th St., Suite 705
Fort Worth, TX 76102
1-817-877-3355, FAX 1-817-877-3396

NVC is a national organization dedicated to reducing the consequences of crime on victims and society by promoting victims' rights and victim assistance. Among NVC's many programs are a legislative data base of over 15,000 relevant statutes, which serves as a resource for individuals and organizations; support of the passage of state amendments protecting victims; networking with many other organizations and individuals concerned with victims' rights; training for professionals and volunteers in the field; and public awareness and educational programs. One of NVC's primary services is providing victims and witnesses with timely referrals to direct assistance in their own communities. A computerized organizational data base of about 7,000 organizations links victims with crisis intervention, information, assistance through the criminal justice system, counseling, support groups, and legal counsel. NVC will also direct potential volunteers to local victim centers. For information, call or write to the Fort Worth office.

## Victim Services (VS)

2 Lafayette St.
New York, NY 10007
1-212-577-7700
Contact: Personnel Director, ext. 1286

VS is a local New York City nonprofit organization dedicated to helping people in crisis. It provides immediate help to crime victims and works to prevent violence and to ensure compassionate treatment of victims through advocacy, research, and public education. VS has a full range of services to crime victims and their families, including hotlines and programs for battered women and children, rape and incest survivors, families of homicide victims, and abused elderly. Volunteers help by escorting victims through the court process, serving as hotline counselors, working as trained mediators (page 160), providing support for battered women in the VS shelter system, caring for children while their parents appear in court, offering support to crime victims waiting to see a counselor or judge, escorting homeless youth on recreational outings, and doing office work. VS welcomes volunteers from all backgrounds, from high school students to retired persons. Each volunteer must begin service with clerical/administrative tasks in order to become familiar with the programs. Further training for more skilled positions is given based on a supervisor's evaluation of the volunteer's level of ability, judgment, and commitment. Call the personnel director for more information.

## FEATURED ORGANIZATION: NATIONAL ORGANIZATION FOR VICTIM ASSISTANCE (NOVA)

1757 Park Rd., NW
Washington, DC 20010
1-202-232-6682
Contact: Volunteer Director

NOVA is a private, nonprofit, public interest organization dedicated to helping all types of victims and survivors of crime and crisis, including underserved populations, such as racial and ethnic minorities; gays, lesbians, and other victims of "hate crimes"; the elderly; children; victims of institutional abuse; the disabled; the homeless; the chronically mentally ill; and other groups with special needs. NOVA, the umbrella organization for groups interested in victim issues, has four purposes: nationwide advocacy for victims; direct service to crime and crisis victims; professional development for victim service specialists; and providing its membership with current information in the field of victim assistance. NOVA has also established a national Community Crisis Response Team Project, which involves trained professional counselors—all volunteers—who are sent to communities that have been traumatized by a catastrophe, either natural or man-made. Among NOVA's publications is *The Directory of Victim Assistance Programs and Resources* ($20 for members, $25 for nonmembers), a listing by state of over 7,000 victim service–related agencies, many of which need volunteers. For information about volunteering in victim assistance, call NOVA for a referral in your area. If you live in or near the District of Columbia, NOVA itself uses local volunteers, all trained by NOVA. Call the volunteer director for more information.

# Disaster Relief

Man-made and natural disasters have always been with us and so have vast numbers of people who, throughout the millennia, have volunteered to help the victims. But it was only in the late nineteenth century that a national organization, American Red Cross Disaster Services (page 92), was created to address the specific needs of victims of war, fire, flood, famine, earthquake, and other unforeseeable but equally devastating events. Since then, of course, new organizations of every kind are helping to meet the needs of disaster victims in the United States and abroad. It's been said that volunteers who work at emergency relief for many years become disaster junkies, always eager for the next opportunity to serve those in immediate need and danger, in the most professional way possible. Most volunteers for agencies supplying direct, on-the-scene service receive demanding training, which pays off handsomely during an actual emergency. Check with your local disaster agency to find out how to organize donations of clothing, bedding, food, and other necessities in advance of disaster or to send to communities that have been struck.

---

## American Radio Relay League, Inc. (ARRL)

Administrative Headquarters
225 Main St.
Newington, CT 06111
1-203-666-1541
Contact: Field Services Department

ARRL is a national volunteer organization of 160,000 licensed radio amateurs. Its field organization consists of 5,000 volunteers who perform emergency preparedness functions. Registered ham radio amateurs work for ARRL's Amateur Radio Emergency Service (ARES), which cooperates closely with the National Traffic System (NTS) to facilitate the moving of emergency traffic. The two together form the public service network that provides critical communications support for relief agencies during a disaster when other lines of communication are down. All FCC-licensed radio amateurs are eligible for ARES and NTS, whether they are members of ARRL or not. For ARRL members, there are many additional volunteer opportunities within its fifteen regional divisions, including service as public information assistants, section traffic managers, assistant technical coordinators, official observers, bulletin managers, and more. Contact the field services department of ARRL administrative headquarters for more information.

## American Red Cross Disaster Services

17th and D Sts., NW
Washington, DC 20006

The American Red Cross (ARC) began providing emergency assistance in 1881 when forest fires ravaged Michigan. In 1905 Congress granted a charter to ARC and recognized the organization as the leading provider of disaster relief in the United States—a recognition due in large part to the leadership role of Clara Barton who recruited volunteers and organized disaster relief efforts for the Johnstown, Ohio, flood in 1889, the Galveston hurricane in 1900, and the 1906 San Francisco earthquake.

Today Red Cross Disaster Services help meet the emergency needs of disaster victims by providing shelter, vouchers for new clothing, essential medications, bedding, and other necessities to meet basic needs. Volunteers prepare meals, run shelters, interview clients to determine their immediate needs, and perform support functions that make the operations run smoothly.

One chapter director of disaster volunteers wrote to say that "Disaster volunteers are a particularly interesting group of people who come from a wild variety of cultural and educational circumstances. On different jobs I've met a cattle rancher, treasury agent, psychiatrists, solar experts, ham radio operators, computer wizards, beauticians—people from almost every profession and ethnic background." A three-week commitment is required from disaster volunteers. If you want to become involved in ARC's Disaster Services, call your local ACR chapter.

## AmeriCares Foundation

161 Cherry St.
New Canaan, CT 06840
1-203-966-5195
Contact: Volunteer Coordinator

AmeriCares is a nonprofit private relief organization that provides immediate response to emergency medical and nutritional needs worldwide. Through the personal business connections of AmeriCare's founder, Robert Macauley, the organization solicits medicine, hospital supplies, and nutritional supplements from major pharmaceutical companies, along with food and whatever else is needed from other sources. AmeriCares then arranges for the shipment of these supplies to a disaster area and has volunteers and staffers accompany the deliveries of supplies to clinics, hospitals, and orphanages in the disaster region. AmeriCares also has a list of professional medical volunteers from across the country and can call on them in times of emergency. Nonprofessional volunteers are needed as well. Call the volunteer coordinator for information about opportunities.

AmeriCares, along with several other social service agencies, sponsors the annual Christmas in April (CIA, page 176) in ten cities and towns in Fairfield County and Southern Connecticut, where as many as 2,800 volunteers join together on the last day of April to renovate the homes of elderly and handicapped people.

**Concern/America (page 186)**

**International Rescue Committee (IRC, page 188)**

**National Organization for Victim Assistance, Community Crisis Response Team Project (NOVA, page 91)**

## National Voluntary Organizations Active in Disaster (NVOAD)

American Red Cross Disaster Services
17th and D Sts., NW
Washington, DC 20006
1-202-737-8300

NVOAD is a national umbrella organization for many local disaster agencies. Its goal is to foster cooperation at all levels among such agencies in order to provide more effective services, especially at the time of a disaster. NVOAD holds annual membership meetings, convenes special national and regional meetings, encourages the formation of state voluntary organizations active in disaster, and maintains liaisons with the Federal Emergency Management Agency (FEMA). "National Voluntary Organizations Active in Disaster" is NVOAD's national directory of nineteen nationwide organizations, many of them disaster response units of religious bodies, that offer a variety of emergency services. The directory also describes NVOAD's goals and program. For a free copy, write to NVOAD.

**Northwest Medical Teams International (NMTI, page 189)**

## Salvation Army Emergency Services (SAES)

799 Bloomfield Ave.
Verona, NJ 07044
1-201-239-0606, FAX 1-201-239-8441
Contact: Emergency Disaster Coordinator

SAES, a special branch of The Salvation Army (page 201), provides relief to victims of disaster: food, clothing, shelter, and other basic necessities; crisis counseling; rebuilding; and help in restoring lives to normal. SAES cooperates with the Federal Emergency Management Agency (FEMA) and participates actively in National Organization for Victim Assistance (NVOAD, page 93) and with other organizations at the state and local levels. Volunteers serve SAES in many capacities, and everyone is encouraged to learn cardiopulmonary resuscitation (CPR). Some groups in disaster-prone areas have regular training sessions for greater efficiency. To volunteer for emergency service, call the SAES volunteer coordinator at your local Salvation Army. SAES also accepts donations of food, clothing, electric generators, building materials, and other supplies.

## State Bar of California (SBC)

Office of Legal Services
555 Franklin St.
San Francisco, CA 94102
1-415-561-8200
Contact: LeRoy Cordova, Director, or Sharon Ngim, Pro Bono Program Developer, 1-800-628-4858

"Disaster Legal Services: A Guide for the Private Bar" was produced by the Bar Association of San Francisco Volunteer Legal Services Program and a former staff attorney, Thomas M. Roberts, as a response to the earthquake that devastated northern California in October 1989. The guide, a publication of the State Bar of California, is a packet of practical information needed to develop and implement local disaster legal services in California, but it can be replicated throughout the country and adapted to meet different kinds of disasters that can overwhelm individual communities. To obtain a free copy of the guide, write to the State Bar of California. For technical assistance with a pro bono disaster legal services program, contact the pro bono program developer.

**Volunteers of America (VOA, page 202)**

# Education

## Volunteer Educators

Volunteer educators are organizations and individual adults working to educate children (Head Start, page 99, for example) and adults (most literacy programs). Volunteer educational programs for children vary enormously: Some are delivered by individuals working on school-originated projects; others, like Environmental Learning for the Future (ELF, page 112) and GrowLab (see National Gardening Association, NGA, page 119), are adopted by schools but funded and carried out by private volunteer groups; and there are programs not connected with schools at all. Get in touch with schools in your area to find out what programs there are for volunteers.

Professional associations, such as bar associations, science academies, and medical associations very often have educational programs offered to schools and cultural institutions. If you belong to such an organization, check for educational programs, or offer to start one.

### American Association of University Women (AAUW)

1111 16th St., NW
Washington, DC 20036
1-202-785-7700
Member Helpline: 1-800-821-4364

AAUW is a nationwide membership organization working to promote education and equity for women and girls. Its programs include mentoring, action projects, lobbying state legislators and Congress, awarding fellowships and grants, leadership development, networking skills, and recently developed student affiliates. AAUW's membership of 135,000 college graduates work at the grassroots level in 1,800 community branches. For information about membership and the location of the nearest branch, contact the Washington office or call the 800 number.

## Museum of Science, Boston (MOS)

Science-By-Mail
Science Park
Boston, MA 02114-1099
1-800-729-3300
Contact: Joan Stanley, National Program Director

Science-By-Mail is a national, open-ended pen pal mentor program in which children in grades 4–9 receive three science packets a year, each based on a central theme. The kids who get them work within groups of up to four schoolmates, family members, or friends. After completing the activities, the children mail their creative solutions to an assigned volunteer scientist, who responds to their ideas through letters, offering them positive, encouraging feedback. The Science-By-Mail program began in 1988 and has grown to an enrollment of 25,000 children and 2,500 scientists, with nineteen regional chapters. Scientists are recruited with the help of professional organizations, such as American Association for the Advancement of Science (AAAS, page 98), and come from many fields: corporations, colleges and universities, and the government and nonprofit groups. For information, call the national program director at the 800 number.

**Community Board Program (CBP, page 155)**

**Constitutional Rights Foundation (CRF, page 150)**

**Constitutional Rights Foundation/Chicago (CRFC, page 151)**

**Education for Democracy/U.S.A., Inc. (page 187)**

**Environmental Learning for the Future (ELF, page 112)**

## Kids on the Block (KOTB)

9385-C Gerwig Lane
Columbia, MD 21046
1-410-290-9095, FAX 1-410-290-9358
1-800-368-5437

KOTB is a small for-profit company selling educational programs that teach children about people with disabilities by using large, handcrafted puppets. Each hand-and-rod puppet (operated by a trained volunteer) has its own name, character, and distinctive mode of dress, including whatever devices are necessary for the puppet's particular condition—wheelchair, walker, headgear. For each program, KOTB sends a group of puppets, a selection of scripts that is intended to help children and adults understand and appreciate people who are different, a guide to using the program, and educational materials designed to involve the children with the puppets after the performance. There are specially designed programs in over thirty topic areas, including: the mainstreaming of disabled kids; educational differences among emotionally disturbed or gifted children; medical differences, such as AIDS, diabetes, epilepsy, and others; and social concerns, among them fire safety, sexual abuse, and aging. Any of the programs can be used by people with no further qualifications than a commitment to teaching an attitude of cooperation and sensitivity to children aged eight and up. The programs, which are being used by about 1,500 groups in all fifty states, are sold only for nonprofit performances at schools and other noncommercial organizations, such as Junior Leagues (JL, page 85) and Lions Clubs (page 115). KOTB programs can be carried out completely by volunteers. For information about KOTB, contact the director.

**"Law-Related Education: Making a Difference" (pages 152–53)**

**National Association for Mediation in Education (NAME, page 159)**

## National Association of Partners in Education, Inc. (NAPE)

209 Madison St., Suite 401
Alexandria, VA 22314
1-703-836-4880
Contact: Director of Public Relations

NAPE is the result of the merging of two organizations: The National School Volunteer Program and The National Symposium on Partnerships in Education. NAPE's members are schools, businesses, community groups, educators, and individual volunteers who work together as partners to help students achieve educational excellence. In all, NAPE represents over 2.6 million school volunteers through its membership and is a clearinghouse for information on school volunteer and partnership initiatives. The organization serves as an advocate for school partnerships, provides training programs for volunteers and teachers, and publishes a number of books designed to meet the needs of schools, corporate and community partners, and individual volunteers.

NAPE's individual professional members ($60 a year) receive the monthly newsletter "Partners in Education," which describes new and ongoing partnerships and how they work. A $10 individual volunteer membership includes a quarterly newsletter, "School Volunteering," with news about programs nationwide and suggestions for improving your own skills. Write to NAPE for more information about its programs and membership, and for a copy of its publications list.

## National Council of La Raza (NCLR)

Project EXCEL (Excellence in Community Education Leadership)
810 1st St., NE, Suite 300
Washington, DC 20003-4205
1-202-289-1380, FAX 1-202-289-8173
Contact: Project Director or Assistant Director

NCLR's largest national initiative is Project EXCEL, a pilot project for developing and testing innovative community-based education models designed to improve Hispanic education achievement. EXCEL is sponsored at the local level by Hispanic community-based organizations, many of them volunteer-run, that want to play a role in improving education for Hispanic youth. Currently, there are over forty-five model projects in twenty-nine different communities nationwide. For more information on Project EXCEL, contact the project director or assistant director.

### National Gardening Association, GrowLab Program (NGA, page 119)

## The National PTA

700 North Rush St.
Chicago, IL 60611-2571
1-312-787-0977

As distinct from local, unaffiliated Parent-Teacher Organizations (PTOs), the national PTA has more than 7 million members in over 27,000 units. Most of the members are parents, and the remainder are school administrators, teachers, students, grandparents, and other interested persons. In pursuing its goals of promoting the health and educational welfare of children, youth, and families, the PTA offers programs ranging from the arts to prevention of alcohol and other drug abuse. Through its legislative program, the PTA educates, organizes, and provides leadership training for its members to better equip them to actively influence the laws relating to children and youth. The PTA often joins with other local community organizations in projects and campaigns that will benefit students and the community generally.

If you are interested in starting a PTA unit in your child's school or want your local parent group to become part of the PTA, call or write to the national office.

## FEATURED ORGANIZATION: AMERICAN ASSOCIATION FOR THE ADVANCEMENT OF SCIENCE (AAAS)

1333 H St., NW
Washington, DC 20005-4792
1-202-326-6400

AAAS's membership of over 130,000 individuals and affiliation with almost 300 science organizations make it the world's largest network of scientists and engineers, spanning all of the scientific disciplines. AAAS's strong commitment to science education is demonstrated in three volunteer programs in which its membership participates: Science and Technology Centers Project (STCP), Senior Scientists and Engineers (SSE), and Bell Atlantic–AAAS Institute for Middle School Science and Technology Teachers.

STCP, initiated in 1980, encourages AAAS-member scientists and engineers to volunteer in science museums around the country to help expand educational programs, train teachers, and sometimes serve as advisers for exhibits. Volunteers may give demonstrations, provide advice and guidance to children working on group projects, serve as mentors for individual high school students working on special science fair projects, describe other sources of learning to students, explain exhibits, and help develop and design activities. STCP also helped the Museum of Science, Boston (MOS) start a Science-By-Mail program (page 96), which links students and scientists through correspondence.

*Using Scientist Volunteers at Museums: Guidelines for Coordinators* is a booklet describing the STCP program and, in two appendixes, discussing the successful use of people with disabilities as museum volunteers and the accessibility of science museum exhibits and programs to disabled users, including a list of resource organizations that can provide consultants to assist museums in improving exhibit access for the disabled. *Using Scientist Volunteers: Proceedings from a Workshop* relates the experiences of some of the science museums working with STCP. For information about STCP, write to Patricia Curlin, project director.

The SSE program is a national cooperative effort of scientific, engineering, and medical societies to apply the knowledge and experience of senior professionals to three areas of public service: public policy, education, and community service. The program is available for different kinds of organizations: community groups, government agencies, and educational institutions. SSE volunteers at Recording for the Blind (RFB, page 141) help record technical information for people with visual impairments. Other volunteers work with congressional committees to help develop reports. Schools can use SSE for hands-on science-training demonstrations in classrooms, advice on curriculums for teaching, preparing teaching aids, tutoring and mentoring university students, planning and conducting science fairs and field trips, and providing students with insight on science and engineering careers. For information about SSE, contact Patricia Curlin.

The Science Institute provides teachers of science and technology, especially those working with minority and disabled students, with a year-long enhancement program to improve their skills and curriculums. AAAS member scientists and engineers who live near the teachers' communities serve as mentors for new teachers and also cooperate with the schools in reviewing curriculums and in other activities. For information, contact Betty Calinger, project manager.

The Natural Guard (TNG, page 110)

## New York City School Volunteer Program, Inc. (NYCSVP)

443 Park Ave. South
New York, NY 10016
Volunteers: 1-212-213-3370, 1-718-858-0010, FAX 1-212-213-0787
Contact: Recruitment Assistant

NYCSVP, created in 1956, was the first school volunteer program in the country. Its success provided a model for thousands of similar programs and ultimately led to the creation of the National School Volunteer Program (NSVP), one of the components of National Association of Partners in Education (NAPE, page 97). Today, almost 5,700 school volunteers provide tutorial and other services for 65,000 students in 514 New York City public schools. Volunteers work primarily with young children, especially those with the greatest need for individual support, by tutoring English, math, reading, science, and English as a second language. In addition to this core program, NYCSVP has special projects, such as one designed to introduce young students to art and natural history and another to help older students with college planning. Volunteers—students, parents, retirees, corporate employees, and others—must complete a screening process and training for the service they have chosen. Daytime school volunteers give at least two hours of service every week at a school near their home or work. Evening school volunteers give at least one and a half hours of service weekly. For information about volunteering, call either of the numbers above.

**Optimist International (page 82)**

## U.S. Department of Health and Human Services (HHS)

Administration for Children, Youth and Families
Head Start Bureau
P. O. Box 1182
Washington, DC 20013
1-202-245-0560

Head Start was begun in 1965 to give preschool children from low-income families an equal chance as they entered school. The program now serves over 600,000 children and their families every year and is administered by 1,346 community-based nonprofit organizations and school systems. The four major components of the program are:

- Education.
- Health, including medical and dental care, nutrition, and mental health.
- Parent involvement.
- Social services.

Although Head Start services are administered and to a large extent delivered by professional staff, volunteers have always been an important part of the program. High school and college students, parents, retired senior citizens, and a general cross section of the community assist in many ways: by supervising indoor and outdoor play, preparing food, driving or escorting children, reading stories, taking groups on outings, providing health education, doing office work, helping in parent training, assisting with budget preparation, and recruiting and instructing other volunteers. For information about volunteering for Head Start, call your local office or write to the national headquarters.

# Literacy

There are more than 27 million adult illiterates in the United States. Awareness of this crippling problem has been intensifying, and national, state, and local organizations have begun tackling illiteracy with considerable vigor. Literacy programs are devised by professionals, but they are almost completely volunteer-run. Tutors are trained before they can teach. Help another person learn to read, and you're giving more than time: You're offering a whole new world.

## Contact Center, Inc.

The National Literacy Hotline
P.O. Box 81826
Lincoln, NE 68501
1-402-464-0602
National Literacy Hotline: 1-800-228-8813
(1-800-552-9097 TDD)

For people who need help reading and for those who want to volunteer, the National Literacy hotline is a clearinghouse providing information about and referrals to over 12,000 local literacy programs across the country. The hotline is staffed with bilingual Spanish/English operators, and they are assisted by trained professionals and volunteers who provide individualized responses to each caller. Contact's monthly newsletter, "the written word" ($15 for a one-year subscription), has articles on special projects; new approaches; national, state, and local programs. For information about literacy, call the hotline, and for a list of publications, call or write to Contact.

## Laubach Literacy Action (LLA)

1320 Jamesville Ave.
Box 131
Syracuse, NY 13210
1-315-422-9121, FAX 1-315-422-6369
Contact: Maria T. Procopio, Information Center Manager

LLA is the nation's largest network of adult literacy programs providing instruction through trained volunteers. LLA works nationally with other literacy organizations as well as the U.S. Department of Education, and it serves as an advocate of the role of volunteers in adult literacy programs. There are LLA affiliates in almost 1,000 communities in 45 states serving more than 100,000 adults annually. Affiliates, which are autonomous, are initiated by local community groups, including public education agencies, libraries, prisons, mental health centers, and service clubs. Affiliates recruit their own volunteers to tutor or assist with management of the organization. Services, instructional materials prepared by LLA, and volunteer training are provided by LLA field offices. Each volunteer tutor must undergo a workshop training period ranging from ten to eighteen hours before being certified. Volunteers also receive ongoing in-service training.

LLA publishes helpful fact sheets, monographs, and guidebooks for voluntary literacy programs. If you cannot find an LLA affiliate in your phone directory, or to receive information about the LLA's publications, contact the Syracuse office.

## Literacy Volunteers of America (LVA)

5795 Widewaters Pkwy.
Syracuse, NY 13214-1846
1-315-445-8000
Contact Literacy Hotline: 1-800-228-8813

Over 450 LVA affiliates provide tutoring and other educational services to enable 50,000 people a year to achieve their personal goals through literacy. LVA affiliates are involved with family literacy, workplace literacy, homeless shelters, correctional facilities, corporations, and migrant camps. Local affiliates provide direct services, recruiting and training volunteer tutors and matching them with adults in need of literacy or English-speaking skills. Individualized tutoring in reading and writing or conversational English is given both in one-to-one and in small group instruction. LVA calls its approach the "whole language philosophy," which means that the material used for tutoring is applicable to the learner's experience, goals, and interests. Look in your local phone directory for the nearest LVA affiliate or call the Contact Literacy Hotline.

## Reading Is Fundamental (RIF)

Smithsonian Institution
600 Maryland Ave., NW, Suite 500
Washington, DC 20560
1-202-287-3220, FAX 1-202-287-3196

RIF is America's largest reading motivation program, encouraging young people to read by giving them a chance to choose books that interest them and to keep the books as their own. National RIF staff work with local groups and public agencies to develop suitable projects for kids aged three through eighteen, and the organization also arranges substantial discounts with book publishers and distributors. Local volunteer groups raise funds for the books, make the book selections, and place orders directly with the booksellers. Book distributions to the children are then handled as celebratory events. RIF, a national program that honors local wisdom, reaches youngsters in all fifty states through a grassroots network of community-based projects in schools, libraries, community centers, hospitals, Head Start programs, Native American reservations, and homeless shelters. RIF is now offered in over 14,000 sites and has a volunteer staff of more than 140,000 people. "I Want You," a booklet for RIF volunteers, is full of useful suggestions for running successful programs. Write to the Washington, DC, office for information about the nearest RIF site or how to start a project in your community.

## Time to Read (TTR)

Time Warner, Inc.
1271 Sixth Ave.
New York, NY 10020
1-212-522-1212
Contact: Taiga Ermanson, Corporate Community Relations, 1-212-522-1453

TTR is a five-step literacy program based on partnerships between adolescent or adult learners and volunteer tutors, and using Time Inc. magazines such as *People, Sports Illustrated, Life, Money,* or *Southern Living* as the texts. The program is flexible and can be implemented by corporations, community-based organizations, government agencies, trade unions, prisons, and schools and colleges, which individually or in partnerships become cosponsors with Time Warner. Time Warner supplies the local organizations with all materials and a trainer to conduct the volunteer tutor training sessions. "Time to Read: A National Partnership to Improve Literacy" discusses the history of the program, gives details about volunteer training and the learning process, and lists the locations of current TTR projects. Write to the Corporate Community Relations Department for the booklet and more information.

# The Environment

For many of us, action at the community level is the most practical and fulfilling way to maintain a good environment or to upgrade a deteriorating one. Much can be accomplished by reading, attending meetings where environmental issues are discussed, learning the facts, and acting in concert with local like-minded groups. For others who have limited time but a lively interest in the future of the planet, joining national organizations whose aims reflect their own and whose advocacy is an important factor in state and national environmental legislation is the best course. Before you involve yourself with any environmental organization, whether by financial contribution or donation of time or goods, find out about the group's philosophy, goals, and policies to see that they accord with your own convictions.

Environmental volunteer work takes many forms; it can be wholly cerebral or purely physical (and it's one of the areas in which physical labor really counts). You can plant trees, work in a national forest as a trail guide or as part of a maintenance crew, do scientific research, work on beach clean-ups, help protect endangered wildlife populations, be a bird-watcher, or help root out the weeds that clog waterways. Alternatively, it's just as important to raise funds or do office work or public relations for a local or national environmental organization, become an advocate, write letters, or help educate children and others about the environment.

## National Environmental Organizations

### American Hiking Society (AHS)

P.O. Box 20160
Washington, DC 20041-2160
1-703-385-3252
Contact: Executive Director

AHS is a nonprofit membership organization dedicated to preserving and improving America's foot trails. Members receive a subscription to *American Hiker*, a quarterly magazine on hiking; the winter issue contains a listing of Volunteer Vacations across the country—mostly building and maintaining trails in remote and primitive areas. AHS's newsletter, published four times a year, and periodic legislative alerts are also sent to members. To become a member, write to the Washington headquarters for an application. For free information about Volunteer Vacations, send a stamped, self-addressed business-sized envelope to: AHS Volunteer Vacations, P.O. Box 86, Dept. AHS/VV, North Scituate, MA 02060.

As a public service, AHS also publishes *Helping Out in the Outdoors: A Directory of Volunteer Work and Internships on America's Public Lands,* an exemplary annual guide to work in every state, with listings for a diverse assortment of volunteers: campground hosts, nature interpreters, trail builders, park divers, archaeologists, librarians, assistants to highly specialized scientists and technicians, among others. The book is published every November. Send $5 for a single copy, or $15 for a three-year subscription, to AHS's Washington office, and make out the check to "AHS Helping Out."

## Appalachian Mountain Club (AMC)

AMC Volunteer Trails Program
5 Joy St.
Boston, MA 02108
1-617-523-1636
Contact: AMC Trails Program Director

AMC is a nonprofit membership organization devoted to conservation and outdoor recreation. Members receive a discount on AMC's extensive list of publications, including maps and guides; discounts on AMC workshops; and a subscription to *Appalachia Bulletin,* published ten times a year, which has news of activities, workshops, and environmental issues. AMC also publishes *The AMC Outdoors,* a seasonal listing of workshops, guided hikes, and information about the Volunteer Trails Program, which involves the use of more than 800 volunteers every year for the maintenance of over 1,400 miles of trails in the Northeast and elsewhere. Projects range from one-day and weekend stints to ten-day service trips to national parks around the country. People of all ages and from all parts of the country can join AMC's Trail Conservation Corps. Some of the work is strenuous, and applicants should be in good health. Backpacking experience and some equipment may be needed for some of the service trip projects. Minimum age for service trips is sixteen, although younger volunteers may be accepted if accompanied by an adult. If you are interested in volunteering, write to the AMC trails program director for an application and a copy of *The AMC Outdoors.*

Conservation Law Foundation of New England (CLF, page 148)

## Earth First! (EF!)

P.O. Box 5176
Missoula, MT 59806

EF! is a direct-action environmental movement, made up of separate and autonomous EF! groups acting cooperatively with each other and with other environmental organizations to promote their concept of Deep Ecology. The two main premises of Deep Ecology are that all natural things have intrinsic value without any reference to human civilization and that, since all nature is interconnected, the industrial processes of human manipulation must be stopped. One of the organization's mandates is to preserve all the wilderness areas that still exist; another is to recreate vast areas of wilderness that have been tainted by human manipulation and management. Some EF! task forces are Rainforest Action Groups (RAGs) (see Rainforest Action Network, RAN, page 105), the Grizzly Bear Task Force, Wolf Action Group, and Preserve Appalachian Wilderness (PAW). The *Earth First! Journal* ($20 for a yearly subscription), published eight times a year, contains articles about the radical environmental movement and the issues that concern it. Write to EF! for more information.

## Earthwatch

680 Mt. Auburn St.
Box 403
Watertown, MA 02272
1-800-776-0188, FAX 1-617-926-8532

Earthwatch is a nonprofit membership organization that finds paying volunteers for scientific field research expeditions in fifty countries around the world. Earthwatch sponsors over 140 projects a year in rain forest ecology, earth sciences, biological sciences, marine studies, social sciences, and art and archaeology. Projects last from two to three weeks, and volunteers share the costs of the expeditions, the average cost per person being about $1,300, which is tax deductible. Earthwatch members receive *Earthwatch*, a bimonthly magazine that has articles about ongoing projects as well as a section containing inspired and intriguing descriptions of Earthwatch expeditions in need of volunteers. For membership ($25 annually) and volunteer information, write to Earthwatch.

## Educational Concerns for Hunger Organization, Inc. (ECHO)

17430 Durrance Rd.
North Fort Myers, FL 33917
1-813-543-3246
Contact: Linda L. Rath, Office Manager

ECHO is a nondenominational Christian organization providing Christian missionaries and churches, the Peace Corps, and overseas development organizations with technical assistance and seeds for underutilized and hard-to-find tropical plants that are appropriate for small Third World farms. ECHO's quarterly networking newsletter, "ECHO Development Notes," provides information on agricultural research and ideas for growing food under difficult tropical conditions, and offers of free trial-sized packets of seed grown in ECHO's seed bank. ECHO also has an intern program for recent college graduates who have a Christian commitment to involvement in the problems of hunger.

ECHO could not run without volunteers; they work on the farm or in the edible landscape nursery, help in the office, do construction work, and more. Work hours are flexible. Housing cannot be provided. Write or call the office manager for more information.

## Izaak Walton League of America (IWLA)

National Office
1401 Wilson Blvd., Level B
Arlington, VA 22209-2318
1-703-528-1818
Contact: Membership Department

IWLA was founded in 1922 by a group of anglers concerned with combating water pollution and with saving the declining fish population. Among the League's goals are: safe, clean water for drinking and recreation; clean air; preserving wildlife habitats; and the promotion of public access to recreational lands and the concomitant ethical use of the environment. IWLA's major national program is Save Our Streams (SOS), which involves thousands of volunteer groups and individuals in stream adoption projects that include biological monitoring, stream bank restoration, and education on water pollution laws. The award-winning Outdoor Ethics program promotes responsible outdoor recreation such as angling, hunting, and hiking, and through publications encourages responsible behavior by all outdoor recreationists. These and IWLA's regional programs are carried out by the volunteer efforts of the League's 54,000 members, with the assistance of professional staff. If you are interested in joining one of IWLA's 400 local chapters, contact the membership department at the national office.

**National Audubon Society** **(NAS, page 41)**

## FEATURED ORGANIZATION: THE NATURE CONSERVANCY (TNC)

1815 N. Lynn St.
Arlington, VA 22209
1-703-841-5300
Contact: Volunteer Coordinator

TNC is a private nonprofit membership organization committed to finding, purchasing, protecting, and maintaining rare species habitats around the world. Over the course of a year, TNC uses the services of about 20,000 volunteers, many of whom come from the organization's membership of over 645,000.

Volunteer stewards and work crews carry out almost all the work, much of it physical, in over 1,300 nature preserves owned and managed by TNC. TNC coordinates volunteer recruitment of work crews with local agencies—American Association of Retired Persons Volunteer Talent Bank (AARP/VTB, page 36), Telephone Pioneers of America (TPA, page 68), Chevron rctired employees (page 67), offenders sentenced to community service and prison crews from minimum security facilities (in some states), and other groups. Unaffiliated individual volunteers are also welcome.

As part of the stewardship concept, a number of habitats are taken beyond protection and preservation: They are being ecologically restored by thousands of volunteers. Habitat restoration is ongoing at 350 sites across the nation, and more are being added.

Volunteers are also needed in TNC's regional and state field offices to work as fund-raisers, communications people, writers and editors of publications, clerical support, economists, and photographers, among others. Call or write to TNC headquarters for the list of state offices or for information about volunteering to work on one of the nature preserves.

### Rainforest Action Network (RAN)

450 Broadway, Suite 700
San Francisco, CA 94111
1-415-398-4404, FAX 1-415-398-2732

RAN is a national activist organization dedicated to saving the world's tropical rain forests and the human rights of those living in and near them. RAN's primary goal is to halt the destruction of the world's rain forests by banning U.S. tropical timber imports, stopping destructive oil drilling and mining operations, promoting the funding of ecologically responsible projects by world financial institutions, and encouraging sustainable economic endeavors in the rain forests. Working in cooperation with other national and international environmental groups, RAN uses a number of means to achieve its ends: public pressure, direct action (letter-writing campaigns, boycotts, consumer action campaigns, demonstrations), grassroots organizing in the United States, sponsorship of conferences and seminars, research, and other methods. RAN has 150 Rainforest Action Groups (RAGs) in the United States and Europe, informal affiliates that organize local community actions and work with a "twin" group in the Third World. Some of RAN's publications are monthly *Action Alerts,* one-page bulletins about issues that need immediate action and the means of addressing those needs, *World Rainforest Report,* a quarterly magazine, and *Rainforest Action Guide,* with information about rain forests, product lists, and tips on how to get involved. RAN depends on volunteers to do much of the day-today work of the organization, such as answering requests for information and clerical work; it also relies on pro bono lawyers, computer data base experts, and others. Interns, mostly for office work, are also encouraged to help. For more information, contact the San Francisco office.

## Sierra Club (SC)

730 Polk St.
San Francisco, CA 94109
1-415-923-5630
Contact: Sierra Club Outing Department

Working in cooperation with government land agencies, SC's National Service Trips program contributes volunteers to about seventy wilderness projects every year. Trip members, who pay an average of $195 to come on the trip, sign on for ten-day outings and work on building and maintaining trails and restoring the wilderness. Each group is led by a trained SC staff leader and accompanied by a staff cook, trainees, and a doctor. If you are interested in volunteering for a National Service Trip, send $2 to the Outing Department and ask for the most timely Sierra Club Outings Trip List.

SC also has an outreach program called Inner City Outings (ICO), operated on a chapter-by-chapter level, which helps provide wilderness adventures for diverse groups of people, among them urban youth, seniors, hearing or visually impaired people, and the physically disabled. ICO volunteer leaders, trained in recreational and safety skills, make their knowledge available to local agencies such as schools, churches, and outdoor clubs that want to develop outing programs for their members. For more information, write to the ICO coordinator at the SC San Francisco headquarters.

## Smithsonian Research Expeditions (SRE, page 61)

## Student Conservation Association(SCA)

National Office
P.O. Box 550
Charlestown, NH 03603
1-603-832-4301

In 1955, Elizabeth Titus wrote a college thesis in which she proposed a plan for using student volunteers to maintain the national parks. Two years later, Titus founded SCA with fifty high school and college students who spent a month living in the wilderness and building trails in Olympic, Washington. Today, SCA places 1,400 to 1,600 volunteers a year in wilderness work projects in more than forty states, the District of Columbia, Puerto Rico, the Virgin Islands, and Canada. It also conducts international exchange projects involving students from Mexico, Russia, and the United States.

SCA has two main programs: the High School Program (HSP), for volunteers sixteen to eighteen years old, who live and work in the wilderness for a month, then spend a final week backpacking or canoeing; and the Resource Assistance Program (RAP), which places volunteers (who must be high school graduates aged eighteen or older) with federal, state, and private resource agencies such as the National Park Service (page 107) and the U.S. Fish and Wildlife Service (FWS, page 43). RAP volunteers spend twelve weeks training intensively and working with environmental professionals. Some of the work is technical and may require prior training or experience. RAP offers year-round opportunities, while HSP field volunteers work only during the summer.

SCA also publishes *Earth Work*, a monthly magazine dedicated to advancing the careers of those who work to protect the land and the environment. It includes JobScan, a national listing of permanent and seasonal jobs and internships in the field of conservation. Write to SCA for information about any of their programs or publications.

### U.S. Department of Agriculture, Forest Service

Human Resource Programs
12th St. and Independence Ave., SW
P.O. Box 96090
Washington, DC 20090-6090
1-703-235-8855
Contact: Program Manager

Almost 70,000 people volunteer every year to work in the national forests. The work is extremely varied, calling on a wide range of skills and interests. Volunteers conduct interpretive natural history walks, assist in fire protection activities, maintain trails, and write and edit Forest Service publications. There are volunteer opportunities in administration, research, and forestry. Touch America Project (TAP) is a special program for volunteer youths who are sponsored by a partnership of organizations to do conservation work on public lands. For information write to the Forest Service program director.

### U.S. Department of the Interior

National Park Service Volunteers in Parks (VIP)
1849 C St., NW
Washington, DC 20240
1-202-208-3100

The VIP program was created by Congress in 1970 as official authorization of the role that volunteers have played from the beginning of America's national parks. Over 22,000 volunteers now work every year in more than 330 sites in all 50 states and U.S. territories. Some of the locations ring with the sound of American history: famous battlegrounds like Antietam in Maryland, Little Bighorn in Montana, and Vicksburg in Mississippi. Others are archaeological sites like Mound City Group in Ohio and the Native American ruins in the Southwest. VIP workers range from highly trained specialists to trail builders, docents, and office staff. Work is seasonal, weekly, or full-time, and hours are flexible.

If you already know the national park where you'd like to volunteer, call or write to the volunteer coordinator. Or write to VIP in Washington for a brochure and information, then contact the appropriate National Park Service regional office.

## Citizen Environmental Monitoring Groups

Citizen environmental monitoring groups are made up of volunteers who use scientific instruments to track local environmental conditions, such as air and water quality, acid rain, soil erosion, wildlife populations, various kinds of beach debris, and polluted habitats in urban, rural, and wilderness settings. There are presently over 130 such groups, and the number is increasing. Many of them are instituted locally by universities, government agencies, private laboratories, and nonprofit organizations, which provide protocols (plans for the experiments) and training for accurate measuring and recording of data. Environmental monitoring groups have extremely diverse memberships, which can include whole families, members of church groups, school classes, children's organizations, professional scientists, in fact anyone who believes that accurate information about the environment is the foundation of effective advocacy.

An important function of voluntary citizen monitors is reporting environmental abuses. Here are two hotlines:

## HOTLINES

National Parks and Conservation Association Hotline: 1-800-448-NPCA (1-800-448-6272) For reporting animal poaching in a national park.

National Response Center: 1-800-424-8802 For reporting oil spills or the release of other hazardous matter.

### American Littoral Society (ALS)

Baykeeper Volunteer Citizen Water Quality Monitoring Project
Sandy Hook
Highlands, NJ 07732
1-800-8-BAYKPR (1-800-822-9577), 1-908-291-0055
Contact: Beverly DeAngelis, Citizen Water Monitoring Coordinator

ALS, a nonprofit membership organization of professional and amateur naturalists, was founded in 1961 to promote the study and conservation of marine life and coastal areas. Chapter members take part in beach and shoreline clean-ups and monitor sites for pollutants. ALS has the largest volunteer sports fishing tag-and-release program in the country, and its data is stored in the National Marine Fisheries Service at Woods Hole, Massachusetts. ALS's volunteer water monitoring project, with protocols developed by a private environmental service, is ongoing at twenty-four stations around the New York–New Jersey harbor, and its participants include high schools, junior high schools, a youth-at-risk program, an urban canoe club, local citizens, and members of civic and environmental organizations. Call or write for information about these and other ALS programs.

### Association of American Weather Observers (AAWO)

P.O. Box 455
Belvidere, IL 61008
1-815-544-5665
Contact: Steven D. Steinke

AAWO is a nonprofit citizen environmental monitoring organization of people interested in the study of weather at a nonprofessional level. Most of AAWO's 2,100 members participate in measuring one form or another of the elements—rainfall, temperature, sunshine, cloud cover—at their homes, their workplaces, and other locations. The information is then shared with local businesses, newspapers, and other interested organizations, and with other members through regional and local networks. Some chapters record weather information on answering machines for easy access to direct callers. AAWO publishes a monthly newsletter and an annual membership directory containing weather statistics for the year and a list of weather highlights observed by members. Becoming a weather watcher does not require a major investment; $50 to $60 should cover all the equipment needed to start. Membership in AAWO is not expensive, and people of all ages can join (there are some ten- and eleven-year-old members). Contact AAWO for more information.

# Planting Trees

Planting trees not only improves the atmosphere and the landscape, it has a ritual significance as a renewal of life. Tree planting is not at all difficult to do, and if you'd like to involve your school or another group in a program, or would prefer to start a program of your own, contact any of the following organizations.

## American Forestry Association (AFA)

P.O. Box 2000
Washington, DC 20013
1-202-667-3300

Founded in 1875 and America's oldest conservation organization, AFA has been active in creating the nation's system of public lands and parks and continues to promote positive conservation.

AFA's national Global Releaf campaign arranges partnerships among businesses, corporations, conservation groups, and neighborhood citizen associations to create or improve forests locally, nationally, and internationally through tree planting, involvement in conservation activities, and legislative reform.

AFA membership includes opportunities to participate in rural and urban tree planting, conservation action, and forest education programs; advice and information on tree planting; special tours with AFA guides; *American Forests*, the AFA magazine; and discounts on a variety of publications in the field of forestry. Write to AFA for a free brochure describing their membership benefits and programs.

## American Free Tree Program (AFTP)

P.O. Box 9079
Canton, OH 44711
1-216-456-TREE (1-216-456-8733)
Contact: David A. Kidd, President

AFTP, an award-winning program, started giving away free trees in Stark County, Ohio, in April 1989, financed by Rotary (page 116) and other local organizations. By April 1992, over 840,000 free trees had been distributed and planted by 100,000 volunteers in Stark County alone, and about 400 more free tree projects were under way across the United States. The goal is to have 1,000 countywide projects and 1 billion trees planted by the year 2000.

AFTP discovered that the biggest expense in any tree planting was labor, and that the cost of the trees themselves was incidental, about ten or twelve cents for a two-year-old seedling. AFTP's theme is: "A responsible citizen is one who will plant one tree every year of his life," and until the year 2000 the organization will show people how to start their own programs using volunteer labor and local funding. Call or write to AFTP, which will send you a kit with instructions on setting up a new free tree project or will refer you to an existing program near you. Ask for "How to Start a Free Tree Planting Program in Your Area," an excellent mini-guide to creating a local organization.

## National Arbor Day Foundation (NADF)

100 Arbor Ave.
Nebraska City, NE 68410
1-402-474-5655
Contact: Member Services

NADF has three nationwide programs to encourage people to plant and care for trees. Each is enacted at the local level by volunteer groups set up for that purpose. The first is a citywide or community Arbor Day Celebration, for which NADF will send a free booklet with suggestions on how to plan and bring off the event. As part of the Trees for America campaign, NADF will provide ten trees for planting along with instructions for planting and care to each person who joins the Foundation. Tree City USA is a designation NADF accords a town or city that fulfills certain standards, among them celebration of Arbor Day. For information, write to the national headquarters.

## TreePeople

12601 Mulholland Dr.
Beverly Hills, CA 90210
1-818-753-4600

TreePeople is a California-based environmental group whose focus is largely on tree planting and maintenance in the Los Angeles area. The organization encourages people to take individual, active responsibility for conserving and improving the environment. A core group of 900 active volunteers, joined by thousands of others as the occasion warrants, participate in tree planting, in both urban and mountain settings. They take the TreePeople message to people at local fairs, community groups, and other agencies; grow seedlings; work on park maintenance; and do office work. The *TreePeople Events Calendar,* published six times a year, lists every scheduled volunteer activity for the next two months.

TreePeople offers training programs for many of its volunteer activities, including Citizen Forester training, recognized nationally as a model instructional program for people who want to organize tree plantings in their own communities. The "Citizen Foresters Training Manual" has been expanded into a full-length book, *The Simple Act of Planting a Tree,* published in 1990 by Jeremy Tarcher and sold nationwide.

TreePeople also conducts an environmental education program in area schools. For information about TreePeople programs call the Beverly Hills office.

# Toxic Waste

## National Toxics Campaign Fund (NTCF)

National Office
1168 Commonwealth Ave.
Boston, MA 02134
1-617-232-0327
Contact: Executive Director

NTCF is a member organization, a coalition of citizens, consumer organizations, environmental groups, family farmers, scientists, educators, lawyers, public health officials, and others. NTCF's objectives are the implementation of citizen-based solutions to the country's toxics and environmental problems and making toxic prevention the ethic of the United States. Members receive a quarterly newsletter, "Toxic Times," with information about the organization's national and local activities and campaigns, advice about organizing in your own community, and latest developments affecting you. There are eight NTCF offices nationwide. The group is also a resource for technical assistance in setting up local antitoxics groups. The Citizens' Environmental Laboratory is a part of NTCF. For information, contact the Boston headquarters.

# Environmental Education

## The Natural Guard (TNG)

2631 Durham Rd.
North Guilford, CT 06437
1-203-457-1302, FAX 1-203-457-1302
Contact: Diana E. Edmonds, Executive Vice Chairman

TNG, founded by the entertainer Richie Havens in 1990, is a national environmental organization for school-age youth. Initiatives for kids' service projects such as recycling, pollution patrols, litter clean-up, tree planting, weather watches, community gardens, and wildlife classification have been developed by TNG and can be implemented in the local community and in cooperation with existing community-based programs. TNG chapters, which are autonomous and must generate their own funds, have been established in Connecticut, Baltimore, Belize (Central America), Brooklyn, Los Angeles, Honolulu, Washington, D.C, and Toms River and Leestville, New Jersey. For information about starting a chapter, write to the executive director.

## FEATURED ORGANIZATION: CITIZEN'S CLEARINGHOUSE FOR HAZARDOUS WASTES (CCHW)

P.O. Box 6806
Falls Church, VA 22040
1-703-237-CCHW (1-703-237-2249)

CCHW was founded in 1981 by Lois Gibb, the leader of the Love Canal residents who successfully forced New York State to relocate their homes because of toxic waste. CCHW serves as a resource for over 7,400 grassroots community groups that organize around local toxic waste issues. Services include: training for organizing and outreach, technical assistance and training to demystify the scientific issues, information services, and a resource center that covers all aspects of hazardous and solid water management. CCHW also cooperates with traditional environmental groups, multi-issue neighborhood groups, and others.

CCHW also provides yearly Community Leadership Development Grants and Community Training Grants.

One of CCHW's major projects is the McToxics Campaign, which became international in scope as individuals and groups took on the issue of banning plastics in packaging. The campaign ultimately led to the banning by the Coast Guard and Navy of Styrofoam use on ships at sea, and the announcement by McDonald's and, subsequently, other fast-food chains that they would end their use of Styrofoam.

CCHW has written and published over fifty handbooks covering organizing, funding, and maintaining a grassroots environmental organization, as well as publications on hazardous wastes and related issues. Members of CCHW ($25 for a basic individual membership) receive *Everyone's Backyard*, published six times a year ($5 for a single copy), an excellent journal with articles and features describing the struggle for a cleaner world.

Contact the Falls Church office for more information and a list of publications.

## FEATURED ORGANIZATION: VERMONT INSTITUTE OF NATURAL SCIENCE (VINS) ENVIRONMENTAL LEARNING FOR THE FUTURE (ELF)

P.O. Box 86
Woodstock, VT 05091
1-802-457-2779
Contact: Education Director

In the winter of 1973, a group of parents in Woodstock, Vermont, approached the staff of the newly founded Vermont Institute of Natural Science (VINS) and asked them to conduct an outdoor nature workshop for elementary school kids. From those beginnings Environmental Learning for the Future (ELF) has grown to include 8,000 Vermont schoolchildren and 800 volunteers, with the strong possibility that there will be a nationwide ELF program in the future.

Here's how the ELF volunteer training program works:

It's a sunny day in mid-October, and sixteen volunteers have gathered in an empty meeting room of the Dorset Elementary School for their training in Habitats, the concept the school has selected for exploration in eight monthly workshops given over the course of the school year. The subject for this month is the forest floor, which, according to the literature handed to each volunteer, is a habitat for millions of seen and unseen plants and animals.

Linda Garrett, an education staffer from VINS who is leading the workshop, runs through the warm-up, a short puppet show with starring roles for mother and daughter salamanders and walk-on parts for a leaf, a worm, and a mole. It's meant to grab the kids' attention while demonstrating some of the multitude of living and dying organisms that can be found on the forest floor.

Next, Garrett asks the volunteers to split up into two circles and begin passing a brown paper "mystery bag" halfway around each circle. "Now, without looking, put your hand into the bag and feel what's in it, then use two words to describe the object and pass the bag to the person next to you. When half of you have done that, the other half has to guess what's in the bag. Remember, this is something that's found on the forest floor."

"It's thin and papery." "It's got a rough, uneven texture." "It's lightweight and crackly." "It's dry and has uneven edges." Then each person in the second part of the group makes a guess: a leaf, a thin shaving of wood, a piece of bark. The last person who felt the object now reveals it: a strip of birch bark!

Soon the group moves outside to a woodland conveniently adjoining the school yard. The volunteers are asked to lie on the ground in a circle with their feet pointing toward the center, first on their backs, then on their stomachs, while Linda questions them about what they see, touch, hear, and smell above, on, and in the forest floor.

As they are led through three more activities—an archaeologists' dig, a forest foray, and a forest fantasy—the volunteers eagerly scan the treetops, nuzzle the earth under fallen leaves, and imagine themselves to be industrious ants tirelessly making their way under twigs and over moss-covered rocks in a trek across a foot or so of the forest floor, all the while encouraged by Linda to observe, question, and appreciate whatever is under scrutiny. As each activity comes to an end,

Linda summarizes it, reviews what has been learned, makes suggestions for alternative activities in case it rains, and recommends modifications that can be made for older or younger children.

After the workshop, the group returns to the meeting room, and the two volunteer leaders, or ELF coordinators, distribute schedules showing which teams of volunteers will present the activities to each class in the school. Team members set up planning sessions so that everyone is prepared and presentations to the children will go smoothly. A week later, the workshop is reenacted with the children, each class led by two or three volunteers. Jenepher Lingelbach, director of ELF, calls the process Hands-on Nature. (*Hands-on-Nature* is also the title of a nationally acclaimed book of 233 ELF activities published by VINS, $18.95 plus $2.50 postage, and edited by Ms. Lingelbach.)

The ELF training program seems quite simple as it leads the volunteers through the same workshop they will be giving the children, but ELF's goals are sophisticated and its effects long lasting. A ten- or eleven-year-old child who has attended ELF workshops since kindergarten will have accumulated a considerable body of knowledge about the natural world. Through the ripple effect, this knowledge is brought home and shared with other family members, who in turn can be expected to become more cnvironmentally aware themselves.

The key ingredient in ELF's success, Jenepher Lingelbach says, is a dynamic local volunteer, a person with enough energy to bring the program into the school and to act as liaison with VINS, a person who is warm and open and reliable, someone who knows the area well enough to recruit a group of enthusiastic volunteers—the people who are at the heart of ELF.

At the present writing, ELF costs each school about $3,000 a year, which covers training staff and materials. For information, write to the VINS director of education.

# Resources

## NATIONAL ENVIRONMENTAL ORGANIZATIONS

*Environmental Opportunities* is a monthly bulletin that lists job openings in private-sector environmental groups. Most of the listings are for salaried staff, but in fact some of the wages offered are low enough to qualify as stipends. Internships and a few volunteer positions are also listed. Subscriptions are $24.00 for six months, $44.00 for one year, and $4.50 for a single copy. Write to Box 4957, Arcata, CA 95521, or call 1-707-839-4640.

*Environmental Vacations: Volunteer Projects to Save the Planet,* by Stephanie Ocko. Santa Fe, NM: John Muir Publications, 1990. Written for paying volunteers interested in working on and helping to subsidize environmental projects (volunteers assist scientists in their fieldwork—on land, at sea, and, in some cases, serving people in need), the book answers questions about money, discusses physical, social, and skill requirements, describes specific projects in fascinating detail (a number of them illustrated with photographs), and gives firsthand reports from volunteers in fields ranging from archaeology to oceanography. Includes a list of organizations sponsoring field projects, a list of endangered species by country, and an index. $15.95.

*Helping Out in the Outdoors: A Directory of Volunteer Work and Internships on America's Public Lands,* an annual publication of the American Hiking Society (AHS). (See box, page 103).

*The Rainforest Book,* by Scott Lewis with the Natural Resources Defense Council. Venice, CA: Living Planet Press, 1990. This book explains what rain forests are and how they benefit the earth, tells how the forests are being destroyed, and discusses steps that can be taken individually and collectively to save them. $5.95.

## CITIZEN ENVIRONMENTAL MONITORING GROUPS

*National Directory of Citizen Volunteer Environmental Monitoring Programs,* by Virginia Lee and Eleanor Ely. This is a comprehensive register of state and national programs that is updated yearly. The 1990 edition contains descriptions of 133 programs, including the purpose of each program, the parameters being measured, and the means of doing so. For a free copy of the directory, call or write to Rhode Island Sea Grant (1-401-792-6842) and send $1 for postage to EPA/Rhode Island Sea Grant, University of Rhode Island, Narragansett, RI 02882.

## ENVIRONMENTAL EDUCATION

*This Planet Is Mine: Teaching Environmental Awareness and Appreciation to Children,* by Mary Metzger and Cinthya P. Whittaker. New York: Fireside Books, 1991. Using clear language, this guide for parents and teachers describes and explains the major elements of the environment and the forces that impact upon them and then presents ways of adapting the information for children of different ages. Environmental projects involving adults and children, everyday ways of making a difference to improve the environment, resource organizations for every major topic and subtopic, an excellent list of resources for parents, environmental hotlines, a glossary, and a state-by-state list of recycling resources all make the book a useful primer. $8.

# Fraternal and Service Clubs

Fraternal and service clubs have long been known for their generosity and their responsiveness to community needs. Devotion to service is part of their credos, and members are encouraged to participate to whatever extent they can in volunteer projects. Each organization has its requirements for membership. In addition to those listed here, check the phone book for the Eagles, the Elks, and other fraternal clubs.

## Kiwanis International (KI)

3636 Woodview Trace
Indianapolis, IN 46268
1-317-875-8755

KI is a worldwide association of Kiwanis Clubs, service clubs for professional men and women concerned with improving their communities. There are more than 8,800 Kiwanis Clubs and 330,000 members in seventy-seven nations and geographic areas. Each club sponsors a variety of fund-raising and service projects chosen by the club to meet community needs as determined by its members. Once a project is selected, the club raises the funds needed and provides the hands-on volunteer services to accomplish the goal. One special area of interest to Kiwanis is getting young people involved in community service and leadership development. Key Club International has 135,000 members in 3,800 high schools, and Circle K International has 10,000 members on 600 college campuses. Membership in Kiwanis is by invitation. For more information, consult your local phone directory, or write to the national headquarters in Indianapolis for the location of the club nearest you.

## Lions Clubs International

300 22nd St.
Oak Brook, IL 60521-8842
1-708-571-5466, FAX 1-708-571-8890

The Lions motto is: "We serve." There are over 40,000 Lions Clubs worldwide, with a total membership of 1.4 million men and women. Clubs participate in many activities, initiating projects in their own communities and sponsoring a very broad spectrum of services, including drug awareness, diabetes education and research, and environmental projects. The Lions' sight conservation programs are international in scope and renown. They encompass free glaucoma screenings, glaucoma education, funding for clinics and other medical facilities, and the establishment and support of a majority of the world's eye banks, among many other services. Membership in a Lions Club is by invitation only. Check the telephone directory for the club nearest you.

## Moose International, Inc.

Supreme Lodge Bldg.
Mooseheart, IL 60539
1-708-859-2000

Moose International is a nonprofit fraternal organization with a membership of 1.8 million men and women dedicated to the improvement of community life, with special emphasis on children, health, and the elderly. Mooseheart, a self-contained city of 1,200 acres, was founded in 1913 as a home for children from orphaned or distressed families. Generally, such children must have a parent or close relative who is a member. Moose International also maintains Moosehaven, a retirement home in Orange Park, Florida, for elderly members and their spouses. Moose Community Services, carried out in over 2,200 lodges nationwide, includes sponsorship of youth athletics and Scout troops. For Operation Santa Claus, lodges collect and distribute about 1 million toys every year to needy children. Volunteers work in behalf of hospitals, blood banks, and other local agencies. Almost every lodge sponsors individual projects geared to fit the needs of the area in which it is located. Look for the local Moose lodge in the phone directory, or contact the Mooseheart office for information.

**Optimist International (page 82)**

## Rotary International

One Rotary Center
1500 Sherman Ave.
Evanston, IL 60201-3698
1-708-866-3000, FAX 1-708-328-8554

Rotary was the world's first service club, formed in Chicago in 1905. Today there are more than 25,000 Rotary Clubs, with a combined membership of over 1.1 million people, all of them volunteers. Rotary's membership is by invitation only, and the organization's goals include humanitarian service, high ethical standards in all vocations, and peace in the world. Each Rotary Club determines its own service activities, some of them based on Rotary International's programs relating to the environment, literacy, substance abuse, and concern for the elderly. Volunteer opportunities abound: hosting Rotary Youth Exchange students; community service of the widest possible range; the Rotary Volunteers in Action (RVIA), a pilot program designed to match individual volunteers with situations in which their specific skills can be used. RVIA works within the clubs to meet the community's needs—transporting elderly or disabled people, providing expert agricultural advice to farmers, planning a water system, tutoring illiterate adults, or setting up a prenatal clinic for expectant mothers. Rotary also maintains a computerized Donations-in-Kind Information Network, which links offers of donated goods, supplies, and services with requests for these items. For information, call your local Rotary Club.

## Sertoma International

1912 E. Meyer Blvd.
Kansas City, MO 64132-1174
1-816-333-8300, FAX 1-816-333-4320
Contact: International Sponsorships Director

Sertoma is a civic service organization with a membership of about 35,000 men and women in more than 950 autonomous chapters in the United States, Canada, and Mexico. Sertoma's primary focus is helping people with speech and hearing problems through individual clubs' affiliations with local facilities that specialize in communicative disorders. Such projects range from having volunteers work with mobile screening units to clubs that fund tuition, professional training, and essential equipment. Public education about hearing problems, much of it carried out by Sertoma volunteers, is another successful program used by a number of the clubs. Each club also sponsors local programs focusing on youth, freedom, and democracy and other human concerns. Anyone interested in joining Sertoma, which stands for "Service to Mankind," should contact the director of international sponsorships.

## Soroptimist International of the Americas (SIA)

1616 Walnut St., Suite 700
Philadelphia, PA 19103
1-215-732-0512, FAX 1-215-732-7508

Soroptimist International is a membership organization of professional and executive businesswomen from diverse backgrounds and occupations. SIA has 50,000 members in 1,500 clubs in 21 countries. Soroptimist programs promote economic and social development, education, human rights and the status of women, health, the environment, and international goodwill and understanding. Local projects, which are undertaken to address the needs of the community, are supported by donations of money, time, or talent, or a combination. Typical Soroptimist projects include working for literacy, participating in community gardens and environmental clean-ups, promoting student exchange programs, sponsoring legislation, and financing substance abuse centers. Membership in a Soroptimist Club is by invitation. Check your phone directory or contact the Philadelphia headquarters for the club nearest you.

## The United States Junior Chamber of Commerce (JAYCEES)

P.O. Box 7
Tulsa, OK 74121-0007
1-918-584-2481, FAX 1-918-584-4422

Jaycees is an international nonprofit organization, with about 4,500 autonomous U.S. chapters and a membership of 225,000 men and women aged twenty-one to thirty-nine who are interested in leadership training and personal development. Jaycee members are recruited at the community level, and their programs are implemented locally. Four priority areas are the environment, prevention of substance abuse, work with the homeless, and governmental affairs. For information, consult your local phone directory for the nearest Jaycee chapter, or get in touch with the national office.

## USO World Headquarters (USO)

601 Indiana Ave., NW
Washington, DC 20004
1-202-783-8121, FAX 1-202-638-4716

Since its founding by President Franklin D. Roosevelt in 1941, USO has been serving the unique needs of transient military groups and their families all around the world. USO helps servicemen and -women with such problems as language difficulties, flight delays, and meeting family members; provides information on travel, transportation, and currency exchange; and assists families in finding housing, day care, and other services. USO operates at airports, fleet centers, and family and community centers, which serve as recreational facilities for the whole family. USO has a paid staff of 700 and over 25,000 volunteers serving the off-duty needs of more than 2 million service members at over 160 locations worldwide. If you're interested in volunteering, contact your local USO or write to the world headquarters and ask for the Directory of Locations.

# Gardening and the Enrichment of Community Life

Gardening—so pleasurable that it is understandably one of the country's most popular leisure pursuits—is a wonderfully satisfying way to help others. Gardeners, both amateur and professional, have ample opportunities to put their skills to good use for the enrichment of community life. You can:

- Help elderly or disabled gardeners with some of the heavier chores.
- Donate part of your own vegetable harvest to a community organization that cooks and distributes food.
- Donate your flowers regularly to nursing homes and other residences.
- Help start a community garden.
- Become a Master Gardener.

## Master Gardeners

If you want to increase your own knowledge of gardening and serve the community at the same time, you might want to become a Master Gardener; that is, a volunteer trained to answer questions from the public about gardening. The Master Gardener program began in Washington State, was further developed by the U.S. Department of Agriculture Extension Service, and now is implemented by county extension agents in forty-six states. Master Gardening courses are also given by some botanical gardens.

Applicants are given 30 to 120 hours of instruction (some of the courses are given free; others require a nominal fee) about all aspects of horticulture, especially as they pertain to local growing conditions—soil chemistry, pest control, climate, how to select and grow vegetables and ornamental plants—and the course includes classroom, laboratory, and hands-on field experience. Master Gardeners are then expected to return to the community at least 40 hours of service by answering questions in person at plant clinics run by botanical gardens, garden clubs, or local radio stations, by volunteering to work with horticultural therapists, working in community gardens, or by writing for a local paper—whatever suits the volunteer's background, skills, and interests. Master Gardener certification is awarded once a person has finished the training and completed the community service requirement. For information about becoming a Master Gardener, get in touch with your county extension agent or cooperative extension office, or call a botanical garden. If a program does not exist in your area, perhaps you can work with the extension agent to develop one.

# Garden Clubs

Garden clubs are nonprofit membership organizations. Active members volunteer for programs and events that benefit the community at large: beautification projects, sales and boutiques that support scholarships for local children, outreach to the community with cooperative recycling programs, fostering community gardens, practicing horticultural therapy, working with children's groups, and much more. Check your local phone book for a garden or horticultural club or society near you, or get in touch with any of the organizations that follow.

## The Gardeners of America, Inc (TGOA)

5560 Merle Hay Rd., Box 241
Johnston, IA 50131-0241
1-515-278-0295

TGOA offers membership to any gardener who wishes to increase and share his or her gardening knowledge. Members in TGOA's 150 clubs nationwide may participate in garden shows, clinics, tours, and beautification projects. TGOA's horticultural therapy program, Gardening from the Heart . . . , has been adopted by many affiliated clubs working with horticultural therapists in local nursing and retirement homes and in programs for the handicapped or those with special needs. TGOA also has community service programs, some involving children's classroom gardening groups using the GrowLab program (see National Gardening Association, NGA, page 119), others concerned with beautification projects. For information about joining a local club or about forming a new one, contact the headquarters in Johnston, Iowa.

## National Council of State Garden Clubs (NCSGC)

National Headquarters
4401 Magnolia Ave.
St. Louis, MO 63110
1-314-776-7574, FAX 1-134-776-5108
Contact: Mrs. Charles H. Mantler, Office Manager

The NCSGC is the largest federation of garden clubs in the United States with over 275,000 members and more than 9,200 clubs nationwide and overseas. Each club has its own particular areas of focus—garden design, birds and other wildlife, the environment, recycling, restoration, landscape architecture, public education, and so on, depending on the club's membership. Every two years the national organization sets agendas in special areas such as civic development (beautification), a wide range of environmental concerns, garden therapy (page 124), historic preservation, and junior gardeners. State organizations then work with local clubs to design and carry out projects based on these themes, many involving outreach to local businesses, schools, and other organizations; especially meritorious projects receive awards. An applicant for membership in a federated garden club must be sponsored by two club members. Check your phone book or local newspaper for the number of the garden club nearest you, or write to the national headquarters for information.

## National Gardening Association (NGA)

GrowLab Program
180 Flynn Ave.
Burlington, VT 05401
1-802-863-1308, FAX 1-802-863-5962
Contact: Eve Pranis, GrowLab Program

GrowLab is not a club; it is a garden-based learning program adopted by schools so that kids in grades K–8 can learn science concepts and build environmental awareness through hands-on growing experiences. NGA can provide the basic inexpensive indoor growing equipment, activities lessons for the program, and other assistance. They help match schools with community partners who provide funding, materials, and volunteer technical and curriculum assistance—nursery owners, botanical garden staff, parents, and garden clubs with youth gardening programs. Classroom teachers receive free issues of "Growing Ideas: A Journal of Garden-Based Learning," the GrowLab newsletter.

Youth gardening groups that volunteer their efforts for the community and in support of environmental awareness are eligible for NGA's Youth Garden Grants and annual awards of about $500 in seeds, tools, and educational materials. For information about the grants, or if you are interested in volunteering for a local GrowLab program or would like to see one started in your area, contact the Burlington office.

# Arboreta and Botanical Gardens

### American Association of Botanical Gardens and Arboreta (AABGA)

786 Church Rd.
Wayne, PA 19087
1-215-688-1120
Contact: Sharon Dixon

There are over 300 arboreta and botanical gardens in the United States and all of them rely extensively on the help of volunteers, who act as docents, salespeople, horticulturists, educators, fund-raisers and board members, office workers, speakers, and hosts of special events, among other activities. For the location of the botanical garden or arboretum nearest you, call or write to AABGA.

### Missouri Botanical Garden (MBG)

P.O. Box 299
St. Louis, MO 63166
1-314-577-5187
Contact: Volunteer Office

At MBG, 734 active volunteers (from a list of over 800) contribute 79,000 hours each year in fulfillment of the Garden's mission to disseminate information about plants through research, education, and display. Volunteers work as Master Gardeners, garden guides, volunteer inspectors; historic home tour guides. They assist customers in the plant and gift shops; they aid in research and library activities, including biographical research, pamphlet- and bookbinding, cataloging, foreign language translation, plant mounting, data processing, and organizing collections of maps and other related material; they help maintain natural trails and cultivated areas in the arboretum; and they host special projects. MBG volunteer horticultural work involves gardening and plant maintenance in the conservatories, production greenhouse, and on the grounds, and there are also volunteer opportunities in set design and construction for indoor floral displays. MBG recruits primarily through its membership. For information, call or write to the volunteer office.

# Community Gardens

There are literally thousands of community gardens throughout the United States. In Philadelphia alone, Philadelphia Green, probably the first major urban community garden program, works with about 1,500 different garden projects, some of them started by the Garden Club of America

## FEATURED ORGANIZATION: CHICAGO BOTANIC GARDEN (CBG)

P.O. Box 400
Glencoe, IL 60022-0400
1-708-835-5440, FAX 1-708-835-4484
Contact: Linda Doede, Manager, Volunteer Services

CBG has a roster of about 475 volunteers, 200 of whom are active at any one time, since some of the work is seasonal. Here are some of the projects they work on:

- The Learning Garden for disabled people is maintained by a group of fourteen volunteers who work with a local seniors center.
- Chicago schoolchildren are taught classes at the garden, where they can explore and experience the plants firsthand. The classes are taught by fifty-five trained volunteer docents.
- In coordination with a school course in basic plant sciences, CBG plants and helps maintain a children's vegetable garden. The garden is supervised by a paid CBG staff coordinator and sixty-three trained volunteers.
- Over 100 volunteers work in the garden's educational greenhouses and outside in garden plant collections helping to grow and maintain plants.
- More than thirty volunteers work in the garden's production greenhouse, helping to grow the 50,000 annual plants that are used for CBG bedding plants and plant sales, and for kids to take home.
- Twenty-five volunteers collect and dry wildflowers all year long for the annual Roadside Flower Sale.
- The garden's gift shop is run by volunteers.
- Special events are hosted by over sixty volunteers.
- There are fourteen weekday volunteer tour guides and fifty-five weekend volunteers.
- Finally, three of the four programs run by CBG's urban horticultural department use volunteers extensively. They are:

1. The Plant Information Service, which uses forty Master Gardeners (page 118) to answer questions and diagnose plant samples brought by walk-in visitors.
2. The GROW (Gardening Resources on Wheels) program, which provides technical assistance to groups starting up community gardens.
3. Green Chicago, which works with inner-city groups that want to develop community gardens (page 120). Although Green Chicago is run by a staff of one, the gardening groups themselves are all-volunteer.

CBG recruits primarily by word of mouth from its cadre of volunteers. For more information, call or write to the volunteer coordinator. Internships at CBG are sometimes available in public relations, conservation ecology, horticulture, pest management, horticultural therapy, and education. Get in touch with the internship coordinator for details.

in the 1950s. Community gardens are sponsored by land grant organizations, churches, horticultural societies, civic organizations, and federal, state, or local government agencies, to name a few.

Community gardens flourish in urban, suburban, and rural settings, and all of them are created to meet the specific needs of the gardeners and their neighborhoods. Some are grown only for vegetables to supplement the gardeners' food supply; some are just for flowers. There are gardens that are grown for and by children, and gardens for people who are disabled, abused, or recovering addicts. Any community garden will improve a neighborhood and the lives of those who see and grow it, but there are other practical benefits as well: The leadership skills that neighborhood people develop as they plan their gardens—deciding where the gardens should be, finding out how to acquire the land and how to get hydrant permits, determining what goes into the gardens, learning how to design them and what plants to use, and so on—all spill over into other areas of community life, such as housing, child care, and education.

## American Community Gardening Association (ACGA)

325 Walnut St.
Philadelphia, PA 19106
1-215-922-1508, FAX 1-215-625-8288
Contact: Sally McCabe, Jeff Myers, or Janet Carter

ACGA is an umbrella membership organization of individuals and about 300 locally sponsored organizations that work with neighborhood groups to establish community gardens, parks, and other green spaces. Members receive the ACGA *Community Greening Review*, with information about successful programs and recources and other news as well. ACGA has an annual conference at which members can exchange ideas and network with other people in the field.

For individual volunteers or groups who are interested either in starting or joining a local community garden, write to ACGA for the name and address of an agency in your area.

## Minnesota State Horticultural Society (MSHS) Minnesota Green(MG)

1970 Folwell Ave., #161
St. Paul, MN 55108
1-612-624-7752
Contact: Rick Bonlender, Minnesota Green Coordinator

MG, the statewide community gardening outreach program of MSHS, began in 1988 with a few model sites in St. Paul and Minneapolis, working mostly with groups of Southeast Asians living in public housing in run-down areas. The residents began by starting small gardens on blocks near porno houses and in the rubble of torn-down buildings, their purpose being to attract and impress developers, and ultimately to bring jobs to the neighborhood. Since then, MG has become one of the largest and fastest-growing community gardening programs in the country, coordinating horticulture-related organizations and community groups across the state.

MG, like other Green organizations, provides technical assistance and training in all aspects of community gardening, from site selection and preparation, to recruiting and training volunteers, to building local networks and promoting the projects, to referrals for gardening information and workshops, to assistance in developing local sources of seeds, plants, and garden supplies.

MG defines community gardening broadly to include front yards; "blooming boulevards" (the spaces between sidewalks and curbs), which in turn have engendered "blooming blocks"; entryway enhancements; wildlife landscaping; vegetable gardens; tree planting; children's gardens; and so on. MG assists groups that get part of their food from food banks, trains them, and ultimately

## FEATURED ORGANIZATION: NEW YORK BOTANICAL GARDEN (NYBG) BRONX GREEN-UP PROGRAM (BGU)

Bronx, NY 10458-5126
1-212-220-8995
Contact: Terry Keller, Program Director

In 1988, NYBG decided to initiate a community garden program in the Bronx, one of New York's poorest boroughs. The idea was to beautify the Bronx by helping residents to reclaim some of the 10,000 abandoned lots in the borough and turn them into green spaces. BGU began with three vacant-lot gardens, and by now it is a model program for other cities with more than 150 gardens that are planned, designed, built, and maintained by over 4,000 community residents and ninety-five BGU volunteers. The gardens are grown near schools, public housing projects, rehab centers, and senior centers, and, of course, in vacant lots.

BGU operates with two full-time and two part-time staff, two interns, and ninety-five neighborhood volunteers who participate in an eight-week program and are taught the specifics of urban gardening, particularly as they relate to conditions in New York City. For instance, although there is no instruction about pesticides or chemical gardening, the volunteers are told about potential lead contamination from demolished buildings. In return for their training, the volunteers contribute forty hours of their time to their neighbors, working in community gardens, assisting with street tree plantings, helping neighborhood groups organize, and working with schools, training teachers to keep gardens active and providing lectures and workshops for schoolchildren. Volunteers have provided 5,000 hours of service.

BGU does not seek out neighborhood groups and suggest to them that the nearby trash-strewn vacant lot, presently frequented by drug dealers and their customers, could be transformed into a beautiful and productive vegetable garden. Instead, a group must organize itself for the purpose of making a community garden, delegate responsibility, and come to BGU with a proposal.

BGU sponsors each garden for three years. The first year is an intensive training process for the neighborhood group, some of it in horticulture and some of it in negotiating the city bureaucracy. The average person in the Bronx has no idea of how to tie together all the services that are available, and BGU is there to provide that expertise. BGU works with the group on a weekly basis, providing leadership training and supplying technical advice and materials to get the garden started, including fencing, material for signs, tools, seeds, soil (a major need in an urban setting, where everything is either concrete or contaminated), and compost—whatever is required for the site. During the second year, there are monthly sessions with additional instruction on how to keep the garden going and more technical and material assistance. During the third and final year of sponsorship, BGU meets quarterly with the garden group, helping to work out strategies for fund-raising, saving seed, and so on. Even after the third year, BGU and its staff and volunteers will offer advice and assistance when asked.

Each garden group makes its own rules as to how to protect the garden, what is grown there, who has keys to get in, what people are allowed to drink, how people are allowed to speak to one another. The gardens are created by many different ethnic groups who work together and get to know each other. The culmination is a huge garden party every August held in a different Bronx

*Continued*

*Continued*

community, where gardeners from all over the borough bring their produce and flowers to show off what they grow and share it with their neighbors, accompanied by music, contests, crafts, demonstrations, and so on.

BGU has served as a model for several other community gardens sponsored by botanical gardens, notably the Brooklyn Botanic Garden. Contact the BGU program director for information about becoming a trained volunteer, starting a Bronx community garden, or starting a program similar to BGU.

helps them grow part of their crops for donation to the food bank. Duluth has a community food garden project directly linked to a food bank and a soup kitchen.

MG's Resource List includes educational publications, slide sets, videos, and films to assist people interested in starting community gardens. *Creating Community Gardens* ($5, including shipping and handling) is a twenty-page booklet about how to plan and create the gardens, useful information for any community garden group. To learn more about MG and its programs, and to obtain its Resource List, write to MG's coordinator.

# Horticultural Therapy

Horticultural therapy has been around for thousands of years as a means of calming mental patients and alleviating their symptoms. Today, it is broadly defined as the use of garden-related activities to aid in the recovery of handicapped people. Programs involving horticultural therapy are often planned and supervised by accredited professionals, while the programs themselves are carried out largely by trained, dedicated volunteers.

Horticultural therapy is now practiced in nursing homes, schools for the emotionally and physically disabled, hospitals, veterans' facilities, and in people's own homes, among other places. Some programs are on a grand scale, like the Enid A. Haupt Greenhouse at Rusk Institute in New York City, which uses volunteer horticulturalists to maintain the separate parts of the greenhouse—orchids, begonias, roses, and others—and volunteers who serve the patients directly. Others, like the Federated Garden Clubs of Vermont, have developed simple kits containing bulbs, potting soil, pots recycled from garden club members, and instructions for planting. Such kits can be adapted for diverse populations, such as alcoholics, people in nursing homes, and schoolchildren.

## American Horticultural Therapy Association (AHTA)

362A Christopher Ave.
Gaithersburg, MD 20879
1-800-634-1603, 1-301-948-3010
Contact: Steven Davis, President

AHTA is the only national organization in the United States dedicated to the promotion and development of horticultural therapy and rehabilitation programs, with a membership comprised of organizations, individual professionals, and some volunteers. AHTA responds to 1,500 calls a year from the general public—inquiries about education, publications, and facilities involved with horticultural therapy. AHTA's publications list includes *An Annotated Bibliography of Horticultural Therapy*, the *AHTA Membership Directory*, and other books and papers. For information about the garden therapy program nearest you, or for literature on membership, call the 800 number.

## William Breman Jewish Home

3150 Howell Mill Rd., NW
Atlanta, GA 30327
1-404-351-8410
Contact: Sandra Epstein, Horticultural Therapist, or Camille Hammond, Director of Recreational Therapy

The William Breman Jewish Home has about 120 residents, many of them disabled physically or mentally. In 1986, the home built a greenhouse, which, although run by professional horticulturalists, is for the residents' use. The home has several successful programs and projects, devised by the horticultural therapist and the director of recreation therapy and carried out by a few volunteers.

In the intergenerational program, second-grade students from a nearby school come to the home to work on various horticultural projects with the elderly residents. The kids call the residents "friends," to show that your friends don't necessarily have to be your own age. All plants, whether decorative or edible, are used by the home or taken by the children to their own homes. Activities include:

- Making tussie mussies (flower bouquets), which the children take home to give to someone they love.
- Twining wire hearts with ivy for Valentine's Day.
- A dish garden program that culminates when some of the gardens are entered in the Atlanta flower show.
- Planting snow white bulbs, which bloom through the winter holiday season.
- Planting miniature flower boxes with spring seeds.
- Residents and children getting together and sharing pictures of their own relatives. Just as people have families, so do plants, and this activity encourages the discussion of the differences and similarities in any kind of family.
- Packaging trees for the city of Atlanta to plant on Arbor Day.

In another project, residents grow vegetable seedlings in peat pots for later planting in a garden plot at a camp for inner-city children. The children tend the garden and when it's harvested, as a way of thanks, campers invite residents to come for lunch and eat the produce. Residents also grow flowers and make weekly arrangements for the Sabbath dining room. Most residents have contact with plants, either at the greenhouse itself or on rolling "plantmobiles," which are brought to immobilized patients.

Volunteers work directly with the residents, transporting them, and helping with bulb planting and other tasks. For instance, the intergenerational program uses ten volunteers for every fifty people (twenty five children and twenty five residents). Volunteers are carefully trained to work and interact with the residents: They are taught how to speak to them without being condescending or demeaning, they learn how to push a wheelchair safely, and are given other practical guidance. For information, get in touch with the horticultural therapist or the director of recreation therapy.

# Health

Ordinary delivery of health care in America is inconceivable without the contributions of millions of volunteers, from every age range and every walk of life, who serve in hundreds of ways. Individuals who want to volunteer for organizations specializing in a single disease should either check the phone book or ask a local doctor or hospital for the address of the national headquarters. All hospitals need volunteers, although each uses them differently, depending on the size and needs of the hospital and the population it serves. Call the volunteer offices of the hospitals in your area to see what's available. In some towns, rescue squad and transportation services are provided (and partly funded) by volunteers. For organizations that work with sick children, see pages 73–77.

### HOTLINE

**National Bone Marrow Donor Program Hotline: 1-800-654-1257**

**Agency for International Development (AID, page 193)**

## American Heart Association (AHA)

7272 Greenville Ave.
Dallas, TX 75231-4596
1-800-AHA-USA1 (1-800-242-8721), 1-214-373-6300

AHA's goal is to reduce death and disability from cardiovascular diseases and strokes, which claim as many lives as all other causes of death combined. AHA is a leading funder of research in the field of heart disease. Through the efforts of 3.5 million volunteers, AHA provides public and professional education and community services that reach over 25 million Americans every year. Volunteers participate in various ways at the grassroots level, from presenting educational programs in elementary schools to blood pressure and cholesterol screening to advocating proper nutrition labeling and tobacco regulation to public affairs. For information about volunteer opportunities, call your local AHA chapter at the 800 number.

## Arthritis Foundation (AF)

P.O. Box 19000
Atlanta, GA 30326
1-800-283-7800

AF supports research to find the cure for and prevention of arthritis and works to improve the quality of life for those affected by the disease. There are over seventy chapters nationwide serving as resource centers for individuals and families whose lives are changed by arthritis and offering a variety of programs and services depending on local needs and resources. AF services rely heavily on volunteers, who work in over ten educational programs; exercise and recreation projects; social support; advocacy; and local fund-raising events. All volunteers must be trained by AF before they begin to work.

If you are interested in volunteering for AF, check your local phone directory for a listing or call the 800 number for the chapter nearest you.

**Brass Ring Society, Inc. (page 76)**

**Clara Barton Camp for Girls with Diabetes, Inc. (CBC, page 74)**

**Concern/America (page 186)**

**Delta Society (DS, page 42)**

**Department of Veterans Affairs (VA, page 232)**

## Epilepsy Foundation of America (EFA)

4351 Garden City Dr.
Landover, MD
1-800-EFA-1000
1-301-459-3700

EFA is the primary national organization involved with a full range of national and local programs designed to help people with epilepsy. National programs include research grants, fellowships, patient services that address the effects of the disease/disorder on all family members, and community services delivered by EFA's eighty-three affiliates. Each affiliate is independent, but many of them offer the following services: information and referral, educational activities and programs such as Kids on the Block (KOTB, page 96), counseling, sponsorship of self-help/support groups, advocacy, and many other programs to help people with epilepsy enjoy a full life. Volunteers are needed to carry out many of these programs. For information about volunteering, or the location of the affiliate nearest you, call the 800 number.

**Famous Fone Friends (FFF, page 76)**

**Grant-a-Wish Foundation (page 76)**

**Health Volunteers Overseas (HVO, page 188)**

## Hospital Audiences, Inc. (HAI)

220 W. 42nd St., 13th Fl.
New York, NY 10036
1-212-575-7677
Contact: Volunteer Coordinator

HAI was founded in 1969 to provide disabled persons and others confined in a variety of institutions with access to the rich cultural life, especially the performing arts, in the New York metropolitan area: plays, sports events, concerts, movies, spectaculars, parades, Fourth of July fireworks, and other public events. Currently, HAI arranges for over 300,000 individuals to attend 9,000 cultural events by acquiring low-cost or free tickets to performing arts events (donated by theater, concert hall, and sporting arena managements). HAI transports clients from their facilities—such as nursing homes, hospitals, prisons, mental health and mental retardation facilities—to the events, looks after the clients during the performances, then transports them back to their facilities. Although clients are accompanied by facility staff members who then remain with their clients, trained HAI volunteers serve as hosts to groups attending an event and act as liaisons between HAI and the theater management. They distribute tickets, provide assistance during the event, and help to make the experience as pleasurable and safe as possible. Volunteers receive orientation and are trained on the job, first by working as assistants to experienced volunteers, then by taking on more responsibilities as time goes on. HAI needs lots of volunteers for its summer program, which takes clients to hundreds of outdoor events. For information, get in touch with the volunteer coordinator.

## International Child Health Foundation (ICHF)

American City Bldg., P.O. Box 1205
Columbia, MD 21044
1-301-596-4514, FAX 1-410-992-5641
Contact: Charlene B. Dale, Executive Vice President

ICHF is a worldwide organization dedicated to improving the lives of children, with an emphasis on the prevention and treatment of disease through better health care. Among ICHF's priorities is the practical application of effective, low-cost solutions to children's health problems in developing countries and in areas of the United States that are medically underserved. ORT (oral rehydration therapy) is one inexpensive means of treating diarrheal disease, a leading killer of children, and ICHF, working with existing agencies and institutions, has a continuing Nutrition and ORT program to prevent infant mortality. ICHF is looking for volunteers with special technical expertise in medicine and public health and those with editorial or writing skills. Contact the executive director for more information.

Make-a-Wish Foundation of America (page 76)

## March of Dimes Birth Defects Foundation

1275 Mamaroneck Ave.
White Plains, NY 10605
1-914-428-7100

The March of Dimes works to improve the health of babies by preventing birth defects and infant mortality through research, community services, education, and advocacy. There are over 130 chapters nationwide, each responsible for community leadership in its territory. Volunteers set the course for and govern the Foundation, and they are active in every aspect of the organization, working as partners with staff in leadership, delivering March of Dimes programs, fund-raising, and working in communications. In addition to a voluntary advisory committee of health and social service professionals, educators, and medical specialists, each chapter has an office of volunteers. March of Dimes programs and projects offer volunteers the opportunity to use many of the skills they have acquired through life experience and education in the following ways:

- Fund-raising. Almost 2 million volunteers are involved with two countrywide events, WalkAmerica and Mother March, which raise more than half of all Foundation funds. Volunteers also stage other special events fund-raisers.
- Community service. Volunteers help out in nurseries, clinics, hospitals, and other care facilities; they counsel pregnant teens and help pregnant women get prenatal care. Some chapters have a "granny program," in which older women are assigned as mentors to women who are pregnant for the first time. The mentors keep in touch throughout the pregnancy, reminding the women of clinic visits and providing transportation and other services.
- Education. A health education program, presented by volunteer health professionals, called Babies and You, is provided at work sites for pregnant women and their husbands and potentially pregnant couples.
- Advocacy. March of Dimes volunteers conduct public affairs activities at all levels of government, often in partnership with other health care and community organizations. Volunteer advocates write letters, testify before Congress, and meet face to face with legislators and other officials.

March of Dimes take its volunteers seriously, as people and as professionals, and has developed guidelines for volunteer development. Check your local chapter for more information.

## FEATURED ORGANIZATION: AMERICAN RED CROSS (ARC)

National Headquarters
Washington, DC 20006
1-202-737-8300

We've come to expect so much of the Red Cross that we can no longer imagine our lives without it, and we are right. The American Red Cross is a humanitarian organization, led by volunteers, that provides relief to victims of disasters and helps people prevent, prepare for, and respond to emergencies. The ratio of Red Cross volunteers to staff is 50 to 1, and volunteers serve in every capacity: governance, management, and direct service of the broadest scope. American Red Cross has 2,700 chapters throughout the United States and its territories as well as field stations on U.S. military installations worldwide. Of the more than 1.5 million volunteers, approximately 16 percent are youth under eighteen. Here are some Red Cross services, almost all of them delivered by volunteers:

- American Red Cross Disaster Services (page 92).
- Community education.
- Blood services, including collecting and testing it.
- Transplantation services; that is, the collection, processing, and distribution of human tissue products.
- Health and safety services, including blood pressure screenings, first aid stations at public events, home health care education, and certifying people in Red Cross health and safety courses such as CPR, first aid, lifeguard training, and swimming.
- HIV/AIDS education.
- Military/social emergency–related services to members of the armed forces, veterans, and their families.
- International services provide emergency health, humanitarian, and educational services in partnership with sister Red Cross and Red Crescent societies and other organizations. The International Red Cross Movement is linked with each chapter through the national office.
- American Red Cross Program for Youth (page 79).
- Community-based programs that respond to the immediate needs of the area, such as transportation services, training volunteers to care for the elderly, and providing shelter to homeless people. ARC encourages its local units, no matter how small, to recruit a diversity of volunteers in order to meet the community's needs effectively. Call your local chapter to ask about volunteer opportunities.

Based on a study of projected trends in volunteerism, ARC published *Taking Volunteerism into the 21st Century*, (ARC4707) and you can order the first copy free, with additional packets of twenty-five booklets for $25.

## National Hospice Organization (NHO)

1901 N. Moore St., Suite 901
Arlington, VA 22209
1-703-243-5900
Hospice HelpLine: 1-800-658-8898

Hospice's purpose is to provide support and care for people in the final phase of a terminal disease so that they can live as fully and comfortably as possible. NHO is a national clearinghouse for locating hospice programs and for information about hospice care. Most of the nation's 1,700 hospice programs belong to NHO, which also publishes the annual *Guide to the Nation's Hospices*. Hospice care addresses the needs of patients and family members through an interdisciplinary team of medical professionals and volunteers under the direction of a physician. Specially trained volunteers are a critical component of the hospice team, providing clerical assistance to staff and such direct services to patients and families as assistance with household tasks, shopping, or transportation. Volunteers often read to patients or sit quietly with them to help ease the loneliness. Hospice programs differ in scope of care and organization, but most programs offer home-care services and arrange for in-patient care when needed. Call the Hospice HelpLine for information and referral.

**Northwest Medical Teams International (NMTI, page 189)**

**Physicians for Human Rights (PHR, page 147)**

**Project Concern International (PCI, page 191)**

**Ronald McDonald House (RMH, page 74)**

**SKIP of New York, Inc. (page 75)**

**Starlight Foundation (SF, page 77)**

**Sunshine Foundation (page 77)**

**Surgical Eye Expeditions International, Inc. (SEE, page 191)**

## United Hospital Fund of New York (UHF)

55 Fifth Ave.
New York, NY 10003
1-212-645-2500
Contact: Susan Wyant, Director of Voluntary Initiatives

UHF has been working for over 100 years to address critical issues affecting health care in New York City. It does so by organizing and consolidating philanthropic activities; by initiating and concluding research, demonstration projects, and health policy development; and by bringing together professionals and volunteers. UHF, which is a distributing agent of United Way of America (UWA, page 38), works with forty-seven beneficiary not-for-profit hospitals in New York City. Mobilizing and channeling the energies of health care volunteers is a major concern, and in 1991, UHF launched a New York City–wide hospital and nursing home volunteer recruitment campaign, "Give a Little—Get a Lot." Over 2,000 individuals responded and a data base of volunteers with particular skills, preferences, and schedules, which could be matched with corresponding needs from individual institutions was created.

UHF has over 300 volunteers who serve as board, committee, and task force members, with about two-thirds of them working on voluntary initiatives' committees and task forces. Committees provide volunteers with an opportunity to actively explore a particular facet of the city's health care system, such as nursing homes, legislation, and the municipal hospital system. Task forces research a particular health care problem in depth, using information from medical specialists, administrators, and other professionals. For instance, the task force on the needs of hospitalized children oversees the Bedtime Story Project (page 76). Volunteers include in-service volunteers, health care professionals, community leaders, retirees, and others who have a special interest in health care needs or a commitment to

New York City's hospitals. For more information, contact the director of voluntary initiatives and ask for "Facts for Volunteers" and other literature.

**Variety Clubs International (VCI, page 83)**

# AIDS

HIV/AIDS is a nationwide epidemic that affects all Americans, a fact that until recently we've tried to ignore. The disease is not going away, and it is possible for everyone to make a difference. A vaccine or a cure for people with the HIV virus or AIDS is the primary aim of every organization. Beyond that, and within much closer range for the average person, education about AIDS prevention, information about current testing and treatment studies, advocacy, and, especially, direct service to People With AIDS (PWA) or those with AIDS-related conditions (ARC) are the major concerns. Most organizations serving PWA directly are local agencies, and the easiest way to find one is to call the AIDS Hotline (below) or CDC National AIDS Clearinghouse (page 132), both of which can tell you about the major policy organizations as well.

### HOTLINE

**AIDS Hotline: 1-800-342-7514**

**ABC Quilts (ABCQ, page 57)**

**Lambda Legal Defense and Education Fund, Inc. (pages 151–52)**

## Los Angeles Center for Living (LACFL)

650 N. Robertson Blvd.
Los Angeles, CA 90069
1-213-850-0877

Project Angel Food: 1-213-874-1677
Contact: Volunteer Hotline: 1-213-656-1986

LACFL is dedicated to helping form a community of comfort and love to those who have AIDS or ARC and their extended families. Some of its programs are listed below:

- Project Angel Food (PAF) prepares and delivers gourmet hot meals daily to homebound people with AIDS. Angel Food volunteers work as cooks and other kitchen help and deliver meals.
- LACFL's hospice fund pays for free medical assistance and attendant care for patients at home.
- Outreach program volunteers provide whatever services are requested by the caller: haircutting, massage, phone buddies, and so on.
- The Clean Team is a corps of volunteers who do housework for homebound clients with AIDS.

For information about volunteering, call the volunteer hotline.

**The NAMES Project AIDS Memorial Quilt (page 56)**

## AIDS Clinical Trials Information Service (ACTIS)

P.O. Box 6421
Rockville, MD 20849-6421
1-800-TRIALS-A (1-800-874-2572), International Line: 1-301-217-0023, FAX 1-301-738-6616

ACTIS is a central source providing health care professionals and the public with current information on federally and privately sponsored clinical trials being conducted to test the effectiveness of experimental therapies or new drugs for AIDS patients and others infected with HIV. This free public health service is provided collaboratively with four federal agencies, including Centers for Disease Control (CDC, see

## FEATURED ORGANIZATION: GAY MEN'S HEALTH CRISIS (GMHC)

129 W. 20th St.
New York, NY 10011-0022
1-212-337-3593
Hotline: 1-212-807-6655, 1-212-645-7470 (TDD)
Contact: Volunteer Office

GMHC was founded in 1981 by volunteers in order to establish services to people with AIDS and ARC and their families, loved ones, and care givers, and to make treatments available to all who need them. Services, education, and advocacy are the organization's mission. Services include support, financial advocacy, recreational opportunities, and legal, ombudsman, and crisis intervention assistance. GMHC's education department is the world's largest nongovernmental distributor of AIDS information. About 2,000 volunteers help carry out these programs, performing the most varied tasks. Over 1,000 of them work in every phase of the client services program, acting as intake clinicians, making outreach calls to clients, providing pro bono legal services, working as ombudsmen, and giving crisis management, support, hope, and help. For information about volunteering, contact the Volunteer Office.

below). ACTIS health specialists are available to answer questions from individuals infected with HIV, their families, and health professionals. For more information call the 800 number.

### Centers for Disease Control (CDC)

CDC National AIDS Clearinghouse
P.O. Box 6003
Rockville, MD 20849-6003

Information for AIDS Professionals
Health Care Professionals: 1-800-458-5231, FAX 1-301-738-6616
International Number: 1-301-217-0023

Consumer Hotlines
CDC National AIDS Hotline: 1-800-342-AIDS (1-800-342-2437)
Spanish Access: 1-800-344-SIDA (1-800-342-7432)
Deaf Access: 1-800-AIDS-TTY (1-800-243-7889)

The Clearinghouse was created in 1987 by CDC, a division of the U.S. Department of Health and Human Services, as part of its national information and education program to respond to AIDS and HIV. The Clearinghouse is a comprehensive information source for health professionals and other professionals working to fight the spread of HIV by making referrals and distributing up-to-date publications on AIDS. For material about resources and services available through the clearinghouse call the appropriate 800 number.

### Pets Are Wonderful Support (PAWS)

P.O. Box 460489
San Francisco, CA 94146-0489
1-415-824-4040

For people with HIV disease, their pets are a special source of companionship and affection, providing real emotional and psychological benefits. PAWS of San Francisco was the first program to offer volunteer services and financial assistance to address the particular problems and needs of pet owners infected with the HIV virus. Some of the many ways volunteers can help are:

- Client services, such as pet food delivery, transportation to vet's appointments, home pet care—dog walking, changing a cat's litterbox—and finding foster or permanent homes for pets of clients who can no longer care for their animals.
- Office work.
- People with writing or graphic design skills are needed to provide education and outreach.
- Fund-raising.

People in the Bay Area interested in volunteering can call the San Francisco office.

### Pets Are Wonderful Support/Los Angeles (PAWS/LA)

7985 Santa Monica Blvd., Suite 109-239
West Hollywood, CA 90046
1-213-650-PAWS (1-213-650-7297)

PAWS/LA is similar to, but not affiliated with, PAWS of San Francisco (page 132). PAWS/LA offers the following services for people with HIV disease: dog walking, hygiene/grooming, and puppy housebreaking and training; cat hygiene and exercise; transport to and from the vet; aquarium and terrarium maintenance; bird care and nail clipping; delivery of pet food and supplies; and finding donation sources of pet food, supplies, groomers, and vets. PAWS/LA needs volunteers to supply foster and permanent homes for pets of owners who are either temporarily hospitalized or no longer able to care for their pets. For information, contact the West Hollywood office.

### San Francisco AIDS Foundation (SFAF)

P.O. Box 426182
San Francisco, CA 94142-6182
1-415-864-5855, FAX 1-415-552-9762
Contact: Director of Volunteer Services

SFAF is a nonprofit organization founded in 1982; its purpose is to educate the public about AIDS to prevent the transmission of HIV, help people make informed choices about HIV-related issues, and assure the protection of the human rights of those infected with HIV. SFAF provides client services for those affected by HIV and cooperates with other organizations in creating educational programs, services, and public policy initiatives. About 500 volunteers work for SFAF at any one time, and about 1,000 are processed annually. A recent Volunteer Classifieds for SFAF included ads for people to answer the SFAF hotline in English, Spanish, and Filipino; do office work, technical writing, and data entry; assist with mailings; work on a client advocacy project; help organize meetings between Bay Area legislators and AIDS service providers; maintain an active AIDS-related media archive; and help with production and assembly of media kits. For information about the many volunteer opportunities at SFAF, get in touch with the director of volunteer services.

## The Fight Against Cancer

Scarcely any American life is untouched by cancer, so pervasive is the disease. Counselors, support group leaders, researchers, board and committee members, word processors, publicists, and fund-raisers are just a few of the many volunteer opportunities that exist for people who want to help. Cancer Information Service (CIS, page 135), National Coalition for Cancer Survivorship (NCCS, page 135), and American Cancer Society (ACS, page 134) can put you in touch with organizations in your area.

## American Cancer Society (ACS)

1599 Clifton Rd., NE
Atlanta, GA 30329
1-404-320-3333
Contact: Local Unit or Division, or for more information, call toll free 1-800-ACS-2345, (1-800-227-2345).

ACS is a nonprofit volunteer organization dedicated to the control and eradication of cancer. There are 57 ACS divisions and more than 3,300 local units. Programs include: public education about prevention and early detection of cancer, education of medical professionals to ensure support of ACS programs, service and rehabilitation programs for cancer patients and their families, cooperation with other organizations concerned with cancer, and funding for research and development of information data bases about all aspects of cancer. These programs are carried out by over 2 million volunteers, recruited from every occupation and age level, and including professionals, homemakers, retired persons, young adults, and children. Volunteers are trained by paid staff (the ratio of volunteers to staff is 600 to 1) and also receive technical assistance as required. Check your phone directory for the nearest ACS and ask about volunteer opportunities. For more information, call the 800 number.

## Candlelighters

Childhood Cancer Foundation (CCCF)
1312 18th St., NW, Suite 200
Washington, DC 20036
1-202-659-5136
1-800-366-2223

Candlelighters is an international network of over 400 peer support groups for parents of children with cancer. Other family members and health or education professionals also belong. The groups help by offering emotional support, trying to lessen families' isolation, exchanging information, and finding other ways to cope with childhood cancer's effect on the child, on the parents, and on the entire family. Membership in Candlelighters is free, and each group is run by its members on a completely voluntary basis. Local groups present speakers and panels, maintain libraries, publish newsletters, and work in concert with other cancer organizations such as the American Cancer Society (ACS, page 134) and the Leukemia Society of America. CCCF is the coordinator, information clearinghouse, educational arm, and advocate for the organization. CCCF publishes various newsletters and will provide free, or almost free, publications useful for families and health professionals, including an annotated bibliography (also available in Spanish), and the directories *Wish Fulfillment Organizations* ($.50, page 76) and *Camps and Vacation Retreats for Children with Cancer and Their Families* ($1, page 84).

Some local CCCF groups welcome volunteer help for their activities. To protect members' privacy, contact names are not released to the public. Interested parties may send an introductory letter to the CCCF office to be forwarded to the appropriate person. The District of Columbia office considers volunteers with general office or graphic design/illustration skills. Lawyers, law students, and insurance industry professionals in any location are welcome for the Ombudsman Program on insurance and employment issues. For information, write to the Washington office.

### Corporate Angel Network (CAN, page 66)

## National Cancer Care Foundation

Cancer Care, Inc. (CCI)
1180 Sixth Ave.
New York, NY 10036
1-212-221-3300
Contact: Coordinator Volunteer

CCI is a social service agency that effectively helps cancer patients and their families and friends cope with the impact of cancer. CCI has six offices in the New York metropolitan area, and their services include counseling, supplemental financial assistance, bereavement counseling, information about services available to the cancer patient, a volunteer visitor program, and an educational program for the community and cancer professionals. CCI's volunteer service program consists of transportation services—driving patients to and from medical appointments, chemotherapy, and radiation therapy—and volunteers who visit homebound or frail cancer patients, helping to alleviate the feelings of isolation and abandonment that cancer patients and their families often experience. CCI is supported entirely by contributions from the public. The organization recruits volunteers through corporations, churches and synagogues, and newspaper ads, and in libraries. Volunteers who work with patients receive four hours of training. Potential volunteers in the area can get in touch with CCI for more information.

## National Coalition for Cancer Survivorship (NCCS)

1010 Wayne Ave., Suite 300
Silver Spring, MD 20910
1-301-585-2616

NCCS is a nonprofit organization whose mission is to improve the lives of all cancer survivors, whether diagnosed recently or years ago. NCCS is dedicated to the idea that these survivors and their families and supporters are a growing constituency who are a powerful, positive force in society. Its members are cancer survivors and their loved ones, health care providers and medical centers, and support and survivorship organizations. NCCS serves as a clearinghouse for information, publications, and programs on survivorship, providing facts about community and national support groups in response to inquiries from individuals and organizations. As an advocate for cancer survivors on issues such as insurance coverage and job discrimination, NCCS addresses public policy through expert testimony before congressional committees and access to the media. Community organizations and those who want to start support groups can get technical assistance from NCCS. Members receive the quarterly publication *NCCS Networker*, with up-to-date news of cancer survivorship. NCCS will direct people interested in volunteering for a survivorship organization to local agencies and support groups.

## U.S. Department of Health and Human Services (HHS)

Cancer Information Service (CIS)
National Institutes of Health (NIH)
National Cancer Institute (NCI)
Bethesda, MD 20892
1-800-4-CANCER (1-800-422-6237)
Contact: Project Officer, CIS, 1-301-496-8664

Supported by NCI, CIS is a network of 23 regional offices that provide accurate, up-to-date information on over 100 types of cancer to patients and their families, health professionals, and the general public. Each CIS office:

- Operates a toll-free telephone service (the 800 number above), which automatically connects callers to the office serving their area.
- Has a resource directory of cancer-related services and programs for the area, and can make referrals, depending on a caller's needs.
- Develops and implements cancer information

and educational programs through the mass media, intermediary organizations, and direct community educational programs.

CIS offices have over 200 paid professionals and volunteers, who use a variety of printed and computerized resources to answer over 500,000 questions a year. Information specialists must contribute a minimum of twelve hours a week. CIS regional offices will refer potential volunteers to other cancer agencies in the area.

## Y-ME National Organization for Breast Cancer Information and Support (Y-ME)

18220 Harwood Ave.
Homewood, IL 60430-2104
1-708-799-8338, FAX 1-708-799-5937
Hotline: 1-800-221-2141 (9–5, CT, weekdays); National Crisis Hotline 1-708-799-8228 (24 hours)

Y-ME is a nonprofit consumer organization and the largest and most comprehensive breast cancer support program in the United States. Its services include:

- Serving as a clearinghouse by providing unbiased information (but not medical advice) about choices in breast cancer treatment.
- Hotline counseling by trained volunteers and staff who are breast cancer patients. In some cases, women can be matched with one of more than 200 trained volunteers nationwide whose condition and treatment are similar.
- Free monthly educational meetings, for women who have had breast cancer or are concerned about it.
- Educational programs for nonsymptomatic women.
- Referral and counseling services for presurgical patients.
- Workshops for organizations and businesses.
- Technical assistance and training for qualified groups that want to develop similar activities.
- Educational support meetings for breast cancer patients and their families and friends.

Y-ME has a number of chapters nationwide and will provide referrals to other organizations across the country. Volunteers and staff, who have experienced breast cancer themselves, are rigorously trained. Call the 800 number for the location of the nearest Y-ME chapter or the names of similar organizations in your area.

# Helping the Mentally and Physically Challenged

The rights of individuals with mental retardation, psychiatric illness, or physical disabilities increasingly are being acknowledged. Today, a disabled person has a far greater chance of living a fulfilling and useful life than ever before, although much still has to be done before the disabled are fully empowered. This new environment is due partly to changes in medicine and technology and partly to the efforts of volunteer advocates, many of them disabled themselves, who have helped enact new laws, especially the Americans with Disabilities Act, which became law in July 1990.

Many opportunities exist for serving the disabled in one's own community. Start with your local hospital, call the nearest volunteer action center (VAC) (see National Volunteer Center, NVC, page 37), check with a veterans' hospital to find out about programs for mentally and physically disabled vets, or ask your local Veterans of Foreign Wars (VFW, page 233). Try local schools for organizations that work with disabled children. Sports organizations for people with many kinds of disabilities offer unique ways to volunteer (see pages 208–216), and consider horticultural therapy (pages 124–25) as well.

## Mental Disabilities

### Compeer

259 Monroe Ave.
Rochester, NY 14607
1-716-546-8280
Contact: Bernice Skirboll, Executive Director

Compeer is a friendship program that matches adult volunteers, one to one, with children and adults who suffer from mental illness. Clients are referred to Compeer by a mental health professional as an adjunct to therapy. Volunteers offer their Compeers a caring and supportive relationship, visiting with them, going to the movies or a concert with them, inviting them home. Compeer's volunteer recruitment flier begins: "Wanted: Men and women to work for no pay for at least one hour per week for a minimum of one year. Experience with loneliness, failure, loss of self-esteem is helpful but not essential. Kindness, gentleness and patience a must. Challenging opportunity to bring another human being back into the world where we live by helping him find the love and trust he has lost." After an extensive screening process, a volunteer is trained and matched with a Compeer friend. Very often the friendships last for years. There are over 100 Compeer programs in thirty-two states, Canada, and the Netherlands. For information about becoming a Compeer volunteer or starting a new chapter, contact the Rochester headquarters.

## Fountain House (FH)

425 W. 47th St.
New York, NY 10036-2304
1-212-582-0340
Contact: Executive Director

FH is a New York City–based clubhouse open to a membership of those with severe and chronic psychiatric illnesses, and FH believes that a fulfilling life is a reasonable and attainable goal for all its members. FH serves as a supportive and rehabilitative base for men and women seeking to overcome their illness, rejoin the community, and return to work or school. Some 400 Fountain House members attend each day and participate, alongside staff, in daily clubhouse activities, which include preparing and serving food, cleaning, office work, horticultural projects, and hosting visitors. FH has several interesting programs that help give members enough training and self-

## FEATURED ORGANIZATION: THE ARC

500 E. Border St., Suite 300
Arlington, TX 76006
1-817-640-0204
Contact: Director

The Arc is a national organization concerned with mental retardation and dedicated to improving the lives of all people with mental retardation and their families. Through advocacy, education, job training and placement, and other programs, the Arc helps people realize their goals of where and how they learn, live, work, and play. There are about 140,000 members and 1,200 state and local chapters of the Arc nationwide, and most of the programs are wholly dependent on volunteers. Here is a roster of volunteer help sought by one (rather large) chapter in Oregon:

- Computer people to design and maintain data bases, enter data, design a spread sheet.
- Clerical people to file, stuff packets, work at mailings.
- Media people to illustrate mailings, do publicity, work at computer graphics, catalog photos, design and build tabletop displays, take photographs.
- "People people" to be citizen advocates, serve on an advisory committee, act as a community representative, work as a general assistant, be a hospitality aide, become a legal guardian to a person with developmental disabilities, assist at national conventions, coordinate programs in schools, help clients find apartments, take clients shopping, plan and run social events for clients, tutor, help out at workshops.
- Writers and researchers to update a bibliography, do research, develop and organize an information and referral file, assist with a newsletter.

Of course, in smaller chapters, a single volunteer very often serves in several roles. For information about The Arc chapter nearest you, contact the national headquarters in Arlington, Texas.

confidence to reenter the work force. Through the Transitional Employment (TE) programs, which involve TE agreements with forty of New York's most prestigious firms, an average of 140 members a day go to work for pay in jobs as mail clerks, data entry personnel, and newsroom assistants, and in other positions.

FH uses volunteers with specific skills to participate in many of its programs: tutors, people to take part in a wide variety of social and recreational activities, volunteers to recruit employers for members who are ready to go out and work, and fund-raisers. Because FH's mission is to help its members develop marketable skills, many of the functions usually performed by volunteers in other institutions are undertaken by members as part of their own restoration.

Since its founding in 1948, FH has pioneered in the development of community-based programs of psychiatric rehabilitation. Although FH is based locally in New York, it has served as a model program, helping to set up more than 260 similar programs all around the country by giving training sessions for staff and club members eight to ten times a year. For information about becoming an FH volunteer or to learn of other programs in your area, get in touch with the executive director.

## Goodwill Industries of America, Inc. (GIA)

Goodwill Industries Volunteer Services (GIVS)
9200 Wisconsin Ave.
Bethesda, MD 20814-3896
1-301-530-6500

GIA helps disabled and disadvantaged individuals and others with special needs expand their opportunities and occupational capabilities by offering vocational training services and job opportunities at over 179 community-based autonomous Goodwill organizations. More than 10,000 volunteers work for Goodwill Industries Volunteer Services (GIVS). They solicit donations of goods for sale, raise funds, work with disabled people, present vintage fashion shows, assist at book sales, and much more. For information about becoming a volunteer, check your local phone directory for the location of the nearest Goodwill, or contact the Bethesda office and ask for a copy of GIVS's most recent yearly directory.

Kids on the Block (KOTB, page 96)

## National Mental Health Association (NMHA)

1021 Prince St.
Alexandria, VA 22314-2971
1-703-684-7722, FAX 1-703-684-5968
Contact: Director, Information Center

NMHA is a citizens' volunteer advocacy organization concerned with all aspects of mental health and mental illness. It works to prevent mental illness, to provide services for the mentally ill, and to educate the public. There are 500 NMHA affiliates in forty-three states, each trying to achieve the organization's goals within the framework of local community needs. At the national level, NMHA is an advocate for the rights of people with mental illness. On the local and state levels, affiliates:

- Recruit, train, and place thousands of volunteers in mental health programs.
- Act as clearinghouses for information and referrals, responding to more than 20,000 personal inquiries every year. NMHA is the nation's primary source of information on what is known about prevention.
- Advocate locally and statewide for people with mental illness.
- Organize self-help groups.
- Coordinate programs with other organizations having the same goals of alleviation of the stigma and public misconceptions about mental illnesses and the people who have them.

NMHA publishes a quarterly newsletter, *Focus*, which keeps staff and volunteers up to date on activities at the national headquarters. In turn, each affiliate publishes its own reports and newsletters about issues, organizations, and events that impact on mentally ill people. Volunteers are the life and breath of NMHA, serving in a broad scope of functions: organizing town meetings and celebrity events, advocating for a rape response advocacy program, counseling high-risk youth, running an Alzheimer's support group, and suicide prevention. Teenage volunteers work at a summer camp for emotionally conflicted children. For information, check your local phone directory for Mental Health Association, or contact the director of the information center in Alexandria.

**National Resource Center on Homelessness and Mental Illness (NRC, page 177)**

# Physical Disabilities

**Breckenridge Outdoor Education Center (BOEC, page 209)**

**Disabled Ski Program at Ski Windham (DSI, page 210)**

**Dwarf Athletic Association of America (DAAA, page 210)**

**Guide Dog Foundation for the Blind, Inc. (GDF, page 44)**

**Guiding Eyes for the Blind, Inc. (GEB, page 44)**

## Mobility International, USA (MIUSA)

P.O. Box 3551
Eugene, OR 97403
1-503-343-1284
Contact: Exchange Coordinator

MIUSA, a membership organization, is the U.S. affiliate of Mobility International, an international organization with offices in over thirty countries. MIUSA promotes and facilitates international travel and educational exchange for people with disabilities and sponsors international educational exchanges and community service programs. MIUSA actively advocates for people with disabilities and assists organizations that wish to accommodate such people. Individual membership costs $20 a year, and members have free use of MIUSA's information and referral services, receive discounts on resource publications and international exchange programs, and receive the newsletter, "Over the Rainbow." Call or write for more information.

**National Foundation of Wheelchair Tennis (NFWT, page 210)**

**National Handicapped Sports (NHS, page 211)**

***A World of Options for the 90's: A Guide to International Educational Exchange, Community Service, and Travel for Persons with Disabilities,*** written and edited by Susan Sygall and Cindy Lewis, is essential reading for any person with a disability interested in international travel or exchange—and essential reading, too, for the hundreds of organizations described and frankly assessed for their accessibility and availability to people with disabilities. The book opens with an annotated directory of organizations for student exchange, international work camps, and community service projects, continues with a directory of organizations—some nonprofit, others that are businesses connected with travel—concerned in one way or another with disabled persons, and concludes with the personal experiences of travelers with disabilities. Send $16 to Mobility International, USA (MIUSA, page 140) for a copy.

## National Society to Prevent Blindness (NSPB)

500 E. Remington Rd.
Schaumburg, IL 60173
1-708-843-2020, FAX 1-708-843-8458
NSPB Center for Sight (NCS): 1-800-331-2020

NSPB is a national volunteer health organization dedicated to ending blindness in America. Among NSPB's programs and services are:

- Public and professional educational programs about eye diseases, eye care, and eye safety.
- Publications, videos, and other educational materials on over forty topics tailored for different ages and ethnic groups.
- NCS (the 800 number), a toll-free information service on eye health and safety.
- Community vision screenings.
- Funding innovative eye research.
- Advocacy.

NSPB has a network of state affiliates and about 35,000 volunteers implementing the programs. Volunteers initiate membership drives, do fund-raising, run community awareness and workplace-safety campaigns, and organize support and self-help groups. If you'd like more information on volunteering, call the 800 number for the location of the affiliate nearest you.

**National Wheelchair Athletic Association (NWAA, page 211)**

**Paralyzed Veterans of America (PVA, page 212)**

## Recording for the Blind, Inc. (RFB)

20 Roszel Rd.
Princeton, NJ 08540
1-609-452-0606

RFB was founded in 1948 to record textbooks for blinded veterans attending college under the G.I. Bill. Since then it has expanded its services to include all those with visual, physical, or perceptual difficulties. RFB serves more than 27,000 people a year, most of them students from fourth grade through postgraduate levels, and other persons with print disabilities working in a wide variety of occupations. Nationwide, recording studios at thirty-one sites are operated by 4,800 volunteers. Most RFB volunteers are college graduates, many with advanced degrees or expertise in specialized fields. Recruiting is through word of mouth among academic and professional colleagues, and networking with such organizations as the American Association for the Advancement of Science (AAAS, page 98). Each recording unit recruits its volunteers, raises its own funds, and has its own subject areas of specialization. Volunteers read and monitor the educational texts, check and duplicate tapes, maintain equipment, recruit and train other volunteers, and raise funds. For information about volunteering, get in touch with the Princeton headquarters.

**United States Association for Blind Athletes (USABA, page 212)**

**United States Cerebral Palsy Athletic Association (USCPAA, page 214)**

**Veterans Administration, National Veterans Winter Sports Clinic (VA, page 215)**

# Resource

### PHYSICAL DISABILITIES

*A World of Options for the 90's: A Guide to International Educational Exchange, Community Service, and Travel for Persons with Disabilities,* by Cindy Lewis and Susan Sygall. (See box, page 140.)

# Holidays

There are lots of ways to volunteer during holidays, and here are a few, just to start. Hospitals, especially children's and veterans' hospitals, nursing homes, residences for disabled persons, jails and prisons—any facility with a shut-in population—need all the volunteer help they can get at holidaytime. Volunteers help put on parties or entertain; cook festive meals; decorate dining rooms and wards; create, donate, wrap, and distribute presents at Hanukkah and Christmas. Church and synagogue congregations stage holiday events, choirs sing at nursing homes or give free public concerts, Scout troops give parties for needy children, service organizations collect toys and clothing and give parties of their own. Send holiday letters and cards through organizations like Mail for Tots (MFT, page 94) or The Box Project (TBP, page 173), volunteer for holiday Meals on Wheels (MOW page 205), or offer to baby-sit for a needy couple.

---

The Box Project, The Santa Program (TBP, page 173)

## First Night International

20 Park Plaza
Boston, MA 02116
1-617-542-1399
Contact: Volunteer Coordinator

First Night is a major New Year's Eve family entertainment arts festival that originated in Boston during the mid-1970s as an alternative to the traditional alcoholic carousing that makes New Year's Eve one of the unsafest nights on the road. The festival is a spectrum of events that might range from puppet theater to an organ recital to African dancing, drumming, and singing, to fireworks. The indoor/outdoor celebration shows the city's diverse history, people, and cultural richness. First Night is supported by the sales of admission buttons and by donations from civic organizations, businesses, and individuals. Over 500,000 people attend First Night in Boston, where more than 700 volunteers assist in jobs that range from managing performance locations to handling button sales, face painting, and answering the telephone. There are First Night celebrations in fifty-five cities in the United States and Canada. For information about volunteering at a First Night organization, or for starting a chapter in your own city, contact the volunteer coordinator in Boston.

## United States Marine Corps Reserve (MCR)

### Toys for Tots (TFT)

In 1947 MCR began collecting new toys for needy children in the Los Angeles area. Today, TFT is an international program collecting over 8 million new toys every year and buying still more. Thousands of volunteers participate annually in TFT as:

- Donors of new, unwrapped toys. Donors are individuals, businesses, or other groups.
- Workers in other phases of the campaign such as publicity and collection and delivery of toys to social welfare agencies. Volunteers research organizations and people who request toys to see that the groups are legitimate.
- Business sponsors who offer public sites for toy collection.

Because December is the busiest month for TFT, the time when it uses the most volunteers, anyone who wishes to volunteer should do so early in November so that MCR knows how many people it can rely on. Check the U.S. Government listings in your phone book for the nearest Marine Corps Reserve station; if none is listed, call your local Marine Corps recruiting station, which will be able to direct you to the Reserves.

## United States Post Office (USPO)

New York Division, General Post Office
Operation Santa Claus (OSC)
Eighth Ave. and 33rd St.
New York, NY 10001
1-212-330-3859
Contact: Dead Letter Office, Operation Santa Claus

OSC began over sixty years ago, when post office clerks in Manhattan's General Post Office used their own money to buy food and toys for needy children who wrote to Santa with little prospect of getting an answer. By now this program has expanded and is an official New York Post Office project. More than 26,000 letters in a year are received from around the world, and nearly all of them are answered. This is how it works: The letters are sorted and boxed by areas and counties. Newspapers, radio, and television alert the public, who go to the dead letter branch of the General Post Office to read through these touching and hopeful appeals and take away as many as their pocketbooks will permit. Then these generous volunteers respond by buying the children presents and sending them with letters from Santa Claus. People living in the New York metropolitan area can look over Santa's letters beginning on the first working day in December, during regular post office hours. For those who live out of the region, get in touch with the Dead Letter Office in sufficient time to make arrangements. Santa Claus Clubs have been formed by such groups as the Women's Media Group, the Fashion Group, and modeling agencies, which send out hundreds of presents every year.

## FEATURED ORGANIZATION: FROM VERMONT WITH LOVE TOY, MITTEN, AND CLOTHES PROJECT

R.F.D. Box 192
South Windham, VT 05359
1-802-874-4182
Contact: Carolyn Partridge

*Carolyn Partridge is a seamstress and fiber artist. She and her husband, who is a contractor, and their three children live on a sheep farm in South Windham, Vermont. Carolyn uses the fleeces; she cleans, dyes, and cards them, then sells them to spinners to make into yarn. She also sews kimonos and pants—anything anyone wants,—and works as a free-lance seamstress for a local fabric store.*

I began the Toy, Mitten, and Clothes Project in 1987 when I was visiting my parents in New Jersey. It was near the holidays, and there were so many television and newspaper stories about the homeless. I remember one especially that Jennifer McLogan, an NBC news reporter, did on the Holland Hotel. It was a welfare hotel and it blew me away; I was so appalled by the horrible conditions in which mothers and children were living. It made me so depressed that I wondered if I could do something. Living in Vermont, I'm so blessed. Then I came home and looked at my children's toys, and I knew they were getting more, so I thought the old ones could be reused.

Toys for Tots wanted only new toys, but mine were in excellent condition and I thought they really should go to some kids who'd want them. So many people ask how I got started: I picked up the phone, called NBC, and asked for Jennifer McLogan. She was on assignment, so I spoke with her assistant, who gave me the name of the New York City agency working with welfare hotels. That's how it started.

We're working now with two hospitals and we provide one of them with seventy to seventy-five new hand-dressed dolls. Each doll gets a dress, a pinafore, a nightgown, and a blanket, then we pack them in shoe boxes that we've already covered with prepasted wallpaper. All those people who cut and sew for the dolls and cover the boxes are volunteers. The other hospital gets new and old toys, and we also send down used adults' and children's winter clothes.

There are a lot of volunteers; I have another battalion of women who knit and crochet hats and mittens. The women will call and ask for yarn, and I leave it at drop-off places. The yarn comes from yarn shop donations, and I've collected yarn over the years; I prefer wool. We have about 150 to 200 volunteers who help out. I always announce the project in church, and the newspapers do stories too. We work sporadically through the entire year. It's very intense October through Thanksgiving. Then my husband and I fill up the truck and we deliver to the hospitals ourselves.

I try to help local people, but being poor in Vermont is different and perhaps easier to take than being poor in New York. I remember a while ago I read an article, an interview with Mother Teresa. Someone wrote to her from Wisconsin, "I really want to come to India and help you," and Mother Teresa answered, "Find your own Calcutta." That had such a powerful impact on me that I did.

## FEATURED ORGANIZATION: THE HOLIDAY PROJECT

P.O. Box 6347
Lake Worth, FL 33466-6347
1-407-966-5702
Contact: Sally Cooney, Executive Director

The Holiday Project was founded in 1971 in San Francisco, when a small group of coworkers wanted to do something together on Christmas Day. They decided to go to a local hospital, where they visited with patients and had Christmas dinner. This happy experience has now expanded to groups in over 400 communities nationwide. Each year more than 15,000 Holiday Project visitors, many of them families with children, share their holidays with 150,000 people in nursing homes, hospitals, women's shelters, and other institutions. Volunteers organize gift-wrapping parties for donated or handmade presents and give the presents to staff and patients at Christmas and Hanukkah. Other volunteers organize the activities of the local committee, and still others donate gifts in kind, including holiday presents.

Holiday Project chapters can be organized by any community group or coalition of groups: schools, churches, service organizations, businesses, and clubs. Each team makes its own choice about which holidays to celebrate and which facilities to visit. Smaller chapters begin with Christmas and Hanukkah; larger ones include as many holidays as the chapter can carry. Businesses that foster employee volunteering on a year-round basis have adopted Holiday Project's monthly celebration program, which includes Mother's Day and Father's Day, Easter, Passover, Valentine's Day, Martin Luther King, Jr.'s Birthday, St. Patrick's Day, and so on, depending on the facility.

To get the location of the Holiday Project nearest you, or for information about starting a group, write to the executive director.

# Human Rights

*All human beings are born free and equal in dignity and rights. They are endowed with reason and conscience and should act towards one another in a spirit of brotherhood.* This is Article 1 of the "Universal Declaration of Human Rights," and for decades human rights organizations have been working to make the nations of the world live up to it and to the remaining articles of the declaration. They've still got their work cut out for them. Although a number of human rights groups work with a small staff of policymakers and researchers, the organizations in this section, especially Amnesty International (AI, page 146), use volunteers as an important tool in accomplishing the groups' goals.

American Civil Liberties Union (ACLU, page 149)

## Amnesty International

Urgent Action Network (UA)
P.O. Box 1270
Nederland, CO 80466-1270
1-303-440-0913, FAX 1-303-258-7881

UA is a network of volunteers who agree to be "on call" to send immediate appeals regarding impending or actual torture, capital punishment, disappearances, inadequate medical care, and other cases of emergencies relating to prisoners of conscience all over the world. Based on well-researched information from the London headquarters, UA compiles a case sheet for each appeal. Case sheets include the names of the people being threatened or harmed, background information, recommended actions, and the individuals to whom appeals should be made. UA volunteers receive one or two case sheets a month. Children's Special Editions (CSE) of UA are case sheets intended for children six to twelve years old, written in simple language and with no graphic details offered. CSEs are sent out once a month to volunteers who request them. For information on becoming a UA volunteer, get in touch with the Colorado office. Membership in Amnesty International (AI, page 146) is a requirement.

## Amnesty International USA (AI)

National Office
322 Eighth Ave.
New York, NY 10001
1-212-807-8400

AI is a worldwide independent human rights organization whose most important mission is to bring about the release of prisoners of conscience—individuals who have been imprisoned for their beliefs, color, sex, ethnic origin, language, or religion, provided they have not used or advocated violence. AI also advocates fair and prompt trials for political prisoners and an end to torture and executions in all cases. A membership of over 1.1 million participates in a number of volunteer programs, including: local groups that meet regularly to write letters and work in human rights campaigns; campus groups; the Urgent Action Network (UA, page 146); networks of freedom writers, health professionals, legal support, and human rights educators; and individual letter writers. "Amnesty Action," is AI's bi-monthly newsletter. For information, contact the national office.

## Lawyers Committee for Human Rights (LCHR)

330 Seventh Ave., 10th Fl.
New York, NY 10001
1-212-629-6170
Contact: William G. O'Neill, Director of Pro Bono Projects

LCHR is a nonprofit organization founded in 1978 to protect and promote fundamental human rights. The committee has two distinct but complementary programs: the advancement of international human rights, with special focus on the abuse of local human rights lawyers and organizations, and the international protection of refugees. Because LCHR maintains close connections with indigenous legal groups, it often acts as liaison between these groups and other larger influential groups, such as the U.S. Congress, the UN, and the American Bar Association. LCHR's Lawyer-to-Lawyer Network is composed of over 5,000 lawyers, law professors, students, bar associations, and other legal groups in ninety countries. Each month Network members are asked to write to governments on behalf of colleagues who are endangered for their human rights activities. LCHR's Refugee Project involves monitoring refugee populations, writing and disseminating public reports about conditions, and advocacy in Congress and internationally.

Volunteer lawyers are involved with over 500 asylum cases, sometimes working with other organizations such as American Civil Liberties Union (ACLU, page 149). Each case can take from fifty to several hundred hours of an attorney's time, and can last from six months to three to four years, all of which means that lawyers working pro bono for LCHR are deeply committed to the cause of human rights. LCHR has two unpaid internships: a summer program and academic year internships in the human rights program, and summer and academic year internships in the Refugee Project. For information about LCHR and a copy of its publications catalog, get in touch with the New York office.

## Physicians for Human Rights (PHR)

100 Boylston St., Suite 620
Boston, MA 02144
1-617-695-0041
Contact: Claire Frances, Office Manager

PHR, a national organization of health professionals, finds teams of physicians, attorneys, and members of other human rights groups to conduct investigations of human abuses around the world and to bring the knowledge and skills of the medical sciences to the investigation and prevention of violations of international human rights and humanitarian law.

PHR works to prevent the participation of doctors in torture and other inhumane practices and to report on the condition of detainees in prisons and refugee camps. PHR is strictly impartial in its mission to protect political victims, and is concerned with the medical consequences of human rights abuses whatever the ideology of the victimizer. The organization works closely with other human rights groups, such as Amnesty International (AI, page 146) and Human Rights Watch Committee. PHR's membership of over 2,500 receives "Record," the quarterly newsletter with news of ongoing investigations and a list of new Medical Action Alerts. Medical Action Alerts are sent to members on a monthly basis as situations arise. The suggested action is often for each member to write a letter of concern on his or her own stationery. Contact PHR for more information.

# Pro Bono Legal Services

Lawyers who do pro bono work donate their services to needy individual clients and nonprofit agencies, they serve as mentors to students and newly released offenders, and they develop and carry out law-related education (LRE) (See Resources, pages 152–53). Nonattorney law professionals, students, and interns can also volunteer their skills. After you've found out about the pro bono clients at your own law firm, try state and city bar associations, which all have volunteer programs, a number of them concerned with LRE, then call the local volunteer action center (VAC) (see National Volunteer Center, NVC, page 37), a good source of nonprofit agencies in need of legal assistance.

---

## The Association of the Bar of the City of New York

Community Outreach Law Program (COLP)
42 W. 44th St.
New York, NY 10036-6690
1-212-382-6629
Contact: Director of COLP

COLP's credo is: "Working with communities to improve access to the legal system." COLP directs the majority of pro bono efforts sponsored by the New York City Bar Association by providing free legal assistance to individuals who can't afford lawyers and to community-based organizations. COLP projects focus on immigration, family, and housing law as well as programs to train over 500 lawyers a year for pro bono representation. Among COLP's other activities are:

- The Pro Bono Mentor Panel, which provides volunteer legal advice to other volunteers involved with pro bono clients.
- The Homeless Project, a demonstration program that conducts a clinic staffed by volunteer lawyers to provide legal services to the homeless.
- Legal Information Service, which asks pro bono lawyers to take phone calls from the public and provide general legal information.
- Community forums, which are held on diverse areas of the law, such as welfare reform, landlord and tenant issues, and senior citizens.

A core group of about 250 lawyers, experts in their specialties, volunteer for COLP programs. They are recruited through notices in the Association's monthly newsletter, "44th Street Notes," and in the *New York Law Journal.* Other lawyers are recruited from over 150 Association committees.

## Conservation Law Foundation of New England (CLF)

3 Joy St.
Boston, MA 02108-1497
1-617-742-2540, Fax 617-523-8109

CLF, a public interest environmental advocacy group operating in the six New England states, is the oldest environmental law organization in America. CLF brings lawsuits against the government or industries to halt projects that might endanger the environment, and it seeks cost-efficient and environmentally responsible alternative approaches to problems. CLF has three offices: Boston; Rockland, Maine; and Montpelier, Vermont. Although each office has paid staff, CLF also uses volunteers, many of whom work in development (fund-raising), and interns, who work on legal issues and science/policy matters. CLF has compiled the resource guide "Internships and Jobs in Environmental Advocacy and Protection." Write to the Boston office for information about interning or volunteering at CLF and ask for the resource guide.

## FEATURED ORGANIZATION: AMERICAN CIVIL LIBERTIES UNION (ACLU)

National Headquarters
132 W. 43rd St.
New York, NY 10036
1-212-944-9800

Founded in 1920, the ACLU is a nationwide nonpartisan organization dedicated to preserving and defending the principles of individual liberty and equality embodied in the Constitution and the nation's civil rights laws.

The list of cases in which the ACLU has participated resonates with the history of twentieth-century America: the Scopes trial in 1925; Sacco and Vanzetti in 1927; the *Ulysses* case in 1933; test cases challenging the government's right to evacuate and relocate Japanese American citizens in 1942; the successful defense in 1943 of the right of children of Jehovah's Witnesses to refuse to salute the flag; numerous civil rights suits, beginning with the first lunch counter sit-ins in 1960; the 1963 Supreme Court decision that every state must, if requested, provide an attorney for a person too poor to hire one; the Court's 1967 ruling that interracial marriage was not a crime; in 1977 the defense of the rights of American Nazis to demonstrate; and, during the 1980s, suits demonstrating that at-large voting plans in many Southern counties diluted minority voting power.

The ACLU is composed of two separate entities: the ACLU Foundation, which handles essential legal work, conducts public education programs, and is supported by large contributions and grants; and the ACLU, which is concerned with legislative lobbying and is supported by dues and contributions from over 250,000 members.

The ACLU has its national headquarters in New York, and there are two regional offices (in Atlanta and Denver), a legislative office in Washington, DC, fifty-one affiliates, and hundreds of local chapters. Affiliates and the national office cooperate in setting and working together on common goals in such broad areas as civil rights, political rights, the right to privacy, and other issues.

The ACLU could not function without volunteers. A national and affiliate staff of fewer than 100 attorneys is able to handle as many as 6,000 cases a year because of the contributions of volunteer attorneys. Nonlegal volunteers help the ACLU lobby Congress and state and local legislatures, recruit new members, and do fund-raising and office work.

Consult your local telephone book to see if there is an ACLU chapter near you, or call or write to the national headquarters for information.

## FEATURED ORGANIZATION: CONSTITUTIONAL RIGHTS FOUNDATION (CRF)

601 S. Kingsley Dr.
Los Angeles, CA 90005
1-213-487-5590
Contact: Elenor Taylor

CRF is a California-based organization founded in 1962 to help young people become active, responsible participants in American society through an understanding of the values expressed in the Constitution and the Bill of Rights. Some of CRF's volunteer-intensive law-related programs include:

- Youth Action Center for Positive Change (YAC), an after-school leadership development program in Compton, California, involving local justice officials and community leaders who volunteer as workshop resource persons and participate in youth action projects.
- Sports and the Law, a program currently used by schools in the Los Angeles County area that draws on kids' interest in sports and athletics and is designed to teach students how rules relate to society. Volunteer sports and legal professionals visit classrooms to personalize the discussions of sports and law issues.
- Mock Trials, a statewide program with over 7,000 students participating. In a Mock Trial, teams of students simulate a criminal court case, playing the roles of the principals in the cast of courtroom characters, activities that increase competence in reading, public speaking, listening, and reasoning. The student teams are coached, scored, and presided over by teachers and volunteer lawyers and judges.
- Lawyer in the Classroom, which brings volunteer attorneys into schools to help students understand laws and the justice system.
- CRF's participation in the national MENTOR program (page 165), pairing law firms and high schools in the Los Angeles area.

CRF's other citizenship education programs include:

- Youth Community Service (YCS), in which over 1,000 student members receive leadership and communication training and learn to work with their peers and adults. In turn, these 1,000 recruit over 20,000 of their classmates to join in YCS projects, which range from tutoring children to spending time with senior citizens to tree planting and neighborhood clean-ups to singing carols during the holiday season.
- Business Issues in the Classroom (BIC), which, by challenging students with actual business and economic dilemmas, helps develop problem-solving skills and promotes understanding of some of the complex social, economic, and ethical issues confronting society. Local business volunteers visit the classrooms to direct lessons and conduct discussions.

All of these programs are offered in California, most of them in southern California, and others throughout the state. CRF, which is discussed as a resource organization in the booklet "Law-

*Continued*

*Continued*
Related Education: Making a Difference" (see Resources, pages 152–53), also provides technical assistance, teacher training, student conferences, classroom volunteer services, and publications. In California, CRF annually uses the services of thousands of volunteer lawyers, business persons, and government and community leaders whom they recruit through local chambers of commerce and bar associations, as well as through the CRF Business Advisory Council and Lawyers Advisory Council, by networking, and by association with other large and small nonprofit agencies. CRF would like to hear from anyone interested in volunteering.

## Constitutional Rights Foundation/Chicago (CRFC)

407 S. Dearborn, Suite 1700
Chicago, IL 60605
1-312-663-9057
Contact: Carolyn Pereira, Director

CRFC is a separately incorporated but philosophically similar affiliate of Constitutional Rights Foundation (CRF, page 150) in Los Angeles. CRFC offers an eighth-grade Constitution program that uses 250 to 350 volunteer lawyers in about 100 elementary schools throughout Illinois. CRFC also recruits justice volunteers—police personnel, lawyers, judges—and law students and graduate students in education to work in the schools as role models and resource persons and to answer substantive questions about the law. The Justice Training and Dissemination Project, carried out jointly with CRF, is a national program that provides training for teachers and justice professionals who wish to participate in law-related education. For information, contact CRFC's director.

## Lawyers Alliance for New York

Community Development Legal Assistance Center (CDLAC)
99 Hudson St.
New York, NY 10013
1-212-219-1800, FAX 1-212-941-7458
Contact: Director of CDLAC

Created in 1980 by the Lawyers Alliance for New York, an organization that promotes law in the public interest, CDLAC provides a full range of corporate, real estate, and tax legal services to nonprofit organizations involved in community development in low-income neighborhoods and among low-income people. CDLAC and about 1,000 pro bono attorneys which it recruits represent clients in developing and operating mutual housing associations, permanent and transitional housing for the homeless and for low-income special-needs populations; low-income housing cooperatives; and community development credit unions and loan funds. Lawyers Alliance recruits attorneys from 100 major New York City law firms interested in pro bono work on community development projects.

## Lambda Legal Defense and Education Fund, Inc.

666 Broadway
New York, NY 10012
1-212-995-8585

Lambda Legal Defense and Education Fund, Inc.
606 S. Olive St., Suite 580
Los Angeles, CA 90014
1-213-629-2728

Lambda was founded in 1973 to serve as an advocate for the rights of lesbians and gay men and to educate the public, the legal profession, and those in government about discrimination based on sexual orientation. Lambda has a nationwide network of cooperating volunteer attorneys who pursue litigation in test cases having to do with discrimination in housing, employment, immigration, and the military; AIDS-related issues; constitutional rights; and other matters of concern to lesbians and gay men and people with HIV/AIDS. In addition to its network of attorneys, legal workers, law students, and law librarians, Lambda requires the volunteer services of professionals in other fields, among them insurance, psychology, anthropology, and medicine. Contact the New York office for more information.

**Lawyers Committee for Human Rights (LCHR, page 147)**

**Legal Action Center for the Homeless (LACH, page 177)**

**National MENTOR Program (page 165)**

## New York State Bar Association

Law, Youth and Citizenship (LYC)
1 Elk St.
Albany, NY 12207
1-518-474-1460
Contact: Dr. Eric Mondschein, Program Director

Sponsored by the New York State Bar Association and the New York State Education Department, LYC seeks to promote law-related education in schools throughout New York State and to encourage such instruction in grades K–12. LYC has two programs similar to those sponsored by the Constitutional Rights Foundation (CRF, page 150): Lawyer in the Classroom, in which volunteer lawyers meet with classes to discuss a variety of legal issues; and annual Mock Trial Tournaments, which give students firsthand knowledge of courtroom procedures. Contact LYC for information about participating schools in your county.

## Volunteer Lawyers for the Arts (VLA)

1285 Sixth Ave.
New York, NY 10019
1-212-977-9270
Contact: Executive Director

VLA provides free legal assistance to artists and arts organizations in all creative fields who cannot afford private counsel. VLA offers pro bono counseling and representation only on arts-related legal matters, including contracts, copyright, moral rights, insurance, labor relations, and small claims court advice. VLA's educational programs for artists and arts organizations encompass nonprofit incorporation seminars, clinics and workshops, publications written especially for artists on taxes and other related issues, and speaking engagements and lectures by VLA lawyers. VLA also offers educational services for attorneys on arts-related legal issues.

National VLA headquarters in New York has a network of over 800 volunteer attorneys. Volunteers for the New York VLA must be members of the New York State Bar and attend a VLA orientation session. VLA also has affiliates in forty-two cities nationwide. For information, contact the New York office.

**Volunteers in Parole (VIP, page 167)**

# Resources

**"Disaster Legal Services: A Guide for the Private Bar,"** published by the State Bar of California. (See page 94.)

**"Law-Related Education: Making a Difference"** is a booklet giving an overview of law-related education (LRE), which encompasses the various programs that educate elementary and secondary students about the foundations of U.S.

law and their responsibilities and rights as citizens. Five national organizations that serve as resources for schools and groups wishing to establish LRE programs are described in some detail, and a state contact list of LRE leaders is included. For a free copy, write to: U.S. Department of Justice, Office of Juvenile Justice and Delinquency Prevention, Washington, DC 20531.

***1991 Directory of Private Bar Involvement Programs,*** American Bar Association, Private Bar Involvement Project, Chicago, IL. Free. This is a state-by-state listing of more than 800 legal programs through which private attorneys offer legal services to poor persons. Many of the programs provide pro bono legal services, and most are sponsored by state or county bar associations.

# Mediation

Dispute resolution (DR), sometimes called alternative dispute resolution (ADR) because it is an alternative to the judicial system, is practiced at every level, from the neighborhood to local agencies to schools to the federal government to international organizations. Mediation is the form of dispute resolution that is most often practiced by trained volunteers. Mediation works by bringing disputants together in an informal way to work out a mutually acceptable settlement. In this they are assisted by a mediator, a trained, neutral volunteer who helps to clarify the issues and structure the discussion, and who writes up the agreement once it is reached. Some kinds of mediation are described as "court-annexed," which means that cases are referred to a mediation center by the courts so that they can be settled outside the formal judicial system.

Mediation is used to resolve an extraordinarily wide range of disputes between and among the most diverse parties imaginable: harassment, assault, criminal trespass, menacing, fraud, breach of contract, landlord-tenant disputes, interpersonal disputes, theft of service, family disputes, barroom brawls, municipal code violations, victim-offender disputes, child custody and visitation issues, farmer-creditor conflicts, truancy, teacher-student and student-student disputes, consumer complaints, domestic violence, employee-employer problems, minor personal injury, problems in nursing homes, and environmental issues. Mediators come from every age group and background.

Here are some of the characteristics shared by good mediators and conciliators:

- Neutrality and impartiality, conveyed in language and demeanor. These attitudes are central to the role of the mediator. A person perceived to be unbiased by both disputants will have a far greater chance of being effective.
- Empathy with all parties, demonstrated by a willingness to listen and to explore feelings.
- An ability to identify and summarize the issues clearly and in language the parties can understand.
- Resourcefulness in helping the disputants propose and negotiate their own solution to the problem. The mediator must be able to structure the negotiation without directing it.
- Patience, flexibility, and the ability to tolerate delay and frustration.
- Discretion. Although mediation is not binding, it is private and confidential, and the proceedings are not documented. The mediator's notes are destroyed at the end of each session.

It is impossible to become a mediator without training. Training programs can last from four to sixty hours, and they may take a day or two to complete or stretch out over a month.

The principle behind mediation—that discussion and an airing of views within a structured setting can lead to agreement—is inherently optimistic, and mediators find the work intense and enormously satisfying.

Most of the organizations discussed in this section are resources; that is, they can be used to locate local organizations that practice dispute resolution.

## American Bar Association (ABA)

Standing Committee on Dispute Resolution
1800 M St., NW
Washington, DC 20036
1-202-331-2200

ABA's Standing Committee on Dispute Resolution acts as a clearinghouse for information and technical assistance regarding dispute resolution. These services are provided to both ABA and external groups. The committee also stimulates state and local bar involvement in dispute resolution, develops and evaluates innovative programs, conducts educational programs, and publishes extensively. Among the publications is the biennial *American Bar Association Dispute Resolution Program Directory*, a listing of local organizations that use volunteer mediators. The directory is not distributed to libraries, but the ABA will send interested persons a printout of community justice organizations for their areas.

## Call for Action (CFA)

3400 Idaho Ave., NW
Washington, DC 20016
1-202-537-0585, 1-202-537-1551 (TDD)
Contact: Shirley Rooker, President

CFA runs a free, confidential consumer hotline service that operates as a nonprofit affiliate of radio and TV broadcasters in twenty-one cities in thirteen states nationwide. Every year, more than 800 CFA volunteers respond to over 150,000 calls, helping with a broad range of problems that people have been unable to solve on their own in such areas as consumer complaints, housing and human services, social security, welfare, abandoned cars, and many others. Trained volunteer mediators listen to consumer complaints, research them for authenticity, then contact the government agencies or businesses involved to arrive at solutions that work well for all concerned. CFA also represents small businesses who believe they have been defrauded.

CFA's Ask the Experts program brings local professionals—accountants, doctors, lawyers, pharmacists, and so on—into the studios to answer consumer questions from the audience. Recently, CFA has expanded its services to help small businesses with consumer problems.

CFA operates almost entirely with volunteer staff. For a list of stations and cities with CFA affiliates, write to the national headquarters.

## Community Board Program (CBP)

149 9th St.
San Francisco, CA 94103
1-415-552-1250
Contact: Public Information Director

CBP is a pioneer in both community conflict resolution and student mediation programs. Since 1977, through its Community Boards of San Francisco, CBP has been training neighborhood volunteers to help solve community problems before they escalate into complaints that can be handled only through formal government channels. Conflicts include harassment, vandalism, noise, money disputes, property damage, landlord-tenant concerns, threats, family disputes, fights, and organizational disputes.

CBSF's approach involves Community Board panel hearings, which are attended by the disputants and a panel of three or four volunteer conciliators, who come from the same neighborhood as the disputing parties, to assist the parties in reaching their own agreement. The intent of the program is to increase self-sufficiency in neighborhoods by individual and group participation in conflict resolution.

About 350 volunteer conciliators a year, aged fourteen to seventy and from different races and walks of life, are active in the CBP, recruited by word of mouth, mail fliers, and neighborhood bulletin boards. Volunteers promise to serve one year. About 50 people a year are trained as conciliators, and some of them receive further in-

*Continued on page 159*

## PORTRAIT OF A SPECIAL VOLUNTEER:

*Danica Wilcox has been described by a colleague as a superb mediator, articulate and compassionate in her perspective. For four years, Danica, now attending college, worked as a comediator at the Community Dispute Resolution Center (CDRC) in Ithaca, New York. Laura Branca, a CDRC trainer, recruited Danica when she was fourteen years old.*

I knew something about mediation before I was recruited because six months earlier I'd been having problems with my parents and we considered family mediation. We worked things out on our own, but when Laura approached me, I thought I'd like to try it.

I was trained in a twenty-hour workshop in basic techniques and skills in family mediation. After that I audited three or four real mediation sessions, mostly listening and watching. Except for the mediator's opening statement and then later the observation, I wasn't fully involved. Then by the beginning of ninth grade I began to do actual mediation, and now I do it more and more, and I've become a youth trainer for youth mediators, training about twenty in a workshop.

Mediation's made a really positive impact on my life. I'd always had a lot of friends with problems, and I was often the person they came to for solutions. They just wanted the solutions handed to them, and sometimes I gave bad advice and I felt terrible about it—it's hard to help people who are unwilling to help themselves. The good thing about mediation is that the people who come to the Center *are* there to help themselves.

The training had a big influence on how I related to these people—it forced me to change my role and become a listener instead of an adviser. There was one specific workshop for youth mediators so we'd understand what it meant to be a young mediator—sharing power with an adult and using that as an example in actual mediation, a kind of role model, to show there can be positive interaction and power sharing.

I love the work. It's frustrating and fulfilling. The fulfillment is in the resolutions you help people make—even the smallest agreement is encouraging. But it's a hard role to play because of the restrictions about giving advice. You always have to remember that you're not a counselor. You're trying to understand everyone's point of view without agreeing—showing people they can make their own decisions and agreements. The frustration comes when you feel there really is an easy solution, but the family doesn't see it, it doesn't occur to them. You can't suggest it; it must be their idea. And it's hard when you've spent a lot of time and feel close to the family and work something out, then you check up every two weeks, six weeks, two months. And when agreements are not holding up and the family won't come back to the Center, it's sad, especially when it's not a hard problem to resolve.

It's emotionally wearing. Older mediators have cried with sympathy—there are so many similarities in people's lives that it's hard not to say, "Oh, I know exactly how you feel," or to suggest a resolution, hard to stay neutral and not openly empathize. If a bigoted person says biased things in mediation, the mediator must set personal feelings aside. Racial hatred is a difficult thing to countenance.

*Continued*

*Continued*

A lot of people we've worked with have called the Center and said they thought the resolution was going to work out, but for many others, even though they try, the conflict is unresolvable. We can suggest more professional help, but the important difference in a lot of these families is that they are living in poverty; some are homeless, school dropouts, absentee parents or teenagers who have been living with grandparents, or in other bad situations. They lead unstable lives, so trying to reach even simple agreements is hard and keeping them is harder, especially where kids don't know what's happening next. Only in stable, higher-income families with smaller problems does conflict resolution have a good chance of sticking. The poorest need mediation the most and have the worst conflicts. Keeping in touch with those families is difficult because they move so often.

But even if families don't stick to the exact agreement, the fact that they came and talked and spoke about how they feel and aired feelings helps. The first agreement they make is that if they're going to fight, they sit down and write it out, agree to use polite language.

Personally, it's had a tremendous influence on my life. I can articulate my feelings much better than before. Now, instead of screaming at once, I can figure out exactly what it is that bothers me and tune in to that rather than side issues. And I can clarify what I want done. I'm much more outspoken about what I need from my parents because I've learned how to use noninflammatory language, and I'm able to explain constructively how I feel without being offensive or overbearing and without making others defensive. I think you can actually get something out of a conflict if you can just focus on one issue and problem, not the person, and ignore all the little things, because basically the only reason you're noticing them is the conflict. Now that I've learned to use language that way, people who would have felt defensive or angry at criticism believe I'm the one who's opening up and making myself vulnerable—not them. Honest!

My family is politically and socially conscientious, so I've been doing volunteer work for a long time. In ninth and tenth grades I did mostly mediation, and of course I'm still doing it now. But this year I got interested in social work; I guess I'm more concerned about people than anything else. My school is flexible, so I've gotten involved in a youth council—a group of kids of varying ethnic and economic backgrounds. We get together once a week to talk about youth—violence, community service work in Ithaca, and lot of the issues.

I went to New York City for a week with Habitat for Humanity, where we worked on an apartment building with the homesteading families who were renovating their apartments over the last two years. I also did some Habitat work in Ithaca for low-income people.

I'm working a couple of days in the Loaves and Fishes soup kitchen where we prepare and serve lunch for about eighty people. And I'm a Big Sister for a little girl in a foster home, so I can use my mediation skills, listen, pick up on feelings.

I've always had an active social life, and I still have a lot of friends, but I feel more fulfilled by the volunteer work, and that's become my social life. It just makes me feel good that I enjoy the work so much and at the same time I can do good.

## FEATURED ORGANIZATION: COUNCIL OF BETTER BUSINESS BUREAUS (CBBB)

National Headquarters
4200 Wilson Blvd.
Arlington, VA 22203
1-703-276-0100, FAX 1-703-525-8277
Contact: Director of Bureau-Manufacturer Affairs,
Alternate Dispute Resolution Division (ADR)

CBBB is an umbrella organization, providing oversight, training, and guidance for the 170 local autonomous Better Business Bureaus nationwide. All told, CBBB and the local Bureaus have a membership of over 250,000 national and local businesses. CBBB promotes ethical business practices and protects the consumer through voluntary self-regulation and monitoring activities.

The BBB Auto Line, designed specifically for the resolution of complaints between consumers and auto manufacturers, began operating nationally in 1982. Since then it has handled over 1 million disputes and has become the largest out-of-court dispute resolution program in the United States, working on over 91,000 complaints a year.

CBBB's ADR (alternative dispute resolution) division provides dispute resolution services to consumers with complaints against companies they have patronized, a program that is offered in a number of local Bureaus. If the business has agreed in advance to ADR, a staff member will first attempt telephone conciliation. If conciliation fails, the complaint is sometimes handled by a mediator (usually staff, but occasionally a volunteer), who assists the consumer and company in reaching a mutually agreeable resolution. If a settlement is not reached, a trained volunteer arbitrator listens to both parties, reviews all relevant evidence, and renders a decision within ten days. The company must accept this decision, but the consumer can reject it. However, if the consumer accepts it, everyone is bound.

Potential arbitrators receive a fourteen-hour training over the course of two days. Certification is based on a quiz, a role play, the examinee's decision based on a videotaped mock hearing, and his or her reasons for that decision. Currently there are about 9,000 certified volunteer arbitrators handling approximately 17,000 arbitrations each year.

Local Bureaus recruit arbitrators through local media, word of mouth, and speeches to civic organizations. Volunteers should have strong communication and analytical skills, write well, and be decisive and fair-minded. There are no educational requirements. Contact your local Bureau for more information or get in touch with CBBB.

CBBB is deeply committed to the ADR process which, it believes, is faster, less expensive, and more satisfactory than legal redress. *BBB Solutions* is a quarterly newsletter devoted to ADR both as it is practiced by BBB staff and volunteers and in a broader national context. To subscribe, write to the national headquarters.

*Continued from page 155*
struction to become trainers themselves.

CBP's Conflict Resolution Resources for Schools and Youth is a national training program offered to elementary, middle, and secondary schools and to juvenile facilities. One of its main features is the Conflict Manager Program, which trains selected students to act as conciliators among their peers. For information, write to CBP.

## Conflict Resolution Center International, Inc. (CRCI)

7101 Hamilton Ave.
Pittsburgh, PA 15208-1828
1-412-371-9884, FAX 1-412-371-9885
Contact: Director

CRCI is a clearinghouse and resource center with a specific focus on community and neighborhood disputes and racial, ethnic, and religious conflicts. An extensive library of conflict resolution materials is partially accessible to subscribers of ConflictNet (page 159), or is accessible by mail. CRCI, which publishes "Conflict Resolution Notes" ($20 annually)—a chronicle of the worldwide conflict resolution movement—also maintains a data base of conflict resolution service providers and trainers and will be happy to provide potential volunteers with information about community-based mediation programs in their own or other areas.

## Institute for Global Communications

ConflictNet
18 De Boom St.
San Francisco, CA 94107
1-415-442-0220, FAX 1-415-546-1794

ConflictNet is a computer-based communications system that can be used by organizations and individuals who need communications services information about dispute resolution (DR). Subscribers, who have access to a computer with a modem, pay a one-time $15 sign-up fee and then are billed $10 monthly. Services include access to information from leading organizations in the field; communication with networks in other countries; electronic mail; and public conferences for sharing information about DR and networking with other individuals and organizations. For mediators or new people in the field, there are calendars of events and information about training, education, and degree programs in conflict resolution. Call IGC for more information.

## National Association for Mediation in Education (NAME)

425 Amity St.
Amherst, MA 01002
1-413-545-2462
Contact: Executive Director

NAME is a membership organization that supports, promotes, and sponsors the development and implementation of school- and university-based conflict resolution programs. It serves as a clearinghouse for information on conflict resolution in education and distributes books and other publications in the field, including its quarterly newsletter, "The Fourth R." NAME also provides resources, technical assistance, and training to existing and developing programs in the schools. Write to NAME for a free information packet.

## National Institute for Dispute Resolution (NIDR)

1901 L St., NW
Washington, DC 20036
1-202-466-4764
Contact: Patrick Piere

NIDR is the only grant-maker in the United States whose sole focus is conflict resolution, with particular support given to the development, testing, and expansion of innovative techniques. NIDR has major programs relating to the courts, public policy, education, and community mediation; publications; and grant-making for new programs. NIDR will send interested persons a listing of dispute resolution centers in any region of the country.

## PACT Institute of Justice

Victim-Offender Reconciliation Program (VORP)
254 Morgan Blvd.
Valparaiso, IN 46383
1-219-462-1127
Contact: Program Coordinator

PACT Institute of Justice is the technical, research, training, and information division of PACT ("Prisoner and Community Together"), a regional, community-based corrections organization founded in 1971 and now running in seven sites in Indiana. The Institute also is a clearinghouse for Victim-Offender Reconciliation and Mediation Program (VORP), which originated in the Midwest in the early 1980s and now is used in at least 100 locations in the United States.

The working premise of VORP is that a face-to-face meeting between a crime victim and the criminal offender will serve both the interests of justice and those of victim and offender. In the course of the meeting, both parties review and explore the facts of the crime and their feelings about it and then work out an agreement about restitution, which can be monetary, or in the form of community service or direct service to the victim. A trained volunteer mediator conducts the meeting and writes up the agreement.

The victim benefits not only by receiving restitution but by participating in the settlement process. In a face-to-face meeting with the offender, a victim is able to vent feelings and get answers to questions, which can reduce anxiety about the crime. For the offender, VORP provides an alternative to incarceration for minor crimes and first-time property offenses and the chance to help decide on the restitution. Just as important, the offender has the opportunity to understand the impact of the crime on a specific individual.

VORP volunteer mediators are usually recruited from the community through newspaper ads and radio announcements, and by local VORP speaking engagements for service groups. Volunteers are screened with care and then undertake a twelve-hour training program, which involves lectures, discussion, and role play in simulated mediation sessions. After the program, the trainee observes skilled mediators at work and later on participates as a comediator.

If you are interested in working as a VORP mediator, call or write to PACT Institute of Justice for the *Victim-Offender Reconciliation and Mediation Program Directory*, $10, which lists the locations of every VORP in the United States and Canada, and overseas as well.

## Victim Services (VS, page 90)

Mediation Center
Contact: Mediation Director

VS, a New York City nonprofit organization that assists victims, has two programs involving the extensive use of volunteer mediators: Project SMART, school mediation projects in four of New York City's five boroughs; and two adult Mediation Centers, which help resolve court-referred cases—conflicts between friends, relatives, neighbors, landlords and tenants—at no charge.

In Project SMART, teachers, school administrators, students, and their parents are taught mediation techniques. VS believes that kids who actually practice peer mediation get more out of the training and give back more to the community. Student mediators serve on panels that resolve such problems as truancy, school violence, and racial issues. Statistics show that student mediation has been correlated with a dramatic drop in suspensions for fighting in the schools.

VS's mediation services are offered as part of the New York State Unified Court System, in which every New York State county offers disputing parties the option of mediation for certain kinds of disputes. VS's Mediation Centers are in Brooklyn and Queens, the one in Brooklyn handling more mediations than any other comparable center in the United States. Potential volunteers send in their resumes and then are interviewed by staff who are looking for people with good listening skills, common sense, and commitment to the program. Volunteers must agree to mediate a minimum of nine hours a month for six months to a year, but more than 40 percent find the work so compelling that they contribute much more time.

Mediators receive an intensive twenty-five-hour training, which includes lectures and class discussions, many group exercises with role play and simulation, instruction on writing the agreement that the disputing parties will sign, and at least four and a half hours of mediation simulation in which each trainee mediates a dispute. The final session closes with a discussion of ethical concerns, the limits of mediation, and the responsibilities of the newly trained mediators. Before working alone, each mediator must observe several real mediations, acting as a comediator in the last two or three of these.

Nationwide, there are hundreds of programs similar to VS's mediation program, many of them offered by Community Dispute Resolution Centers (CDRCs). For the location of a CDRC near you, write to the American Bar Association Standing Committee on Dispute Resolution (ABA, page 155).

# Mentoring

A mentor is any caring person who offers someone younger friendship, emotional support, and guidance within a structured program. Interaction with a mentor can increase self-esteem and help a youth develop the ability to make decisions, plan for the future, and cope with and even overcome the difficulties of personal circumstance. Kids—especially those who have been through the mill of the juvenile justice system or who have received the ministrations of family service organizations, however well intentioned—know that mentors are more fun to be with simply because they *are* volunteers who *choose* to be with children.

Many mentoring programs are designed to meet specific goals—preventing children from dropping out of school, improving their academic skills, helping to prepare them for careers and parenthood. Although the term *mentor* very often describes a one-to-one relationship, organizations such as Junior Achievement (JA, page 164) and the National MENTOR Program (page 165) provide individual consultants to mentor an entire school class.

Mentors come from every walk of life and almost every age group, from teenage, or peer, mentors who work with slightly younger students to retired people. To be an effective mentor, you must:

1. Respect younger people and accept them as they are.
2. Be open and willing to listen without being judgmental.
3. Be committed to spending the time needed to develop and nurture the relationship.

Mentoring programs are run by states, schools and universities, churches, various human service agencies and civic organizations, and businesses. All novice mentors receive some training before they begin work with their junior partners, depending on the program and the individuals being mentored.

---

**American Association for the Advancement of Science (AAAS, page 98)**

### Asian American Journalists Association (AAJA)

National Office
1765 Sutter St., Room 1000
San Francisco, CA 94115
1-415-346-2051, FAX 1-415-931-4671
Contact: Executive Director

AAJA is a nonprofit organization whose aim is to increase employment of Asian American journalists, assist students pursuing journalism careers, encourage fair and accurate coverage of Asian American issues, and provide support for Asian American journalists. AAJA's mentoring program matches experienced journalists one to one with beginning journalists. Mentors discuss career options with students, assist them with assignments, and act as conduits to the profession. There are AAJA chapters in thirteen regions in the continental United States and in Hawaii with a membership of over 1,100 journalists and students. For information about becoming a member, get in touch with the national office.

**ASPIRA Association, Inc. (page 79)**

**Museum of Science, Boston, Science-By-Mail (MOS, page 96)**

## The Breakthrough Foundation (BF)

Youth at Risk Program
1952 Lombard St.
San Francisco, CA 94123
1-415-673-0171

BF is a nonprofit organization that brings together, and acts as a consultant to, community-based organizations, providing programs that address the problems faced by youth at risk. The programs can be adapted to local circumstances—drug abuse, crime, school dropouts, low employment—and they rely to a large extent on trained volunteer Committed Partners, or mentors. Once a community decides to take on a program, BF sends in a staff team to run workshops for professionals and volunteers and provide coaching over the course of one to two years. Individual youth are recommended by schools, clubs, the local justice system, and other nonprofit social agencies. After the initial residential course, each youth is assigned a mentor and sets his or her own goals. Mentors keep in touch with their youth regularly and also help them get work, discuss any problems, assist the youth in sticking to the program, and try to reinforce any breakthroughs achieved. Volunteer mentors receive intensive initial training, and ongoing support from BF. During a typical program, 350 volunteers take on over 650 different jobs. So far, over 2,000 youth have completed the program, which is active in thirty-four communities nationwide. To find out if there is one in your city, contact the San Francisco office.

**Community Outreach Law Program (COLP, page 148)**

**Compeer (page 137)**

**Constitutional Rights Foundation (CRF, page 150)**

**Constitutional Rights Foundation/Chicago (CRFC, page 151)**

## Help One Student to Succeed (HOSTS)

National Headquarters
1801 D St., Suite 2
Vancouver, WA 98663
1-800-833-4678
Contact: Jerald L. Willbur, Ed.D., President and Chief Operating Officer

HOSTS is a national one-on-one program designed to help students in grades K–12 improve their basic language skills. Volunteer mentors—adults from the community and older students—work with a computerized data base that generates lesson plans specific to each child's age, reading level, and learning style. As mentor and student work through the lesson plan together, they share a common learning experience, and the child becomes more confident and ready for success.

The HOSTS program, which has received many awards and has been validated by the U.S. Department of Education as a Chapter I model, is currently being used in over 400 schools nationwide and utilizes the services of more than 100,000 volunteers. HOSTS volunteers are often recruited by school district personnel through their work and social activities. Call your local

## FEATURED ORGANIZATION: BIG BROTHERS/BIG SISTERS OF AMERICA (BB/BSA)

National Headquarters
230 N. 13th St.
Philadelphia, PA 19107-1510
1-215-567-7000, FAX 1-215-567-0394

BB/BSA is the nation's largest mentoring organization, with over 500 affiliated agencies. For nearly ninety years, BB/BSA has provided adult mentors on a one-to-one basis for school-age children at risk, particularly those from single-parent homes, in the belief that such a friendship can enable a child to mature in a positive way. Volunteer mentors come from every background. They can be married or single, have children or grandchildren, be handicapped or disabled. Every volunteer is carefully screened and trained and then matched with a child, based on the child's needs and the interests of the volunteer. In many communities an effort is made to match children with mentors of the same race and ethnicity. Each mentor makes a commitment to spend several hours each week with a Little Brother or Little Sister for at least one year, offering companionship and guidance, sharing experiences, and helping the child develop self-esteem and a sense of accomplishment. In all of this, the agency's professional staff furnishes ongoing support and assistance, and regular contacts are maintained between the parent, child, volunteer, and caseworker.

BB/BSA offers other services as part of the one-to-one mentoring programs. EMPOWER, designed to be used with young children and teenagers, helps identify potentially abusive situations before they become problems. ALTERNATIVES is an education and prevention program created to address the problem of substance abuse. BB/BSA cooperates with other national organizations to develop programs to meet some of the many problems facing children today. Affiliated agencies may have specific programs that focus on school dropouts, AIDS prevention, and adolescent pregnancy prevention programs, as well as programs for the disabled. BB/BSA also forms partnerships with corporations for volunteer recruitment and fund-raising.

BB/BSA is always looking for volunteer mentors and has mounted a special effort to recruit volunteers for their "Pass It On" Minority Mentorship Campaign. Community leaders are needed to serve as board members or as advisers at the local and national levels. For information, check your phone book for the nearest affiliate, or call or write to the national office for the affiliate nearest you.

school district office to see if any of the local schools have adopted HOSTS, or call or write to the national headquarters for a list of HOSTS schools in your area.

### Junior Achievement, Inc. (JA)

National Headquarters
45 Clubhouse Dr.
Colorado Springs, CO 80906
1-719-540-8000
Contact: Vice President of Communications

JA brings the business and education worlds together by sharing economic and business knowledge with students through innovative, hands-on, activity-based programs. There are over 250 franchised JA affiliates nationwide, each composed of sponsoring firms that contribute funds and recruit volunteers from among their employees to serve as business consultants in JA's programs. In the United States alone, over 1 million students participate in these programs, which are provided free to schools. Volunteer consultants receive special JA training, which they use in tandem with their own unique perspectives and business experiences to act as constructive role models in the classroom.

Some JA programs are:

- Business Basics, which pairs consultants with classroom teachers to familiarize fifth- and sixth-grade children with the fundamentals of business organization, practices, and economics.
- Project Business, designed to supplement eighth- and ninth-grade social studies classes.
- Applied Economics, in which consultants advise senior high school students and help them form, run, and liquidate businesses.
- Success Now, a recent pilot program that is part of a continuum of economic education JA is developing for at-risk and minority students from kindergarten through sixth grade.

Although many volunteer consultants are drawn from JA-sponsoring companies, anyone with solid business and work experience who feels comfortable going into a classroom and talking to children is a potential JA volunteer. If you are an individual volunteer or work for a company that wishes to participate in JA, consult your phone book for the JA nearest you, or call or write to the national headquarters.

## National MENTOR Program (MENTOR)

Washington State Bar Association
500 Westin Building
2001 Sixth Ave.
Seattle, WA 98121-2599
1-206-727-8282
Contact: Program Director

MENTOR's goal is to increase high school students' understanding of the U.S. legal system and its impact on their lives, to make students more aware of their rights and responsibilities as citizens, and to provide information on possible careers related to the justice system. In the MENTOR partnership, a high school class is paired with a law firm. The basic program, usually incorporated into social studies or business law classes, includes:

- An orientation, in which lawyers from the sponsoring firm visit the classroom and speak about the legal profession.
- A class visit to the law firm, with an office tour and discussions with people who hold a variety of positions in the firm.
- Courtroom visits to observe civil and criminal trials.
- Electives, which might involve a visit to a judge's chambers, students enacting mock trials, legal writing, and other activities designed to use community resources.

MENTOR is currently available in over 200 schools nationwide in twenty states and in Canada. If you work for a law firm that is already a MENTOR partner, get in touch with the program director. To find out if MENTOR is offered in your community or for information about how to become involved in the program, contact the MENTOR program director at the Washington State Bar Association.

## National Association for the Advancement of Colored People (NAACP)

"Back-to-School/Stay-in-School" Program
4805 Mt. Hope Dr.
Baltimore, MD 21215-3297
1-301-358-8900
Contact: Program Director

The NAACP is acting to combat rising school dropout rates and truancy among black and other minority youth with its national "Back-to-

School/Stay-in-School" Program, which provides at-risk students with tutoring, remediation, guidance, and incentives designed to help them graduate from school. Local NAACP branches organize their own programs based on manuals and materials created by a national technical staff. Branch members work with administrators of school districts that have high dropout rates to establish in-school pilot projects, and local businesses are asked to provide space and/or supervision for after-school tutorial programs. Volunteers are recruited to serve as tutors and role models from the NAACP Youth and College Division, and from fraternities, sororities, and numerous service organizations. Call your local NAACP branch for more information.

## One to One Partnerships, Inc. (1 to 1)

2801 M St., NW
Washington, DC 20007
1-202-338-3844, FAX 1-202-338-1642
Contact: Director of Public Affairs

One to One was formed in 1989 as a catalyst to raise national and local consciousness about the benefits of mentoring to disadvantaged youths, with a special focus on the private sector. By providing advice and materials and helping to develop action plans, One to One serves as a resource for organizations that wish to become involved in mentoring. For information call or write to the director of Public Affairs.

## Partners, Inc.

1675 Larimer, Suite 730
Denver, CO 80202-1629
1-303-595-4400
Contact: Bill Stout, Program Support Director

Partners works to prevent youth already involved in the juvenile justice system from getting into more trouble and to help at-risk youth combat the problems they face before their future is threatened. Partners relies on trained volunteers, called "senior partners," who work one-to-one with each youth, or "junior partner," in a highly structured program customized to the specific needs and situation of the child. Both partners agree to spend at least three hours together every week for a year. Everyone in a partnership is a volunteer, including the child and his or her parents. Senior partners are expected to be open and flexible and to have a good idea of what can reasonably be expected from working with kids at risk. The program also provides professional referral services, counseling, and crisis intervention.

Matchups are always between partners of the same sex, with an occasional exception when a child is matched with a couple. A junior partner often becomes involved in the most meaningful parts of a mentor's life—regular family gatherings, holiday celebrations, religious or spiritual occasions, sports events, and other entertainment—all of which offer the child a model of how a healthy family functions. It is not uncommon for a good senior partner to have a relationship with a junior partner for three or four years.

Volunteers undergo a careful screening process before they are selected. Volunteer training includes six hours of instruction and another fourteen hours of interviews and screening. There are Partners programs in eight sites in Colorado and one in North Carolina, with 1,000 to 1,200 volunteers overall. If you live in either of these states, call or write to the national headquarters to find out if there is an affiliate near you.

Becoming a Partners affiliate: Partners was created in Denver in 1968 to serve at-risk children. Since then it has helped over 20,000 youths, refining its program and making it adaptable to local needs and specific populations. Among the resources the parent organization can provide are the *Partners Training and Resource Manual* (over 250 pages), technical assistance and access to other affiliates' best ideas and experience, and an annual site visit and evaluation (a peer review accreditation process). If you wish to start a Partners in your own community, contact the national headquarters.

Shooting Back Media Center (SBMC, page 61)

### State Bar of California

Volunteers in Parole (VIP)
555 Franklin St.
San Francisco, CA 94102
1-415-561-8217
Contact: Statewide Director, VIP

VIP, originally modeled on the Big Brother/Big Sister mentoring program (BB/BSA, page 164), matches youthful parolees fifteen to twenty-five years old with attorneys and other legal professionals who can help the ex-offenders make a successful adjustment to life outside of prison. Attorneys serve as mentors for VIP because people in the legal profession are not only highly motivated and trained to communicate, they are also knowledgeable about their communities' resources for credit, financial planning, family services, jobs, and housing.

VIP program directors try to match up people who live reasonably close to each other and who have a common interest—the same sports, movies, foods, books—which might be the springboard for a friendship. Volunteers and parolees spend time walking together, going to movies, taking bicycle rides, or going to restaurants. Volunteers try to help parolees find jobs or housing or to fulfill other goals.

VIP is currently available in eight California counties. Volunteers meet with their parolees for six to eight hours a month and must commit themselves to at least six months. VIP cautions that being a mentor to a parolee is not always easy; it requires patience, dedication, and realistic expectations about the speed with which a parolee can change. Volunteer legal professionals are recruited through local bar associations, and by publicity over the radio, in community newspapers, and by word of mouth. Call the San Francisco office for information.

Volunteers in Prevention, Probation & Prisons, (page 183)

# Resources

"Mentor Bulletin," a quarterly newsletter funded by the U.S. Department of Labor, contains current in- formation about mentoring, including news about mentoring programs around the country, reprints of articles from other publications, and previews of future events. To order a copy or to subscribe, call or write to The National Media Outreach Center, 4802 Fifth Ave., Pittsburgh, PA 15213, 1-412-622-1300, Ricki Wertz, Project Director.

"National Mentor Network Contacts" is a state-by-state listing of people who have volunteered to serve as mentoring contacts for their communities. It is published by the National Mentor Network, under a contract with the U.S. Department of Labor. For a free copy, call or write to National Mentor Network (NMW), One PLUS One, PLUS Project on Mentoring, 4802 Fifth Ave., Pittsburgh, PA 15213, 1-412-622-1584, Anastasia Kawalec, Project Coordinator.

"A Youth Mentoring Program Directory" is an annotated sampling of local and national programs. The booklet is designed as a resource for organizations that want to start mentoring programs of their own. Send $5 to One Plus One, The National Media Outreach Center, 4802 Fifth Ave., Pittsburgh, PA 15213, or call 1-412-622-1300, Ricki Wertz, Project Director.

*The Student Pugwash USA Mentorship Guide: A Directory of Resource People and Advisors in Social Change,* edited by Brent Hopkins and Jeff McIntyre. Send $6 to Student Pugwash USA, 1638 R St., NW., Suite 32, Washington, D.C. or call 1-202-328-6555.

# Working with and for Minorities

## Immigrants and Refugees

To get an idea of the kind of help immigrants need, imagine that you are about to resettle in a country whose language you don't know, where housing, family and religious life, pastimes, and education are all very different from your own. Fortunately there are a large number of nonprofit agencies working to help refugees and other immigrants settle comfortably in their new communities, offering exactly the help you'd want yourself: orientation to the community, tutoring in a new language, assistance finding housing, work, and education for your children, and, not least, instruction on your rights as an immigrant and access to those rights. Local agencies working with immigrants very often originate with church or synagogue groups that welcome newcomers and help them adjust to their new homes.

### American Council for Nationalities Service (ACNS)

National Headquarters
95 Madison Ave.
New York, NY 10016
1-212-532-5858
Contact: Assistant Director

ACNS is a network of forty independent nonprofit affiliates working with immigrants nationwide. Paid staff and community volunteers provide services such as counseling; language tutoring; help in setting up a household; donating clothing, furniture, and food; acting as a friend and mentor. All these activities rely heavily on volunteers. For a list of ACNS affiliates, call or write to the national headquarters.

ACNS is one of at least eleven umbrella organizations working with the State Department to resettle refugees. Here are other organizations doing similar work:

### Church World Service (CWS)

475 Riverside Dr.
New York, NY 10115
1-212-870-3300

CWS has about forty-eight refugee service branches, all of them run by Protestant churches and all of them listed in the *Directory of Voluntary Agencies, M-233* (See Immigration and Naturalization Service Examinations Operations Facilitation Program, INS page 169). CWS will answer any request for information about the branch nearest you.

## Lutheran Immigration and Refugee Service (LIRS)

390 Park Ave. S.
New York, NY 10016
1-212-532-6350

LIRS works with immigrants and refugees through twenty-six affiliate offices and twenty-eight suboffices. Although LIRS has paid professional staff, it also uses many local volunteers who are recruited through congregations and community groups. Some of the LIRS affiliates are listed in the *Directory of Voluntary Agencies, M-233* (See Immigration and Naturalization Service Examinations Operations Facilitation Program, INS/EOFP, page 169), or write to LIRS for a list.

## United States Catholic Conference (USCC)

902 Broadway
New York, NY 10010
1-212-614-1277

USCC has forty agencies across the country, all based within the diocesan network. Ask at your local parish about programs to help immigrants.

## Refugee Voices (RV)

3041 4th St., NE
Washington, DC 20017-1102
1-202-832-0020, FAX 1-202-832-5616
Contact: Frank Moan, SJ, Director

RV is a national nonprofit group dedicated to raising consciousness about the plight of refugees here and abroad by documenting refugee lives in taped interviews. Radio shows and public service announcements are distributed to 300 radio stations across the country, and RV videotapes of refugees are distributed to other refugee organizations. "Refugee Voices," RV's quarterly newsletter, is sent free to anyone who wishes it. Membership in RV is by donation. Potential volunteers can call for the names of local agencies involved with helping refugees, as well as for copies of the newsletter and "Support Services to Refugee Voices/Direct Service to Refugees," which has ideas for community groups and individuals wishing to help refugees.

## U.S. Department of Justice

Immigration and Naturalization Service Examinations Operations Facilitation Program (INS/EOFP)
425 I St., NW
Washington, DC 20536
1-202-633-4123, 1-202-514-4123

INS's responsibility is to assist aliens entitled to immigration benefits. Many aliens are unaware of or find it difficult to apply for their benefits. The INS/EOFP works closely with over 800 local nonprofit immigration provider organizations to help people in ethnic neighborhoods who are having problems with resettlement. INS trains the agencies' staffs on immigration procedures and provides technical assistance. These organizations work directly with their alien clients, helping them to understand their rights, filling out forms, counseling them on other problems, and referring the clients to other agencies. EOFP keeps the local agencies up to date on any changes in immigration law and provides regular training sessions as well. Approximately 1,000 agencies are included in the INS listing of community groups working with the EOFP, the *Directory of Voluntary Agencies, M-233,* which is published yearly.

# Ethnic Minorities

There are hundreds of organizations, including federal, state, and local agencies, addressing the issues confronting ethnic minority populations in the United States. Ethnic organizations do more than advocate and educate; they also celebrate shared background, culture, and traditions. In states with large groups of ethnic minorities, ask about volunteer programs at local churches, synagogues, service groups, Scout troops, Ys, and volunteer action centers (VACs). (See National Volunteer Center, NVC, page 37).

### American Indian Heritage Foundation (AIHF)

6051 Arlington Blvd.
Falls Church, VA 22044
1-202-INDIANS, FAX 1-703-532-1921
Contact: Zainab "Peggy" Aljibouri, Director of Resource Development

AIHF is a nonprofit organization working to meet the physical and social needs of American Indians by providing emergency relief and fostering economic development. Through its Gifts-in-Kind Program, AIHF brings corporations with surplus inventory together with American Indian tribes and organizations that need tangible assistance. The program arranges for the distribution of books, food, clothing, and medicine. Other programs involve educating American Indian youth about their own cultures, developing markets for American Indian handcrafts, and working through the media. AIHF needs volunteers at its Falls Church headquarters for all kinds of general office work, telemarketing (soliciting product donations), research, fund-raising, working on community outreach, and writing grant proposals. Contact the Falls Church office for information and a volunteer application form.

**Asian American Journalists Association (AAJA, page 162)**

### Center for Third World Organizing (CTWO)

3861 Martin Luther King, Jr. Way
Oakland, CA 94609
1-415-654-9601
Contact: Alfred DeAvila, Training Director

CTWO offers technical assistance to community organizations and agencies committed to creating social change or providing vital social services, particularly for people of color. CTWO's multilingual and multicultural staff can assist an organization with an individually designed program to research and solve problems, broaden the organization's multicultural diversity, plan and implement community campaigns, and learn how to raise money. CTWO also offers several other services, including a Saturday school for community leaders. The Minority Activist Apprenticeship Program (MAAP) is an internship program for students of color who want to become community organizers. The program lasts eight weeks, six of them spent in the field. For information on MAAP internship, contact the CTWO training director.

### League of United Latin American Citizens (LULAC)

National Office
900 E. Karen Ave., Suite C-215
Las Vegas, NV 89109
1-702-737-1240, FAX 1-702-796-6193

LULAC is a national membership organization working to enhance the lives of Hispanic citizens through better education, employment, and civil rights. There are 500 LULAC councils nationwide, each helping to meet the needs of local Hispanics with job training, advocacy, promotion of women's rights, voter registration, and scholarship aid. Much of this work, including fund-raising, is carried out by member volunteers. For more information about LULAC and the location of the council nearest you, get in touch with the national office.

National Association for the Advancement of Colored People (NAACP, page 165)

## National Council of La Raza (NCLR)

810 1st St., NE, Suite 300
Washington, DC 20003-4205
1-202-289-1380, FAX 1-202-289-8173
Contact: Lisa Navarrete

NCLR was founded in 1968 to improve opportunities for Hispanic Americans by addressing the problems of discrimination and poverty. NCLR national initiatives are to strengthen Hispanic community-based organizations, do research on and advocacy for the Hispanic community, provide accurate information for the public, and involve Hispanics in broader international issues. NCLR is an umbrella for 130 affiliates in thirty-five states, each an independent local organization. NCLR offers affiliate technical assistance on policy analysis, board and staff training, resource development, and advice on programs. Much of this assistance is also offered to nonaffiliated local Hispanic groups, including training and on-site help. For information about NCLR and for referral, contact Lisa Navarrete in the Washington office. See page 97 for NCLR's Project EXCEL (Excellence in Community Educational Leadership).

## National Council of Negro Women, Inc. (NCNW)

1211 Connecticut Ave., NW, Suite 702
Washington, DC 20036
1-202-659-2372, FAX 1-202-785-8733

NCNW is an umbrella organization of over 30 national affiliated organizations, such as Delta Sigma Theta Sorority, Las Amigas, and the National Bar Association. NCNW also has 250 community-based sections nationwide providing programs that serve African American women and their families in the areas of education and tutoring, health, adolescent pregnancy, substance abuse, and others. The organization is assisted by some 1,500 volunteers annually, most of whom implement The Black Family Reunion Celebration (BFRC), a multicity event focusing on the historic strengths and values of African American families. BFRC is held in six major cities nationwide every year and includes service, information, entertainment, workshops, and much more. For information about NCNW affiliates or to volunteer at one of its sections, get in touch with the Washington office.

## Sioux YMCA

Box 218
Dupree, SD 57623
1-605-365-5232
Contact: Myrl Weaver, Executive Director

Sioux YMCAs operate in twenty-eight communities on five reservations in South Dakota, North Dakota, and Montana and they are the only YMCAs operated by and serving primarily American Indian people. Programs focus on youth and leadership development, camping, community recreation, interdenominational religious programs, community development, and sports. Many of these programs are reliant on the efforts of volunteers from across the United States and from Europe and Asia as well. Here are some of the activities in which volunteers participate:

- Summer camp: Twelve volunteers, college age and older, are needed to serve as staff for a ten-week summer term. Volunteers must have skills suitable for primitive camping and be prepared to live in tepees with the campers, without electricity and running water.
- Community work: Skilled and dedicated volunteers, college age and older, are needed in winter, spring, summer, and fall to work for various development projects in remote communities of 50 to 3,000 people. Activities include developing sports and recreation programs and facilities, working at centers for

the elderly, counseling on substance abuse, inspiring teenagers to stay in school, and spending time with the families in the communities. Activities usually take place over an eight- to ten-week period.

- Program administration: Long-term volunteers, who receive a small monthly stipend and serve for at least one year, are needed as program directors.

Volunteers pay for their own transportation to and from South Dakota, and room and board are provided. For information, get in touch with the executive director.

## White Bison, Inc. (WBI)

1556 York Rd.
Colorado Springs, CO 80918
1-719-548-1000
Contact: Don Coyhis, Director

WBI's goal is to see 95 percent sobriety among American Indian youth by the year 2000. WBI combines elements of human development training principles, the 12-step recovery method of Alcoholics Anonymous (page 226), and traditional American Indian culture into programs that can be used by American Indian community leaders to help their youth. WBI provides training and technical assistance to American Indian nations across the United States and is developing a Native American Olympics. Residents in the Colorado Springs area can volunteer to organize games or work as office assistants, fund-raisers, or advocates. For more information, contact the director.

# Resource

### IMMIGRANTS AND REFUGEES

*Working with Refugees: A Guide for Community Involvement* is a free manual, published in 1983, that provides an overview of homelessness and refugees, then takes the reader through the steps that are helpful in resettlement of refugees in small and large communities, explaining the many services volunteers provide. Although written from a Catholic diocesan point of view, the manual will be helpful to any group that wants to assist aliens. For a copy, write to Migration and Refugee Service, U.S. Catholic Conference, 1312 Massachusetts Ave., NW, Washington, DC 20005.

# Helping the Needy

The first way to help needy people is to recognize and acknowledge their humanity. After that, there are hundreds of options: You can personally donate clothing, household articles, or food to shelters and nonprofit agencies for distribution, or you can arrange for donations of goods and services from businesses in the community. You can give as much time as you have or want to volunteer.

There are national advocacy organizations working on behalf of the hungry and homeless, but it is on the local level that food and shelter are funded and provided. Find out about programs through churches and synagogues, which run shelters and soup kitchens and have other services; the area volunteer action center (VAC) (see National Volunteer Center, NVC, page 37); the local United Way (UWA, page 38); service and children's clubs; and newspapers, especially the ones that run a volunteer opportunities section.

---

**Booksellers for Social Responsibility (BSR, page 195)**

## The Box Project (BP)

P.O. Box 435, Dept. Q
Plainville, CT 06062
1-203-747-8182
Contact: Executive Director

There are about 6,000 individuals, families, and groups nationwide participating in BP, an organization that facilitates assistance to families in need through the sending of material aid, information, advocacy, and friendship. BP took its name from one of its principle programs: volunteer "sisters" form ties of friendship by sending letters and boxes of food, clothing, household goods, and toys directly to families in need in the rural United States. Each BP volunteer or volunteer-group helper is matched with a "sister family" with whom to exchange correspondence and to whom the helper sends the packages of goods.

The Santa Program finds donors of special one-time holiday gifts to families still waiting for a helping "sister family" to be assigned. For more information, get in touch with the executive director.

**Community of Caring (COC, page 199)**

**Concern/America (page 186)**

**Fourth World Movement (FWM page 187)**

**National Student Campaign Against Hunger and Homelessness (NSCAHH, page 223)**

## NGA, Inc.

1007-B Street Rd.
Southampton, PA 18966
1-215-322-5759

NGA (formerly The Needlework Guild of America, Inc.) was founded in 1885 to collect new garments and give them to needy people. Through its almost 150 branches in twenty-three states, member-volunteers collect and give to America's needy more than 470,000 new items in the hope that these gifts carry with them not only comfort and warmth but also improved self-image and a promise of better days. The gifts are distributed through agencies such as American Red Cross (ARC, page 129) and The Salvation Army (TSA, page 201). NGA works closely with youth organizations—Camp Fire Boys and Girls (CFBG, page 72), 4-H (page 83), and Girl Scouts (GSUSA, page 73)—who contribute new items and their time. NGA's National Emergency Relief Fund is used in the wake of disasters to provide immediate relief in the form of new clothing and linens. If you would like to join a local NGA (the membership fee is the donation of two items) or start a chapter of your own, get in touch with the Southampton, Pennsylvania, office.

# Feeding the Hungry

## Bread for the World (BFW)

802 Rhode Island Ave., NE
Washington, DC 20018
1-202-269-0200
Contact: Volunteer Coordinator, or Personnel Director

BFW is a nationwide Christian movement that serves as an advocate for the world's hungry. There are 355 local BFW chapters, about 1,000 participating churches, and about 2,500 volunteer leaders. The organization seeks to help redress hunger by using its members' citizenship to affect national policies about hunger, especially by lobbying decision makers, locally and nationally, and conducting research and education on policies related to hunger and development. BFW members are asked to participate in letter-writing campaigns, to meet with their congressional representatives, to respond to targeted legislative alerts, to speak before church and community groups, and to attend educational and training events to support them. For information about volunteering at a local BFW, contact the Washington office, which itself offers six to twelve internships for people of all ages, some of them stipended, and uses ten to twenty volunteers a year as well. Ask the volunteer coordinator for brochures and applications.

## Gleaning Network

Society of St. Andrew
P.O. Box 329, State Rt. 615
Big Island, VA 24526
1-804-333-4597
Contact: Director of Gleaning Ministries

Gleaners are mentioned several times in the Bible as people who go into fields and orchards to pick vegetables and fruits that remain after the harvest. Gleaners share this produce with those in need. Because most farmers find it too labor-intensive and uneconomical to pick the food remaining after the regular harvest is done, 20 percent of the food produced for human consumption in the United States is lost—over 135 million tons worth more than $30 billion. Gleaning groups are scattered here and there throughout the country, most of them unaffiliated but in touch with each other through networking. The Gleaning Network is operated by the Society of Saint Andrew, with groups in Virginia, Pennsylvania, North Carolina, South Carolina, Maryland, and Washington, DC, and its strongest volunteer force is in the DC area. The network asks local extension agents to find farmers willing to cooperate, and groups are scheduled. Gleaning groups come from churches, schools, neighborhoods, Scout troops, senior groups, and other organizations, and can number from as few as 5 people to as many as 250. Gleaners should be able to bend over and to lift about twenty pounds of produce. For information about volunteering for The Gleaning Network, call the Big Island number.

## Second Harvest National Food Bank Network

116 S. Michigan Ave., Suite 4
Chicago, IL 60603
1-312-263-2303, FAX 1-312-263-5626
Contact: Network Services

Second Harvest helps feed the hungry by channeling donations from America's food industry to a nationwide network of more than 180 food banks. The network, which began with a single food bank in Phoenix, now distributes over 500 million pounds of food a year. Here's how it works:

1. Food distributors, manufacturers, processors, retailers, and suppliers donate food to Second Harvest, all under specific guidelines for the storage and handling of food.
2. Second Harvest distributes the food to its food bank network. The food banks are monitored for strict compliance with food handling and warehousing standards.
3. In turn, the food banks distribute the food to nearly 40,000 charitable agencies, such as soup kitchens, day-care programs, shelters, senior centers, and other groups.
4. The food is provided for those who need it.

Opportunities for volunteering are most abundant at the food banks, where volunteers help sort, pack, and inventory food, work in the office, and help with mailings. Most food banks have volunteer coordinators. For information about the nearest cooperating food bank, call Second Harvest.

## Share Our Strength

Prepared and Perishable Food Programs (SOS/PPFP)
1511 K St., NW, Suite 623
Washington, DC 20005
1-202-393-2925
Contact: Jennifer Hadley, PPFP Program Director

SOS is a nationwide network of creative professionals who use their skills to raise funds and awareness for hunger relief. SOS was created in 1984 to organize restaurants and other food industry professionals nationwide on behalf of hunger relief and development agencies. SOS organizes fund-raising events and special projects to fund direct food assistance and long-term self-sufficiency programs in the United States and abroad to help fight the causes and consequences of hunger. SOS is funded by foundations, corporations, restaurants, and individual donors, with most of the funds going to organizations fighting hunger. Fight Food Waste (FFW) is an SOS program that encourages the food industry to salvage leftover food and deliver it to soup kitchens and shelters, which then distribute it to the hungry. A summary of each state's Good Samaritan Law, which establishes a standard of food care, is available from SOS on request, as is a list of PPFPs nationwide.

## SHARE-USA

3350 E St.
San Diego, CA 92102
1-619-525-2257, FAX 1-619-525-2299
Contact: Sr. Beatrice Ryan, Executive Director

SHARE-USA is a nonprofit organization, a division of World SHARE. There are twenty-two SHARE network affiliates nationwide working to promote self-help and resource exchange, a way of allowing people to help themselves meet their food needs in a way that does not perpetuate reliance on emergency programs for the needy. At local host sites across the country, SHARE distributes food at a fraction of its cost—$13 for a bag of food worth close to $35—to more than 375,000 families every month. Before they pick up their food, participants show proof of two hours of community service for every bag of food they take home. Many participants contribute their community service to the food distribution centers; others work as youth mentors, teachers, and telephone volunteers, and in many other ways. A monthly newsletter with news of SHARE community service activities, recipes, and nutrition information accompanies every SHARE food package. For a list of SHARE host sites or for more information, get in touch with the San Diego office.

### U.S. National Committee for World Food Day (WFD)

1001 22nd St., NW
Washington, DC 20437
1-202-653-2404
Contact: Patricia Young, National Coordinator

World Food Day is observed every October 16, a worldwide event designed to increase awareness, understanding, and year-round, long-term action on the issues of eliminating hunger and assuring food security for all. WFD is observed in 150 nations and in hundreds of ways. There are 450 sponsoring organizations in the United States (listed on the WFD letterhead), and WFD planning groups can be found in most communities. Call or write to the National Committee for more information, a copy of the WFD *Resource List,* and other publications, including *Ideas in Action,* a description of successful ideas and programs to combat hunger. The National Committee will also provide materials helpful for WFD organizers, answer questions you have about the program, and can often refer you to volunteer organizations in your area.

### USA Harvest

P.O. Box 1628
Louisville, KY 40201-1628
1-800-872-4366
Contact: Stan Curtis

USA Harvest is an all-volunteer organization whose mission is to feed the hungry. It accomplishes this goal by picking up food donations from restaurants, fast-food chains, hotels, cafeterias, bakeries, army bases, retail stores, and wholesale warehouses and delivering them to nonprofit agencies, such as The Salvation Army (TSA, page 201), soup kitchens, and shelters, which distribute the food to the hungry. USA Harvest began in 1987 as Kentucky Harvest, modeled on similar programs in New York City and Philadelphia. Since then it has grown to sixty chapters, each one a grassroots organization, accepting no money from either the public or the government. Over 50,000 volunteers donate time, skills, and food to USA Harvest. For information about volunteering, call the 800 number.

## Housing Organizations

### Christmas in April * U.S.A. (CIA)

1225 Eye St., NW, Suite 601
Washington, DC 20005
1-202-326-8268
Contact: Patricia R. Johnson, Executive Director

CIA helps low-income, elderly, and disabled homeowners live with safety and dignity in their own homes. One day every year (usually the last Saturday in April, but at other times as well) 62,000 individuals in over 210 cities and towns across the country volunteer to repair and rehabilitate at least 2,400 homes, using donated materials. Anyone interested can volunteer, and although skilled tradespeople are always in demand—especially, carpenters, plumbers, electricians, roofers, and others—so are secretaries, doctors, and policemen. Each CIA community program is responsible for its own fund-raising, publicity, volunteer recruitment, and management. The national office offers advice, training, and technical assistance to all communities that have a program or want to start one. If you want to volunteer for a nearby CIA, or if you want help starting a program in your area, get in touch with the Washington office.

## Habitat for Humanity International, Inc.

Habitat and Church Sts.
Americus, GA 31709-3498
1-912-924-6935

Habitat is a grassroots Christian ministry whose goal is to eliminate poverty housing. Habitat builds and renovates housing in the United States and overseas at no profit and no interest. Habitat describes itself as a hand-up, not a handout, because each family that benefits must invest sweat equity hours in the construction of their home and pay for the material and building or renovation costs (about half normal costs) over a fixed period of time. Habitat offers diverse opportunities for volunteering. For its international projects, experienced administrators, construction people, and community organizers are needed; they must be willing to commit to a three-year term, and it helps to speak a foreign language. At headquarters in Americus, volunteers aged eighteen and older do office work, provide child care and public relations, and work in many other areas as well. The headquarters also hosts one- and two-week work camps for various age groups year-round. There are over 700 Habitat affiliates nationwide, all of them run and staffed by volunteers, and each one largely self-supporting. Affiliates need volunteers of every description, and they usually recruit through local churches, community groups, and volunteer action centers (VACs) (see National Volunteer Center, NVC, page 37). For more information, get in touch with the Americus office.

## Legal Action Center for the Homeless (LACH)

27 W. 24th St., Room 600
New York, NY 10010
1-212-229-2080, FAX 1-212-229-2273
Contact: Volunteer Coordinator

LACH acts as a legal advocate for the homeless in New York City by setting up legal clinics in soup kitchens, educating the homeless about their rights, and representing the homeless at hearings. LACH also pursues law reform and other advocacy, and issues reports based on its research. Lawyers, a small paid staff, and up to forty volunteers work for LACH. Volunteers who represent clients at administrative fair hearings train at LACH's legal clinics. For information about volunteering, get in touch with the volunteer coordinator.

## National Resource Center on Homelessness and Mental Illness (NRC)

Policy Research Associates, Inc.
262 Delaware Ave.
Delmar, NY 12054
1-800-444-7415

NCR is the only national source of information specifically focused on the mental health aspects of housing and service needs of people with severe mental illness. Under contract to the National Institute of Mental Health (NIMH), NRC provides organizations and individuals with key services, which include telephone consultation; a comprehensive data base of information on the homeless mentally ill population as well as data base searches; a free subscription to NRC's periodic bulletin, *Access;* and "National Organizations

Concerned with Mental Health, Housing, and Homelessness," (also free), a current directory of more than eighty federal and national organizations that are concerned with homelessness and mental health. Many of these organizations use volunteers, and for anyone interested in the plight of the mentally ill homeless population, the "National Organizations" directory is indispensable. Call the 800 number for more information.

## Partnership for the Homeless, Inc. (PFTH)

110 W. 32nd St.
New York, NY 10001-3274
1-212-947-3444
Contact: Volunteer Department

PFTH is committed to sheltering and feeding New York's homeless and, ultimately, to helping them move into their own homes and off welfare. More than 14,000 volunteers carry out PFTH programs:

- Coordinating over 150 safe emergency shelters in all boroughs, mostly in churches and synagogues.
- Relocating homeless families from shelters to permanent, affordable housing (Project Domicile).
- Providing over 1 million meals annually.
- Providing vocational training for the homeless and help finding jobs.
- Providing supportive transitional housing for the homeless with special needs.

Volunteers are needed for all these programs; they stay overnight at homeless shelters, attend to the needs of families that have moved into their own housing, cook and serve food at shelters and soup kitchens, assist residents living in transitional housing, and much more. For information about volunteering, get in touch with the volunteer director.

# Resource

## HOUSING ORGANIZATIONS

*What You Can Do to Help the Homeless,* by Thomas L. Kenyon (New York: Fireside Books). This was written for The National Alliance to End Homelessness. It has hundreds of practical suggestions for ways to contribute to the basic needs of the homeless and to educate yourself as well. Succinct chapters recommend ways to understand the homeless, treat them with empathy, educate the public, including your own children, about the homeless, work with homeless children, get your business involved, organize a food or clothing drive, work in a soup kitchen, and employ the homeless. Each chapter has down-to-earth ideas for activities and a list of organizations to contact. A list of major organizations that help the homeless and a bibliography conclude the book, which might have been improved by an index of organizations. $7.95.

# Working with Offenders

Two comon beliefs link the widely diverse organizations working with offenders. One is that offender rehabilitation is possible through positive and constructive interaction with the community, usually one-to-one volunteer/prisoner contact. The second, usually backed up with statistics, is that such contact results in a considerable decrease in recidivism, meaning that these programs are highly cost-effective. Like mentoring, one reason for the apparent success of many of the one-to-one visitation programs is that inmates know their new friends are not part of the system and that they are motivated by a genuine interest in helping.

Although all the organizations that work with offenders are humanitarian in their work and intentions, each has its own unique perspective. Some have a religious mission, and structure their programs and services to that end. Others are secular and simply work with the system as it stands. Still others, in addition to programs that serve the immediate needs of offenders and their families, have long-term goals that include the ultimate reform of the criminal justice system.

Volunteers who want to work with offenders should be very sure of their ideals and convictions and extremely patient as well, with a genuine interest in befriending offenders and realistic expectations for change. Volunteers must also be willing to undergo extensive screening and training.

Although it might seem that local volunteer action centers (VACs) (see National Volunteer Center, NVC, page 37) would be the logical venues for recruiting such volunteers, in fact they are not. Most organizations, even the secular ones, work with local churches and synagogues, whose support for justice volunteerism is founded on biblical example and injunction. Nationwide, many local corrections departments have volunteer programs and can refer you to the volunteer coordinator. Both the International Association of Justice Volunteerism (IAJV, page 179) and Volunteers in Prevention, Probation & Prisons (VIP, page 183) can also refer you to programs in your area.

---

## International Association of Justice Volunteerism (IAJV)

International Headquarters
University of Wisconsin—Milwaukee Criminal Justice Institute
P. O. Box 786
Milwaukee, WI 53201
1-414-229-5630
Contact: William Winter, Director

IAJV was created to improve the juvenile and criminal justice systems through citizen participation. The organization's most important mission is to strengthen, unify, and coordinate efforts of various local volunteer justice programs and to join them with other local programs nationwide and in Canada.

IAJV serves as a clearinghouse and resource for its over 500 members—individuals and organizations—who are involved with the justice system. IAJV establishes guidelines for citizen involvement in local justice programs and conducts an annual training forum that facilitates an exchange of information on justice volunteers. Other information sources are "IAJV in Action," a quarterly newsletter providing news about individual and organization activities; the IAJV Resource Service, a list of publications helpful for designing and managing justice volunteer services; and the IAJV library. In its role as advocate, IAJV works to enhance the image of justice volunteerism.

IAJV has eleven regional offices and one in every Canadian province. Call the international headquarters in Milwaukee for information about membership or for the names of criminal justice volunteer organizations in your area.

## Justice Fellowship (JF)

A Ministry of Prison Fellowship Ministries (PFM)
National Headquarters
P.O. Box 17500
Washington, DC 20041-0500
1-703-478-0100
Contact: Steve Varnum, Vice President

A ministry of Prison Fellowship Ministries (PFM, page 181), JF is a national organization whose mission is to make the criminal justice system more consistent with biblical teaching on justice by enabling concerned citizens to promote reforms that will heal victims, hold offenders accountable, reconcile victims and offenders, and protect the public. JF believes that victims should be given a formal role in the criminal justice system, including the right to pursue restitution, and that offenders who do not pose a threat to society should be sentenced to restitution and community service programs rather than prison. JF operates in twenty-two states, recruiting task forces of fifteen to twenty Christian volunteers from different backgrounds. Each task force becomes a strategic criminal justice reform education and action group that, with information provided by JF, puts together a plan specific for that state. JF works with the legislative, judicial, and executive branches of government to accomplish these criminal justice reform goals. For more information, write to the national headquarters.

Laubach Literacy Action (LLA, page 100)

## M-2/Job Therapy

P.O. Box 293, 205 Ave. C
Snohomish, WA 98290
1-206-568-3268, 1-206-335-0855
Contact: Lou Kaufer, Executive Director

M-2/Job Therapy matches inmates one-to-one with community volunteers who visit offenders while they are in prison and who assist prisoners once they are released. The organization offers several programs designed to meet the diverse needs of offenders and ex-offenders, including Job Search Assistance, Summer Youth Employment and Training, and Anger Management Training. These programs are run by trained staff. But the heart of M-2/Job Therapy is the M-2/W-2 (Man-to-Man/Woman-to-Woman) Prison Visitation Program in which an individual volunteer, or sponsor, visits once or twice a month for one year or more, offering an inmate friendship, encouragement, and a positive role model. The friendship continues after the inmate is released, since that is when a dependable relationship is often most desperately needed to help the ex-offender adjust successfully to the responsibilities of freedom.

M-2/Job Therapy is a program local to Snohomish, WA. There are about 200 sponsors visiting at any one time, and they are recruited primarily from service clubs and churches. Volunteers are carefully screened for character, and their references are checked. For information, write to M-2.

## M-2/Match-Two Prisoner Outreach (M-2)

P.O. Box 447, 500 Main St.
San Quentin, CA 94964
1-415-457-8701, FAX 1-415-457-0221

M-2 is a statewide California program that began in 1971 and was patterned after M-2/Job Therapy (above). Its purpose is to match a community volunteer with a prison inmate, most often one who ordinarily receives neither visitors nor mail. Prison inmates volunteer for M-2 and are screened by the M-2 program director. Community volunteers are interviewed by M-2 staff and then matched with inmates of the same sex with similar interests and compatible personalities. A volunteer must agree to visit at least once a month for a year to allow time for a relationship of mutual growth and change to develop. In a similar program that matches visitors with youthful offenders, volunteers must commit to visit inmates twice a month. Some volunteers continue the friendship during the stressful period just after the inmate is released.

With about 1,600 volunteers visiting inmates every month and about 2,500 visitors matched over the course of a year, M-2/Match-Two is the largest prison visitation system in the country. As is true for many such programs, most of the visitors are recruited through churches and service organizations, with churches contributing the majority of volunteers. Volunteers attend a three-hour training session and then are individually matched and introduced. For information, contact the headquarters at San Quentin.

**PACT Institute of Justice, Victim-Offender Reconciliation Program** **(VORP, page 160)**

## Prison Fellowship Ministries (PFM)

P.O. Box 17500
Washington, DC 20041-0500
1-703-478-0100

PFM was founded by Chuck Colson to bring the Christian faith into the lives of prisoners, ex-prisoners, and their families, and in doing so, to change those lives for the better. A second goal is to promote biblical standards of justice in the criminal justice system. For incarcerated prisoners, PFM works with jails, prisons, departments of corrections, and prison chaplains to set up in-prison programs: in-prison seminars, Bible study, pen pal programs, marriage seminars, life-plan seminars, one-to-one visits, and mentoring plans. In some cases, inmates are released for one or two weeks to stay with PFM volunteers and do community service work. Ex-offenders can participate in the Aftercare Ministry.

PFM is international in scope, with 40,000 volunteers active in over 735 state and federal institutions in the United States and overseas. Depending on the community, volunteers are recruited either directly through churches and community groups, or indirectly, with PFM making presentations to the pastors and elders of various churches and the churches recruiting volunteers from their membership.

PFM has an award-winning twenty-hour training program that includes videos, training manuals, and the active participation of volunteers. The program encompasses an introduction to PFM, its work, and the basic dos and don'ts of prison ministry; an overview of problems faced by prisoners, ex-prisoners, and their families and the ways PFM programs address those needs; exercises for developing listening and responding skills; and, finally, in-depth coverage of the programs selected by the volunteers.

Consult your local phone book for a PFM listing, or check with churches in your community. For further information, write to the national headquarters.

## FEATURED ORGANIZATION: OFFENDER AID AND RESTORATION (OAR)

National Office
301 Park Drive
Severna Park, MD 21146-4415
1-410-647-3806
Contact: Diane Gofoitu, USA Staff Coordinator

OAR has two missions. The first is to use trained volunteers to work with offenders early enough to help them change their direction toward a restoration and reconciliation with the community. The second is to work for systemic change in the criminal justice system through public education and by the promotion of community programs that provide effective alternatives to incarceration wherever possible.

OAR is a national organization with ten sites, all of them east of the Mississippi. Although the local sites all share common goals, each is an independent entity, with its own board of directors, responsibility for its own funding, and a range of services based on community need. All sites focus on early intervention at local jails in the belief that a caring community can help change the kind of behavior that leads to prison terms. A main component of this focus is one-on-one volunteer/offender visitation, provided by each OAR site. Here are some other OAR programs:

- Inmate services include serving as ombudsman between inmate and jail staff, contacting the lawyer or public defender, delivering messages to the inmate's family, arranging for tutoring and counseling, offering transportation to family members, preparing a pretrial or presentence program for the court's consideration, and appearing in court with the offender.
- Community Service Restitution Projects (CSRP), offered in several sites, maintain alternatives to incarceration that can be tailored to community needs either as pretrial or post-trial programs.
- In the Victim-Offender Reconciliation Program (VORP, page 160), mediation between offender and victim is used to settle some minor disputes.
- Work Empowerment helps offenders identify their skills and plan for careers, as well as teaching them job-hunting techniques.
- Family Support, an outreach program for family members of offenders, is provided at several OAR sites. Program services include providing information about the criminal justice system and community resources as well as family support groups.

Volunteers are the lifeblood of OAR. They participate in every program for offenders, ex-offenders, and their families, and they perform numerous assignments that help link the offender with the community. Most important, volunteers provide by example an opportunity for offenders and ex-offenders to see that life can be positive, healthy, and productive. Other OAR volunteers serve as board members, fund-raisers, administrators, and technical advisers.

Each site recruits through public service announcements, free local newspaper spots, and announcements in church bulletins, by sending speakers to community groups, and by word of

*Continued*

*Continued*
mouth from current volunteers. Since all sites send volunteers to work in jails and in some prisons, volunteers are very carefully screened and undergo twelve to twenty-five hours of preservice training, with follow-up in-service training as well. For a list of OAR sites and the services they provide, write to the national office.

**State Bar of California, Volunteers in Parole (VIP, page 167)**

## Thresholds/Decisions

56 1/2 Merchants Row, Room 310
Rutland, VT 05701
1-802-775-3236, 1-802-775-5706
Contact: Leigh E. Adams, President

Thresholds/Decisions teaches prisoners and men and women on probation decision-making skills that will enable them to have more control over their lives. Thresholds/Decision is a ten-week, forty-hour course for prisoners that helps them cope with life, both in and out of prison. The course, which is presented in group and one-to-one sessions by intensively trained community volunteers, is designed to help prisoners change their self-images and to think of themselves in new, more positive ways. The program consists of decision-making training, practice in developing and carrying out short- and long-range plans, work on changing personal attitudes, and consideration of a desirable life-style. Studies have shown that the course is most effective when undertaken by younger prisoners who have less than one year left to serve so that the goal-setting process is timely and meaningful to them.

The Thresholds/Decision program is currently offered in six Vermont community correctional centers, and each program is run autonomously. However, the main volunteer instructional center is in Rutland, where two weekends a year are devoted to training volunteers from Vermont and other states. Once the eighteen- to twenty-hour course is completed, volunteers undergo an orientation and background check by the facility they'll be working in. Volunteers are recruited by word of mouth and through local newspaper and radio ads.

To start a Thresholds/Decisions program in your community, contact Leigh E. Pickering in Rutland.

## Volunteers in Prevention, Probation & Prisons, Inc. (VIP)

15999 W. 12 Mile Rd., #130
Southfield, MI 48076
1-313-559-7223
Contact: F. Gerald Dash, Executive Director

In 1959 the city of Royal Oak, Michigan, spurred by municipal judge Keith J. Leenhouts, began using community volunteers in its rehabilitative probation program. Leenhouts's belief that human conduct can be changed by human contact was the foundation of the program that later became known as VIP. The program was so effective that in 1961 a similar approach was successfully adopted by the Juvenile Court in Boulder, Colorado. These seminal programs have now developed into a national movement to use volunteers, in partnership with the justice system, to help offenders and parolees change their attitudes and behavior and thus become reintegrated into society. Since 1969 VIP has served more as a movement than as an organization. Its primary mission is to stimulate the courts, jails, and juvenile prisons to utilize massive numbers of citizen volunteers in criminal justice probation and rehabilitation programs and to improve community life through the reduction of crime.

VIP is now a clearinghouse of volunteer organizations that work with juvenile and adult offenders and parolees. It provides help in starting new citizen volunteer programs or in expanding existing programs for early intervention, probation, or parole. VIP has produced a twelve-minute videotape showing the many ways volunteers can be used within the court system: as visitors, mentors, administrators, donors of professional skills, presentence volunteers, and conductors of group programs.

VIP also has a National Education-Training Program: Volunteer Court-Correction Movement, a course designed for use by colleges and universities. With International Association of Justice Volunteerism (IAJV, page 179), VIP holds annual forums offering training and other workshops for justice volunteers. The "VIP Examiner" is a quarterly newsletter full of information about current successful and innovative programs.

Working with IAJV, VIP has set up its National Communications Network, a free service for organizations that are committed to the use of volunteers in criminal justice and have a desire to share and exchange information and ideas with other organizations. For more information about VIP or about joining the communications network, call or write to Gerald Dash.

# Overseas Service

Hundreds of private voluntary organizations (PVOs) provide technical, educational, medical, and humanitarian services to countries overseas. Because the United States is technologically advanced, and the developing nations are so needy in that regard, there is some demand for volunteers who are experienced professionals in such fields and services as agriculture and animal husbandry, business and industry, working with children, community development, conservation and environmental issues, providing assistance and training for disabled and handicapped people, disaster relief, education, family planning, providing food, health, housing, refugee aid, rural water development, aid to artisans, vocational education, and women in development. In addition to direct aid—emergency disaster relief, food, medicine, and clothing—overseas PVOs provide technical assistance and training to community organizations within the host nations, helping to develop long-term, self-sustaining programs suitable to the situation at hand.

However, for volunteers looking for a few weeks' or months' hard work in an international setting and willing to pay for the experience, there are archaeological digs, scientific field research expeditions, internships, and work camps all over the world. For overseas religious ministries, see pages 199 and 200.

---

## American Friends Service Committee (AFSC)

National Office
1501 Cherry St.
Philadelphia, PA 19102
1-215-241-7295
Contact: Personnel Department

AFSC offers summer community service projects in Mexico, which are undertaken in cooperation with rural towns and villages, and which develop from the initiative and skills of the participants and the needs of the community. Much of the work is hard and physical; it can include construction and repair of schools, clinics, roads, houses, and irrigation systems as well as reforestation, gardening, and health and nutrition. Each project brings together about twelve volunteers and two leaders, at least half of whom are Latin Americans who speak only Spanish.

AFSC needs about fifteen volunteers from the United States each summer (late June to mid-August) for its Mexican projects. Volunteers must be eighteen to twenty-six years old, fluent in Spanish, healthy, and willing to adapt to group living. Each participant contributes $700 to cover orientation, food, and lodging. Transportation to Mexico is at the volunteer's own expense. For more information, write to AFSC.

**American Red Cross Disaster Services (page 92)**

## Amigos de las Americas (AMIGOS)

5618 Star Lane
Houston, TX 77057
1-713-782-5290, FAX 1-713-782-9267
1-800-231-7796
FAX 1-713-782-9267
Contact: Celdie Sencion, Recruiting Director

AMIGOS is a private voluntary organization dedicated to youth leadership development and cross-cultural understanding, and to providing public health services in Latin America. Some of the services offered by teenage volunteers include community sanitation and dental hygiene, immunizations, eyeglass distribution, and other projects. Projects last from four to eight weeks. Amigo volunteers must be sixteen by June 1 of the program year and must have completed at least one year of high school Spanish or the equivalent. The AMIGOS training program, which is offered at its twenty chapters or training groups nationwide and through the Correspondent Training Program, takes three to five months to complete and prepares volunteers technically and culturally for their roles as health workers who will work alongside local people. Part of the training includes fund-raising for the volunteer's expenses, which are tax deductible and can range from $2,300 to about $3,000 depending on the program and its location. For information, contact the Houston office.

## Citizens Democracy Corps (CDC)

2021 K St., NW, Suite 215
Washington, DC 20006
1-202-872-0933, FAX 1-202-872-0923
1-800-321-1945

CDC is a private nonprofit organization that mobilizes United States voluntary efforts to assist the countries of Central and Eastern Europe and the former Soviet Union in their transition to democratic institutions and free market economies. CDC's programs include:

- In direct response to needs expressed by government, civic, and industry leaders abroad, CDC Field Projects organizes the expertise and resources from the private sector to identify, plan, fund, and implement programs.
- The Business Entrepreneur Program connects American entrepreneurs with small and medium-sized companies in Central and Eastern Europe.
- The CDC Databank is a comprehensive source of information about voluntary activities conducted by United States businesses, nonprofit organizations, foundations, and universities working in the region. The Databank publishes a series of country-specific directories about nonprofit groups and their work and a resource list of specialized topics.
- The Volunteer Registry supplies information on individuals seeking volunteer positions with American and Eastern European organizations looking for skilled personnel.

For information contact the office in Washington, DC.

Community of Caring (COC, page 199)

## Concern/America

P.O. Box 1790, N. Broadway #103
Santa Ana, CA 92702
1-714-953-8575, FAX 1-714-953-1242

Concern/America provides training, technical help, and material support to people in Latin America and Africa who need assistance as a result of natural disaster, civil disruption, forced migration, discrimination, or historically rooted poverty. Among Concern's services to impoverished communities and refugees are: training community health workers to be health resources in their villages, vaccination campaigns, primary health care, literacy training programs, and small-scale agricultural and crafts projects. Some of these programs are carried out in collaboration with local institutions such as the Catholic or Lutheran churches.

Concern services are all provided by volunteer professionals in the fields of health, nutrition, sanitation, economic and agricultural development, and education, and much of their work is in training local workers in the same field. Volunteers must be at least twenty-one years old, have a degree or experience in the field of choice, speak fluent Spanish (except for physicians who wish to serve in Africa), and be willing to serve for at least one year. Concern will provide room, board, transportation, health insurance, a monthly stipend of $50, and a repatriation allowance that depends on length of service. At present Concern uses twenty to twenty-five volunteers a year. Write for information.

## Education for Democracy/U.S.A., Inc. (EFD/USA)

P.O. Box 40514
Mobile, AL 36640-0514
1-205-434-3889 or 1-205-434-3890,
FAX 1-205-434-3773
Contact: Ann Gardner, President

EFD/USA provides volunteer instructors of primary and supplementary conversational English to Czechoslovak, Latvian, Lithuanian, and Estonian citizens who want to either learn or upgrade their English. EFD instructors teach in universities, industries, hospitals, travel agencies, spas, and some secondary schools. The volunteers are considered staff members of those organizations, which also provide housing for the volunteers. Although ideally an instructor's education and work experience are major factors in the assignment to a particular organization, job availability at the time of the volunteer's arrival is just as important. Instructors are expected to bring their own basic teaching materials, many of them suggested by EFD. Scenarios and springboards for teaching conversation are also provided by EFD, some of them based on the experiences of volunteers who have returned from Europe.

EFD is beginning to broaden its base of services to provide U.S. volunteer advisers from various professions and businesses. EFD/USA will send a qualified volunteer's resume to the appropriate agency in Czechoslovakia or any of the three Baltic republics, and assignment will be made from there. For its conversational English program, EFD is looking for highly motivated and responsible people between the ages of twenty-one and sixty-five with outstanding professional and/or academic credentials. Volunteers must agree to serve for at least five months and to pay for their transportation to and from Czechoslovakia or the Baltic states. The screening and selection process is competitive. For information and an application form, write to EFD/USA.

## Fourth World Movement (FWM)

7600 Willow Hill Dr.
Landover, MD 20785-4685
1-301-336-9489

FWM was founded in 1957 by Joseph Wresinski, a Catholic priest who became chaplain to 252 homeless families living in an emergency housing camp near Paris. Determined to end the poverty of these families, Wresinski launched various grassroots projects with them, and the movement they started was eventually joined by other friends and volunteers. One of FWM's main missions is to send international teams of full-time volunteers to work in partnership with disadvantaged families, and FWM now reaches families living in twenty-three countries on four continents. Trained volunteers live within the community they serve, learning from the families how to work with them to overcome persistent poverty. The volunteers help run educational and cultural projects, and they maintain representation at UNICEF and other international organizations, where they serve as witness to the courage and endurance of families in poverty.

Volunteer teams and disadvantaged families set up programs in ghettos, slums, shantytowns, and depressed rural areas. Many of the projects involve education: preschools, literacy, job training, and street libraries. FWM also promotes local meetings that encourage the adults in the families to voice their concerns and to participate in the life of their community.

As a regular activity, all volunteers write daily about the experiences they witness, as well as recording what the families say. These detailed accounts, which have been collected for over thirty years from many countries, are the basis for evaluating programs, writing documents, and representing the persistently poor. FWM currently has more than 300 long-term, full-time volunteers from all over the world, about twenty of them from the United States. Every year, four to twelve new volunteers undergo an intense two-month internship, living and working with full-time volunteers and poor families in Washington, DC, and sometimes New York City. Those willing to commit to a two-year or longer volunteership are sent where their interests lie and where FWM needs them. Interns must be aged nineteen or older and have completed high school at least two years earlier. Interns who have completed the program and full-time volunteers are paid minimal stipends.

The International FWM also runs two-week summer work/information camps in Europe, which give new participants a chance to meet and work with experienced volunteers. Work/information weekends are held throughout the year at the national center in Landover. Write to the Landover office for more information.

Habitat for Humanity International, Inc. (page 177)

## Health Volunteers Overseas (HVO)

c/o Washington Station
P.O. Box 65157
Washington, DC 20035-5157
1-202-296-0928, FAX 1-202-296-8018
Contact: Kate Skillman, Program Coordinator

HVO brings qualified medical volunteers into developing countries to run on-site training programs for people who in turn will train others in a variety of medical, dental, and surgical skills. HVO is a membership organization for health professionals—doctors, dentists, physical therapists, and nurses—who are affiliated with one of five divisions: anesthesia, dentistry, general surgery, oral and maxillofacial surgery, and orthopedics. HVO training programs are realistically designed to fit in with the local environment, addressing its specific pathologies and medical problems with the equipment available. Volunteer opportunities are listed in the organization's quarterly bulletin, "Health Volunteers Overseas." Assignments average one month but can vary in length from two weeks to several months. Volunteers generally pay their own transportation and living expenses, although some support is available. Call HVO for a Volunteer Profile Form or for detailed information about a specific program.

International Executive Service Corps (IESC, page 64)

## International Rescue Committee (IRC)

386 Park Ave. S.
New York, NY 10016
1-212-679-0010
Contact: Overseas Recruitment

IRC was founded in 1933, at the request of Albert Einstein, to help anti-Nazis trapped in Hitler's Germany. Since then, IRC has helped millions of refugees and displaced persons by providing relief and resettlement programs in Africa, Asia, Central America, Europe, and the United States. Through its Women's Commission for Refugee Women and Children, IRC acts as an advocate for refugees. Its first concern is emergency relief and medical aid, with special feeding for malnourished children. Other programs for refugees in resettlement camps involve self-help and education about medicine and public health, child care, food production and agriculture, migration and refugee affairs, and public advocacy.

IRC uses volunteers in all of its overseas programs and in its seventeen resettlement offices around the United States, the number depending on how many refugee emergencies must be met at any one time. IRC needs volunteers in all the health professions as well as sanitarians (people with expertise in sanitary and water systems) and teachers. Volunteer logicians (people with experience in setting up emergency refugee camps) are crucial to IRC's efforts.

Volunteers are recruited through a loyal network of people who have served on earlier projects; many of them call when a refugee emergency arises. IRC encourages potential volunteers to send their resumes with a cover letter listing dates of availability. A six-month commitment is requested, although length of service varies with the program: some last for only a month, others for up to two years. IRC pays for transportation and health insurance and provides minimum stipends.

## International Voluntary Services, Inc. (IVS)

1424 16th St., NW, Suite 204
Washington, DC 20036
1-202-387-5533, FAX 1-202-387-4234
Contact: Tonya Caprarola, Program Officer

IVS's goal is to strengthen the ability of local groups in developing countries to solve critical problems in ways that are self-sustaining. IVS responds to request from organizations in host countries by sending highly skilled technicians who, through workshops, demonstrations, and hands-on training, help local groups and leaders to set up programs for community development, food production and agriculture, medicine and public health, and development of small enterprises. All project initiative and management is the responsibility of the local organization.

IVS currently has thirty-five volunteers working on specific assignments. Volunteers come from the international community and are of all ages—professionals in such fields as agronomy, nutrition, acountancy, and health. Requirements are an advanced technical degree and a minimum of two years' field experience. Most assignments last two to three years, but some are longer. For more information, call or write to the Washington office.

## Northwest Medical Teams International (NMTI)

P.O. Box 231177, 12256 S.W. Garden Pl.
Portland, OR 97223
1-503-624-0229, FAX 1-503-624-0319
Contact: Carren Woods, Director of Support Services

NMTI offers medical and nonmedical help to victims of natural disasters and political upheaval abroad and supplies medicine, equipment, and food for needy people in the American Northwest.

NMTI has three major components:

- Overseas disaster response, which involves treating serious injuries, feeding the hungry, and training nationals to meet their ongoing needs.
- Development assistance overseas and in the United States, including projects in agriculture, construction, and education.
- A Medical and Dental Van that provides care to migrants, the homeless, and working poor people in a nine-county area surrounding Portland, Oregon.

NMTI sends between 450 and 500 volunteers a year overseas, about half of them medical professionals. There are also about 100 volunteers yearly who work on the mobile van, and 30 to 40 working in the Portland office. NMTI needs volunteer physicians, medical technicians, office workers, construction people, agricultural advisers and workers, nurses, dental workers, and fundraisers. Write to the director of support services.

## Partners of the Americas (POTA)

1424 K St., NW, Suite 700
Washington, DC 20005
1-202-628-3300, FAX 1-202-628-3306

Partners of the Americas was founded in 1964 as the "people to people" program of the Kennedy administration's Alliance for Progress. It is now a private nonprofit organization pairing individual U.S. states with regions and countries in Latin America and the Caribbean to work in partnerships on economic and social development and technical training projects. For instance, Vermont is linked with Honduras, Minnesota with Uruguay, and Oregon with Costa Rica. At present, there are sixty partnerships that foster inter-American friendship and cultural and educational exchanges. Private citizens on both sides of the partnership determine the local needs and mobilize people and resources to accomplish work in such areas as agricultural and rural development; natural resource management and environmental conservation; culture, including exchanges of performing, visual, and folk artists and links between museums and other cultural institutions; child health and nutrition; vocational training for disadvantaged groups; emergency preparedness and disaster management; drug abuse; and AIDS education and prevention.

POTA uses volunteers from all walks of life—foresters, soccer coaches, engineers, doctors and other health professionals, artists, high school students, farmers, city administrators, and many others, all of whom share an active concern for inter-American friendship and cooperation. Write for information.

**The Partnership for Service-Learning (PSL, page 221)**

**Peace Brigades International (PBI, page 196)**

## Peace Corps

1990 K St., NW
Washington, DC 20526
1-800-424-8580, ext. 2293

On March 1, 1961, President John F. Kennedy signed an executive order creating the Peace Corps, with the goals of helping to promote world peace and friendship, helping developing countries meet needs for skilled men and women, and advancing mutual understanding among nations. To date, over 131,800 volunteers have served in more than 100 nations, and during the next few years, the Peace Corps anticipates sending an increasing number of volunteers to former Eastern Bloc countries to help in the establishment of free market economies.

At present, there are more than 6,000 volunteers and trainees working in ninety nations on grassroots, self-help development projects in rural health, family nutrition, fisheries, agriculture, teacher training, math and science education, vocational training, small business consulting, forestry, and more. Volunteers must be healthy U.S. citizens, aged eighteen or older. A bachelor's degree or extensive experience in agriculture or a skilled trade is also helpful. College freshmen and sophomores who are planning to serve in the Peace Corps after graduation should contact their local recruitment officers to find out what languages and other volunteer experience will help them gain acceptance. After screening and acceptance, volunteers sign up for twenty-seven months of service, which includes three months of intensive training, some of it in the language and cultural and political mores of the host country, the rest in technical training. Call the 800 number for the phone number of the recruitment office nearest you.

**Physicians for Human Rights (PHR, page 147)**

**Presbyterian Church (U.S.A.) (PC/USA, page 200)**

## Project Concern International (PCI-OPTIONS)

3550 Afton Rd.
San Diego, CA 92123
1-619-279-9690, FAX 1-619-694-0294
Contact: Director of Community Relations

PCI provides medical and development assistance to needy people in the United States and overseas, with a special focus on children and mothers of childbearing age. PCI's OPTIONS Service links volunteer health and development professionals with domestic and international facilities to serve on assignments that range from sending a team of ophthalmologists to perform eye surgery on Romanian orphans to providing primary care to communities in the Appalachians.

PCI-OPTIONS places 200 to 250 volunteers a year, including physicians of all specialties, public health nurses, physical therapists, psychologists, and development specialists. PCI continually expands its resource base of medical and development specialists. Each assignment is unique; however, most short-term assignments (one month to one year) include room and board, and many long-term assignments include a stipend or travel. Project Concern's OPTIONS Service publishes a bimonthly newsletter, *OPTIONS*, listing specific opportunities to serve. Contact PCI-OPTIONS for more information and for a sample copy of *OPTIONS*.

## Surgical Eye Expeditions International, Inc. (SEE)

27C-2 East De La Guerra
Santa Barbara, CA 93104
1-805-963-3303, FAX 1-805-965-3564
Contact: Program Officer

SEE's purpose is to restore vision to disadvantaged people in the United States and abroad through ophthalmic surgery. SEE treats more than 70,000 people and performs more than 7,000 sight-saving surgeries every year. To accomplish this, the organization has created ongoing partnerships with community health care providers, who invite SEE's multinational surgical teams to work with local SEE ophthalmologists, health professionals, and civic authorities. Community sponsorship is found for these expeditions, often through service clubs and their international organizations, and local medical providers screen patients and assume postoperative care for recovering patients. Once these preliminary arrangements are made, visiting SEE ophthalmic teams, using specially developed and field-tested self-contained mobile eye surgery units, screen patients rapidly and perform free sight-restoring surgery. SEE also maintains year-round glaucoma screening, eyeglass clinics, and muscle surgery for children with crossed eyes—all provided free. SEE needs more than 300 health professionals yearly for short-term eye expeditions that usually last less than week. Write to the headquarters in Santa Barbara for more information.

## Volunteers for Peace (VFP)

43 Tiffany Rd.
Belmont, VT 05730
1-802-259-2759, FAX 1-802-259-2922
Contact: Megan Brook, Assistant Director

VFP recruits American and Canadian volunteers to live and work in international work camps in order to promote peace and create a better environment as well as to foster friendships between East and West. Recruitment is through VFP's annual *International Workcamp Directory* (available with a $10 membership contribution), published every April, with 800 to 1,000 listings of summer and fall work camp programs in Europe, Africa, Turkey, and the former Soviet Union. Most programs, which are sponsored by organizations in the host countries, last for two to three weeks, and 40 percent of volunteers register for multiple work camps in the same or different countries. At the camps, participants from several countries form teams to accomplish a variety of different work: helping to renovate a peace museum in Remagen, Germany; cleaning brush from the bed and edges of the Dordogne River in France; archeological excavations on a Roman site in the Pyrenees; working one to one with mentally and physically disabled children and adults on holiday in England.

VFP is a membership organization with a $10 annual fee. About 450 volunteers, aged eighteen and older, are placed every summer on a first-come, first-served basis. The registration fee for each work camp is $125 in Western Europe and $350 to $700 per work camp for those in Eastern Europe. Volunteers pay for and arrange all travel themselves. Write or call for more information and a free copy of VFP's newsletter. Most volunteers register by early May.

## Volunteers in Overseas Cooperative Assistance (VOCA)

50 F St., NW, Suite 1075
Washington, DC 20001
1-202-383-4961, FAX 1-202-783-7204
Contact: Program Recruiter

VOCA provides short-term technical assistance to cooperatives and other small- and medium-scale agriculturally based enterprises worldwide in order to increase their economic opportunities and incomes. VOCA takes on hundreds of projects a year in developing countries and emerging democracies around the world, always at the request of organizations in the host countries. Most projects last for thirty to ninety days and include such highly specialized work as organizing and managing cooperatives; credit union management; farm management; agricultural production; food processing; and pricing, distributing, and marketing farm products. A recently initiated "Share the Experience" program will train 120 returned VOCA volunteers in community education techniques, and these volunteer educators will in turn reach out to more than 42,000 people throughout the Midwest.

In 1992, VOCA will send out about 400 volunteers. Each must be an experienced specialist in some area of agriculture or relating to cooperative and agribusiness development. Volunteers may be former CEOs or senior managers of cooperatives, or accountants, chemists, plant physiologists, veterinarians, farmers, beekeepers, and dairymen. Recruitment is through a network of organizations, cooperatives, land-grant colleges, and so on. Write to the program recruiter for information.

## Volunteers in Technical Assistance (VITA)

1815 N. Lynn St., Suite 200
Arlington, VA 22209
1-703-276-1800, FAX 1-703-243-1865
Contact: Manager of Information

VITA was created in 1959 by scientists and engineers who wanted to share their knowledge, skills, and experience with people in developing countries by designing simple, inexpensive applications of sophisticated technologies. VITA receives and responds to more than 2,000 requests each month for technical information from organizations and individuals in developing countries. Volunteers respond with designs, analyses, guidelines, evaluations—whatever is required—either by designing new technologies or identifying existing ones that are applicable to those needs. Most such questions can be answered by mail from the United States, although there is occasional on-site work in support of field projects. VITA volunteers also help develop low-cost communications networks for use in remote areas of developing countries; they serve on technical panels, write and review publications, brainstorm policy issues, and more. VITA can use volunteers with expertise in small enterprise development, renewable energy applications, agriculture, reforestation, water supply and sanitation, and low-cost housing construction. Call or write for more information.

## Youth Service International (YSI)

301 N. Blount St.
Raleigh, NC 27601-1007
1-919-733-9366, FAX 1-919-733-0309

YSI is a U.S.–based nonprofit organization that conducts and encourages human service and environmental expeditions to remote areas of the world. Approximately thirty to forty volunteers, aged seventeen to twenty-five, participate in the YSI program. The four-part program involves: selection weekends staged at various sites around the country, which are designed to be challenging and arduous; preparation, including team building, perhaps learning a language, and other skills needed for the expedition, as well as raising about $3,800 to cover part of the expedition costs; the expedition itself, which may be in any area of the world, however remote; return from the expedition, at which point each team member is required to participate in 100 hours of community service and/or conservation work in the member's local community. Volunteer requirements are rigorous, and in addition to demonstrating reliability, enthusiasm, and an ability to work well with others, members must be able to speak English and to swim 500 yards. For information, get in touch with the Raleigh office.

# Resources

*Voluntary Foreign Aid Programs* is a directory of private voluntary organizations (PVOs) with overseas development programs that are sponsored in part by the Agency for International Development (AID). Some, but not all, the organizations use volunteers. To receive a copy, write to Agency for International Development, Bureau for Food for Peace and Voluntary Assistance, Washington, DC 20523.

*InterAction Member Profiles* is an annotated directory of 125 member agencies of the American Council for Voluntary International Action (InterAction). Some of the organizations appear in *Voluntary Foreign Aid Programs* (above); others do not. To receive a copy, send $23 to InterAction, 200 Park Ave. S., New York, NY 10003.

*Volunteer Vacations: A Directory of Short-Term Adventures That Will Benefit You . . . and Others,* 2nd edition, by Bill McMillon. Chicago: Chicago Review Press, 1989. This is a guide to volunteer opportunities in the United States and overseas in a broad spectrum of areas—manual labor, gardening, translating, conservation, surveying archaeological digs, and more. Excellent job descriptions include project locations, dates, costs to the volunteer (usually travel, room, and board), and work done by volunteers. Cross-referenced index.

*International Volunteer Program Guide,* published annually by Service Civil International (SCI), $2, is an international listing of work camp opportunities in the United States and many overseas countries. Some of the work is environmental or cultural, other listings involve working with children, and still other camps are political in intention. Application fees vary from $35 to $100, depending on the country and continent.

*Invest Yourself: The Catalogue of Volunteer Opportunities, a Guide to Action.* (See page 39.)

# Public Affairs

Public affairs organizations address some of the major questions facing all human beings. A public issue can be found in or crafted from almost every human activity: creating art, disarmament, feeding the hungry (or not), adequate health care, environmental options, and making crucial moral and legal choices for ourselves and others. Public affairs groups that are basically policy organizations get along with very small staffs, some researchers, and a few extremely skilled advocates to make their case. Groups like American Civil Liberties Union (ACLU, page 149) and League of Women Voters (LWV, page 195) are broad-based, with large and active memberships, many chapters, and dedicated volunteers. Participation in a local organization that's attempting to achieve a particular goal in the community is a very good way to meet your neighbors. To be a useful public affairs volunteer, even if you're stuffing envelopes in a political campaign, it's important to know what you're talking about, what the issue or the candidate means to you and others, who is affected, and what facts are relevant.

---

## Accuracy in Media, Inc. (AIM)

1275 K St., NW, Suite 1150
Washington, DC 20005
1-202-371-6710, FAX 1-202-371-9054
Contact: Don Irvine, Executive Secretary

AIM is a nonprofit organization devoted to monitoring and reporting on the media from a politically conservative point of view. AIM itself publishes *AIM Report* and *Campus Report* and contributes to other publications as well. AIM has an internship program for students who can do research, have strong writing skills, and are politically conservative and self-motivated. School-sponsored internships can be accommodated. Internships last from a minimum of six weeks to a maximum of eighteen weeks and pay $25 a day or $125 a week for a forty-hour week, with housing arrangements left to the interns. For information, write to the executive secretary.

## Architects/Designers/Planners for Social Responsibility (ADPSR)

National Headquarters
225 Lafayette St., Room 205
New York, NY 10012
1-212-431-3756

ADPSR is a membership organization of design professionals and students who are committed to helping the public understand the need for arms reduction, protection of the natural and man-made environment, and socially responsible development. ADPSR activities are conducted principally through its twelve chapters nationwide. Members are encouraged to work toward specific ends with other private nonprofit or government groups at the community level. Chapters also work with university students and faculties to introduce ADPSR's agenda into the education of design professionals: conduct programs with other professional design organizations, and advocate an end of the arms race and conversion of military spending to the basic physical and social infrastructure needs of the United States. Members receive the "National Networker/ADPSR" newsletter with information about chapter activities and national and international campaigns. For information about ADPSR, write to the national headquarters.

## Booksellers for Social Responsibility (BSR)

Guild Books
2456 Lincoln Ave.
Chicago, IL 60614
1-312-525-3667
Contact: Lew Rosenbaum, President

BSR is a fledgling organization whose members are booksellers, people who work in publishing, and other individuals connected with the book community. Part of BSR's mission is to stimulate and involve the community in discussion of, debate about, and possible solutions to some of the nation's more pressing social and cultural issues: homelessness, literacy, education, and censorship among them. One means of fostering discussion is for local book stores, sometimes working as a coalition, to hold readings and sponsor other events about such subjects. For more information, call or write to Lew Rosenbaum.

Call for Action (CFA, page 155)

Center for Third World Organizing (CTWO, page 170)

## Common Cause

2030 M St., NW
Washington, DC 20036
1-202-833-1200, FAX 1-202-659-3716
Contact: Rumi Matsuyama

Common Cause is a nonprofit citizens' lobbying organization with 270,000 members nationwide committed to making the government function more efficiently, more responsively, and more honestly. Common Cause's priority issues are campaign finance reform and stronger ethics legislation. Every year, Common Cause offers college students from across the country the opportunity to participate actively in the political process as interns, receiving up to a full semester's credit through arrangements with their schools. Interns work as grassroots organizers, researchers, congressional monitors, magazine research assistants, and liaisons between the national office and state and local activists, and they answer mail and produce and distribute press releases. Internships are open to undergraduates and graduate students willing to devote two to five days a week for approximately a ten- to twelve-week period during the spring or fall semester; there are summer internships as well. Out-of-pocket expenses, including local transportation, are paid, but there is no stipend. Interns pay their own room and board and transportation costs to Washington. For information, contact Rumi Matsuyama.

## League of Women Voters (LWV)

1730 M St., NW
Washington, DC 20036
1-202-429-1965

LWV is a nonpartisan political organization whose membership works for the full participation of citizens in government, by voter registration and through public discussion of the issues. LWV advocates for universal voter registration and campaign integrity; the right to privacy in reproductive choice; civil rights; clean air and water; and safe, affordable housing and child care. League members volunteer by becoming involved with public service efforts, including: research, civic education, running candidate debates, voter registration, publishing reports on public issues, advocating at the local, state, or national level, public speaking, and working with the media, to cite a few. LWV has over 100,000 members in over 1,100 communities in all 50 states, the District of Columbia, Puerto Rico, and the Virgin Islands. Check your local phone book or contact the Washington office for information about joining.

## Peace Brigades International (PBI)

Box 1233, Harvard Square
Cambridge, MA 02238
1-617-491-4226

PBI is a volunteer organization dedicated to establishing international and nonpartisan approaches to peacemaking and to the support of basic human rights, with programs now in Central America, Sri Lanka, and North America. Unarmed peace teams of trained PBI volunteers are invited to areas of violent repression or conflict, where they work to reduce the violence and to support local social justice initiatives. The peace teams act as nonviolent bodyguards, providing protective accompaniment for people whose lives are threatened because of their work for human rights. In Central America, PBI's Peace Education Program volunteers offer nonpartisan workshops adapted to each group's needs, from making toys and other goods to working with church groups, labor unions, and rural communities on human rights issues. PBI volunteers are trained in two phases. The first takes place in the United States before an individual has been selected to become a team member. At this stage, volunteers learn how to function well in groups, work through some of the problems and situations that can arise, and in general get a taste for what they'll face. Then each trainee is interviewed to see if he or she is still interested and qualified. For volunteers going to Central America who want to work in the Peace Education Program, the second phase of training is given on-site by experienced teams already working at conflict resolution. Volunteers in Central America must be able to speak Spanish and be ready to serve for at least six months. For Sri Lanka, volunteers must speak English. Trainings are currently being held for "ready-response" brigades to respond to disputes between Native Americans and non-native peoples or their governments. All volunteers should be at least twenty-five years old, committed to the cause of nonviolence, able to live with stress, and prepared to live and work in a cross-cultural group.

PBI's Emergency Response Network (ERN) is a group of thousands of volunteers worldwide (with 3,000 in the United States alone) who can be quickly mobilized to respond to gross instances of human rights abuse, especially in emergency situations involving PBI volunteers or the Central Americans they are accompanying. The network provides support by phone calls and telegrams. ERN volunteers, who work out of their homes or offices, are always needed.

For information about either of PBI's volunteer programs, call or write to the Cambridge office.

## The Postcard Activist

Box 660
Yonkers, NY 10710

The Postcard Activist's *Ban Censorship* was put together with the help of People for the American Way, an advocacy group based in Washington, DC. The book consists of thirty postcards, preaddressed to network programming presidents, senators, congresspeople, the chairman of Sony Music Entertainment, the state board of education, various school board presidents, educational publishers, and more. With *Ban Censorship* in hand, you'll have immediate access to people in high places, the people who make decisions regarding censorship. Each card is also preprinted with a message, such as this one for the programming presidents of the major networks: "Please don't bow to right wing pressure in making your programming decisions. Give Americans the freedom to choose what they watch in their homes." There's room left for you to add your own comments, with suggestions for what you might write about. Two other Postcard Activist titles are *Keep Abortion Safe and Legal* and *No Handguns,* both published in the same format.

### United States Public Interest Research Group (PIRG)

National Association of State PIRGs
215 Pennsylvania Ave., SE
Washington, DC 20003
1-202-546-9707

The first PIRG was founded by Ralph Nader in 1971. Today, there are more than 150 PIRG offices in twenty-five states nationwide working on substantive issues regarding the environment, consumer rights, and voter registration. Each state PIRG sets its own agenda. About half of all PIRG members are students, many of whom volunteer in two programs: National Student Campaign for Voter Registration, which has helped register over 1 million students for national elections, and National Student Campaign Against Hunger and Homelessness (NSCAHH, page 223), which has organized students on over 250 campuses. Volunteers are needed in most PIRG offices to work on campaigns, do canvassing, writing, and other activities. For the location of the PIRG nearest you, contact the Washington office.

*Call to Action: Handbook for Ecology, Peace and Justice.*

*(See page 238.)*

# Resources

*Consumer's Resource Handbook,* United States Office of Consumer Affairs, Washington, DC. This free handbook is updated every two years. Part I tells you how to be a smart consumer and gives specific tips for selecting a broad range of goods and services, from airlines to financial institutions to choosing a school. Part II is a consumer assistance directory of organizations in every area that applies to consumer protection. For people seeking information about volunteer opportunities in their communities, the directories for Better Business Bureaus (BBB, page 158), state Agencies on Aging (page 206), and state vocational and rehabilitation agencies will prove extremely useful.

*Directory of National Helplines: A Guide to Toll-Free Public Service Numbers, 1991–1992.* This specialized directory provides immediate access to social, economic, health, and environmental organizations. The helplines provide services to runaway children, consumers, people in search of information about AIDS, victims of domestic violence, and many others. Listings for the handicapped are particularly extensive. To order a copy, send $6 to The Pierian Press, P.O. Box 1808, Ann Arbor, MI 48106, or call 1-800-678-2435.

# Religious Organizations

Religious organizations are a major source of volunteer activities in communities all over the world; they provide health care, education, and disaster relief, minister to prisoners, help the hungry and homeless, and advocate for human rights and political freedom.

If you are an active member of a religious congregation, you'll know all about the programs and volunteer opportunities offered, or you can ask at churches and synagogues in your community about volunteer projects. Missionary programs generally prefer volunteers to be religious, but there are plenty of churches and synagogues eager for anyone to volunteer in community programs.

## American Bible Society (ABS)

1865 Broadway
New York, NY 10023
1-212-408-1200, FAX 1-212-408-1512
Contact: Director, Church Relations/Volunteer Activities

Since 1816 ABS has been committed to making the Scriptures available to as many people as possible, including translations into more than eighty different languages, published in a wide variety of formats and styles, as well as in languages and translations for the visually impaired and blind. Thousands of volunteers contribute time and devotion to ABS, most of them working to meet Scripture needs in the course of their everyday lives by sharing the Scripture personally; working as church volunteers to serve as links between ABS and their own congregations; setting up ABS booths at meetings and conventions; becoming volunteer speakers; operating Scripture centers in their own communities; and recruiting other volunteers. Volunteers, who can contribute as much time as they wish, receive considerable support and recognition. They also receive the "Volunteers Bulletin," which has news about ongoing programs and suggestions for creating local ABS projects. For volunteer information, contact the director of church relations/volunteer activities.

## B'nai B'rith International (BB)

Community Volunteer Services (CVS)
1640 Rhode Island Ave., NW
Washington, DC 20036
1-202-857-6582
Contact: Betty Hilton, Assistant Director, CVS

BB, the world's largest Jewish organization, was founded in 1843, and it is still devoted to the preservation of Jewish culture and identity, and the unity of the Jewish people. BB is an advocate for Israel at the UN and elsewhere around the world. Member volunteers serve BB at every level: They form the governing structure, do fundraising, and play key roles at the Hillel Foundation, BB's college and university student organization, and at the BB Youth Organization (BBYO) for teenage girls and boys.

Thousands of individuals work with BBCVS,

the program that addresses problems experienced by the entire community: substance abuse; hunger and homelessness; combating AIDS; providing adequate services for older adults, veterans, and members of the armed services. CVS also reaches out to the Jewish community, with programs for Ethiopian Jewry and Jewish immigrants from the former Soviet Union, and Jewish prisoner outreach. CVS has developed volunteer training manuals for each of its programs. To find out more about BB, check your local phone book, or contact the Washington office.

**Bread for the World (BFW, page 174)**

## Casa Juan Diego (CJD)

Houston Catholic Worker
P.O. Box 70113
Houston, TX 77270
1-713-869-7376, 1-713-864-4944
Contact: Director

CJD is a Catholic Worker House of Hospitality committed to the immediate relief of those in need. Volunteers live in the community, sheltering homeless Central American refugees and Spanish-speaking battered women and children, distributing food to the hungry in the community and feeding guests at CJD, providing clothing and medical services for the poor, and publishing *Houston Catholic Worker*, a bilingual monthly newspaper. CJD needs twenty-five volunteers a year who are over twenty-one or college graduates and who speak functional Spanish. If you are committed to the values and ideals of the Catholic Worker Movement and interested in volunteering, send a resume and three letters of recommendation. Volunteers receive room, board, medical care, and a monthly stipend of $100. For more information, write to CJD.

## Christian Outreach Appeal (COA)

515 E. 3rd St.
Long Beach, CA 90802
1-213-432-1440
Contact: Pastor Frank Miller, Director of Social Services

COA is an interdenominational Christian relief and development ministry whose objective is serving hungry and homeless people. COA operates in Mexico and in southern California. The California services reach almost 5,000 people each week, some of them from the Hispanic population and others from the largest Christian Cambodian community in the world. Services include various food programs (much of the food is donated); free clothing, counseling, and job skill seminars; holiday celebrations; and cultural events. All COA programs are heavily dependent on volunteers. For information, contact Pastor Miller.

## Community of Caring (COC)

245 E. 8th St., P.O. Box 204
Erie, PA 16512
1-814-456-6661
Contact: Sister Mary Beth Kennedy, Executive Director

COC is a Christian membership organization founded to meet the needs of the hungry, homeless, and sick, both in the United States and in Africa and Latin America. Anyone who makes a commitment to one act of kindness every day is eligible to join COC. The only other requirements are that members love God, love people, and are willing to work hard. Much of COC's work is done by volunteer members: food distribution and hot meal programs, setting up residences for the homeless, and supplying clinics and medicine. For information, contact the executive director.

**Habitat for Humanity International, Inc. (page 177)**

## Lutheran Volunteer Corps (LVC)

1226 Vermont Ave., NW
Washington, DC 20005
1-202-387-3222

LVC offers volunteers the opportunity to spend a year working for social justice, living in a simplified life-style in intentional Christian community. LVC volunteers work for nonprofit social service agencies such as shelters, soup kitchens, food banks, community centers, rape crisis centers, and medical clinics; they assist advocacy and policy organizations working on issues related to the environment, women, Central America, and state and national food policies. LVC is open to people, twenty-one and older, of all Christian traditions. Volunteers live in apartments and houses in the six urban areas that LVC services. There is no special educational background or set of professional skills required of volunteers, but people with particular skills and experience are also welcome. For information, get in touch with the Washington office.

## Mennonite Board of Missions (MBM)

Volunteer Service (VS)
Box 370
Elkhart, IN 46515-0370
1-219-294-7523 (Voice/TTY)
Contact: Berni Kaufman

MBMVS spreads the word of God through compassionate service, sharing of faith, and involvement in issues of peace and justice. Working with church, family, and neighborhood groups, many of them Christian-based, VS focuses primarily on issues of housing, health care, homelessness, refugees, neighborhood economic development, and education in the United States. VS openings are published twice yearly in *Opportunity to Serve,* a booklet listing current service assignments in wide-ranging fields: community and social work, administration, education, health, and home repair and construction. Most assignments are for at least one year, and frequently longer. A VS worker must be prepared to participate in the issues and activities of a local community and a local Mennonite congregation, and willing to share in a group household where a simple life-style is the rule. Contact Berni Kaufman for more information.

National Council of Jewish Women (NCJW, page 86)

## Presbyterian Church (U.S.A.) (PC/USA)

Global Mission Unit (GMU)
100 Witherspoon St.
Louisville, KY 40202-1396
1-502-569-5295, FAX 1-502-569-5018
Contact: Mission Recruitment Office

Mission Volunteers (MV) and MV/International are programs of PC/USA's Global Mission Unit, offering opportunities for people of all ages who are willing to contribute service and live a simple life-style while helping to meet needs locally and globally. MV serves full-time for terms ranging from two months to three years, and it is matched by GMU to meet the needs and requests of churches and other institutions, most of them connected to Christian groups. Opportunities in the United States include: working with diverse ministries; serving at Christian camps, conference centers, and churches; teaching; working with health-related organizations; assisting with social and human services; and working with refugees. MV/International focuses on education, health services, and community development assignments, and for these placements, professionals in those fields, as well as engineers, construction workers, computer experts, and others, are needed. Special skills in such areas as music, arts, crafts, recreation, leadership, and accounting are useful for U.S. and overseas service. PC/USA requests that all volunteers be active church members, although not necessarily of the PC/USA, and display a willingness to accept the disciplines of a Christian community. For an application packet and more information about MV and MV/International, write to the Mission Recruitment Office.

## St. Vincent Palloti Center for Apostolic Development, Inc.

Box 893, Cardinal Station
Washington, DC 20064
1-202-529-3330

St. Vincent Pallotti Center for Apostolic Development promotes all phases of Catholic volunteerism, encouraging the laity to full participation and collaboration in the Christian mission. *Connections*, the Center's annual directory of lay volunteer opportunities, has listings that are extremely varied in terms of skills, experience, and length of service. There are six St. Vincent Pallotti Centers nationwide, and each of them serves as a clearinghouse of information about church-oriented volunteer programs. The Centers also offer skills assessment, referrals, and consultation for people interested in lay ministry. Write to the national office for a free copy of *Connections* and any other information you require.

## The Salvation Army (TSA)

National Headquarters
799 Bloomfield Ave.
Verona, NJ 07044
1-201-239-0606, FAX 1-201-239-8441

TSA, founded in England in 1865, describes itself as an international religious and charitable organization organized and operated on a quasi-military pattern and as a branch of the Christian church. Its membership consists of officers (clergy), soldiers (laity), and members of TSA activity groups, volunteers, and advisers. Most of TSA's national and regional programs are administered through over 1,000 local corps community centers, which tailor programs to their areas' special needs. All TSA programs are open to anyone who wants to use them. Projects range from religious services and evangelistic campaigns to family counseling, day-care centers, youth activities, helping young single mothers, working with offenders and ex-offenders, summer camps, emergency disaster service (see Salvation Army Emergency Services, SAES, page 94), programs for the elderly, women's residences, and much more. TSA's League of Mercy, dedicated groups of volunteer men and women, makes hospital and nursing home visits to distribute toilet articles and magazines, to chat with the patients and residents, and to distribute hand-wrapped gifts at Christmas. Famous for its services to the sick and needy during the winter holiday season, TSA provides festive dinners, music, trees, and good cheer. TSA Service Units, men and women who know their home communities well, make local, regional, and national services available in places where TSA has no corps community center. For information about TSA and volunteer opportunities, call your local TSA unit.

SHARE-USA (page 175)

SIOUX YMCA (page 171)

## Unitarian Universalist Service Committee (UUSC)

130 Prospect St.
Cambridge, MA 02139
1-617-868-6600, FAX 1-617-868-7102
Contact: Citizen Action Department

UUSC is an independent, nonsectarian membership organization that promotes peace, social justice, and freedom worldwide. UUSC's work is inspired by the underlying religious belief in the worth and dignity of every human being and the interdependence of all people. UUSC assists grassroots organizations in self-help projects in fifteen countries, supports human rights all over the world, and coordinates educational and social justice activities in the United States. More than 800 UUSC volunteers help conduct education and action campaigns, organize study groups, sponsor demonstrations, distribute educational materials, work with the news media, and arrange speaking engagements. UUSC has two structured volunteer groups. The first, the Volunteer Network, organizes activities in hundreds of Unitarian Universalist congregations. The second, UUSC's Units, are active in ten states and the District of Columbia and organize community activities on issues such as hunger, criminal justice, and Central America. For more information about volunteering, contact your local Unitarian church or the Citizen Action Department at UUSC's Cambridge headquarters.

## Volunteers of America (VOA)

National Office
3813 N. Causeway Blvd.
Metairie, LA 70002-1784
1-504-837-2652

VOA is an interdenominational Christian organization founded in 1896 "to reach and uplift all people." One of the country's largest human services agencies, VOA delivers joyful, compassionate service, with a focus on the individual as a whole person—body, mind, and spirit. VOA programs focus on child care, adoption, shelter for the homeless, alcohol and drug abuse, the elderly, families, people with mental and physical disabilities, and prisoners. These services are provided in partnership with local governments, businesses, churches, and volunteers working with VOA to solve community problems. Although VOA programs are operated by paid, professional staff, volunteers are needed for many phases of the work. For more information, check your local telephone directory for the nearest VOA or get in touch with the national office.

# Resource

*The Response: Lay Volunteer Mission Opportunities Directory* is an annual publication of International Liaison of Lay Volunteers in Mission (ILLVM), the U.S. Catholic network of lay mission programs. Many of the listings are for work overseas, and most of them require a religious commitment. There are opportunities for married couples, married or single parents with children, the elderly, and people aged eighteen and younger. Most of the placements are for long-term commitments, but there are some short-term and summer programs. Each entry has a full rundown of pertinent information about the program so that volunteers will have a good idea of what to expect. For a copy of *The Response,* send a $10 voluntary contribution to ILLVM, 4121 Harewood Rd., NE, Washington, DC 20017, or call 1-800-543-5046.

# Senior Volunteers and Volunteering for Seniors

## Senior Volunteers

Senior volunteers bring a lifetime of experience, knowledge, and skill to any work they do. Since the elderly are a cross section of America, as a group they are the most versatile volunteers, capable of and interested in every possible kind of service and at every organizational level. There are older volunteers working for most of the organizations in this book, but for an agency looking for senior volunteers, try Retired Senior Volunteers Program (RSVP, page 204), your local volunteer action center (VAC) (see National Volunteer Center, NVC, page 37), American Association of Retired Persons (AARP, page 203), or your local Area Agency on Aging, which can be located through the state government listings in the phone book.

**American Association for the Advancement of Science (AAAS, page 98)**

### American Association of Retired Persons (AARP)

601 E St., NW
Washington, DC 20049
1-202-434-2277
Contact: Chapter Records Office

There are over 4,000 chapters and more than 33 million members of AARP, one of the nation's most powerful and effective advocates for the elderly. Among the more than twenty AARP volunteer programs providing service for older persons are state legislative committees representing the interests of older people in all fifty states; Tax-Aide, provided in 10,000 sites nationwide which, in cooperation with the IRS volunteer service (see IRS Volunteers, page 87), offers state and federal tax return counseling to low- and middle-income persons over sixty; a workforce education program in which volunteers work with businesses and other organizations to prepare employees and members for retirement; advocacy volunteers, who work on problems of age discrimination; 55 Alive/Mature Driving, a refresher driving course for people over fifty; and health advocacy volunteers. AARP members also work individually and in groups for local community interests and causes. Membership costs are very reasonable. Consult your telephone directory for the AARP chapter nearest you or write to the Chapter Records Office in Washington. (See also AARP's Volunteer Talent Bank, VTB, page 36).

**Chevron USA, Chevron Retirees (page 67)**

## Foster Grandparent Program (FGP)

ACTION
1100 Vermont Ave., NW
Washington, DC 20525
1-202-606-4855

FGP is ACTION's (page 35) intergenerational program, in which low-income persons aged sixty and older volunteer their services to children with exceptional needs. Volunteers receive a small tax-free stipend, transportation costs, meals, accident and liability insurance, and an annual physical exam. Foster grandparents (FGs) commit four hours a day five times a week to spend with children—kids in state hospitals, acute-care facilities, juvenile correction centers, and other residential settings; children with mental retardation or suffering from child abuse and neglect, learning disabilities, and other special problems. FGs receive forty hours of preservice orientation and training, plus four hours of in-service training monthly. There are about 23,000 FGP volunteers serving over 70,000 children annually nationwide. For information, call a local FGP (see the U.S. Government listings in the phone book) or contact ACTION.

**International Executive Service Corps (IESC, page 64)**

**National Executive Service Corps (NESC, page 65)**

## Older Women's League (OWL)

730 11th St., NW
Washington, DC 20001
1-202-783-6686

OWL is a national grassroots membership organization whose focus is exclusively on women as they age. Among the issues OWL addresses nationally are a national universal health care system, reform of Social Security benefits, and combating discrimination in the workplace. Each of OWL's more than 130 chapters in thirty-six states work on these and other programs at the local level, often in cooperation with other voluntary organizations. For a chapter directory, write to the Field Services Division.

## Retired Senior Volunteers Program (RSVP)

ACTION
1100 Vermont Ave., NW
Washington, DC 20525
1-202-606-4855

RSVP is one of the most successful volunteer projects initiated by ACTION (page 35), with more than 427,000 volunteers assigned to about 275 local sponsoring organizations nationwide. RSVP offers opportunities for citizens aged sixty and older to use their talents and experience in community services that respond to local needs. Services and jobs are wide-ranging and include adult basic education, consultancy services, Meals on Wheels (MOW, page 205), tour guides, tax aides, classroom aides, home visitation, telephone reassurance, substance abuse counseling and education, literacy, youth services, and many others. RSVP "volunteer stations" are located in courts, schools, libraries, day-care centers, hospitals. Volunteers receive a brief orientation and, after placement, get in-service instruction. Check the U.S. Government pages of the phone book for the nearest RSVP station or get in touch with your regional ACTION center (page 35).

### Senior Companion Program (SCP)

ACTION
1100 Vermont Ave., NW
Washington, DC 20525
1-202-606-4855

SCP, another ACTION (page 30) program, offers person-to-person volunteer opportunities for low-income Americans aged sixty and over. Just as foster grandparents (FGs) (see Foster Grandparent Program, FGP, page 204) help children with special needs, SCP volunteers provide personal assistance and peer support, primarily to older adults who are homebound and physically or mentally challenged. Volunteers, who are recruited through local health and social service agencies designated as "volunteer stations," usually commit four hours a day five days a week to helping their clients. Senior Companions (SCs) are trained for forty hours before they begin service and receive another four hours of in-service instruction a month. Like FGP, SCP offers its volunteers a tax-free allowance, or stipend, as well as reimbursement for transportation and meals, on-duty insurance, and an annual physical examination. For information about volunteering, check the U.S. Government listings in the phone book, or get in touch with your regional ACTION office (page 30).

**Service Corps of Retired Executives (SCORE, page 65)**

**Telephone Pioneers of America (TPA, page 68)**

# Volunteering for Seniors

We need more services for older Americans, especially for those who are dependent on others for help in maintaining life with dignity. Individually, most of us do help elderly people just in the ordinary way, without thinking of it as volunteering, whether it's shoveling out a neighbor's driveway, grocery shopping for a housebound friend, driving an older person to a doctor's appointment, calling to check in, or returning books to the library. It's a reflection of our lives today that there are so many intergenerational programs for senior persons, usually involving groups of children who spend time in nursing homes and similar residences helping the residents, playing with them, working together on projects. However, you need not be a child to work for older people. Call your state Area Agency on Aging to find out about local programs, then try a volunteer action center (VAC) (see National Volunteer Center, NVC, page 37) or United Way (UWA, page 38).

**Magic Me (MM, 220)**

### Meals on Wheels (MOW)

Meals on Wheels is not the name of a program, but rather the generic term for a service: one free hot meal a day delivered to low-income homebound elderly people or served to them in a communal setting. MOW is always locally organized and implemented, usually under the auspices of one of the federal government's 670 regional Area Offices on Aging (check the U.S. government pages in your telephone directory) or a state agency on aging (see *Consumer's Resource Handbook*, page 197). Some programs are completely privately funded; others receive money and food donations from state and local governments along with donations of food and other goods from businesses. Any MOW program that receives federal funding pays local community agencies to carry out the program under the supervision of professional nutritionists and other paid staff. Each program works somewhat differently, depending on its funding and the region and population it serves, so that work for volunteers varies greatly. Most programs rely on volunteers to deliver the meals on weekdays and for additional services on weekends and holidays. Check the phone book for your local Meals on Wheels.

### Meals-on-Wheels-America (MOWA)

280 Broadway, Suite 214
New York, NY 10007
1-212-964-5700
Contact: Director

MOWA is a technical assistance project under the auspices of the New York City Department for the Aging (NYCDFTA). MOWA is currently helping over thirty-five selected meal programs nationwide develop local public/private partnerships to raise funds for home-delivered meals to the elderly for weekends, holidays, or in times of emergency. MOWA "Recipes" are single-topic master plans for fund-raising revolving around a specific holiday or issue—Valentine's Day, bidding for big donations, supermarket "round-ups," emergency meal packages, and so on—each recipe leading the reader (or organization) step by step through a series of activities culminating in a successful campaign. *More Meals for the Homebound Through Public/Private Partnerships: A Technical Assistance Guide* is a manual for community fund-raising, and although its purpose is to assist local Meals on Wheels (MOW, page 205) programs, the advice it provides is valuable for any organization working for community improvement. *More Meals for the Homebound* and MOWA's "Recipes" have been distributed free to all 670 federal Area Agencies on Aging as well as to several thousand meal providers nationally. For information, contact the director.

**New York City Department for the Aging, Intergenerational Work/Study Program (NYCDFTA/IWSP, page 220)**

**U.S. National Senior Sports Organization (USNSSO, page 217)**

**William Breman Jewish Home (page 125)**

# Ombudsmen

Ombudsmen are trained and certified volunteer advocates for residents in nursing and adult homes. The ombudsman's job is to visit the homes regularly, spend time with the elderly residents, hear their comments and complaints, and investigate and resolve problems. By federal law, each state is required to have an ombudsman program, administered from the state Office for the Aging or from an Area Agency on Aging. Check the state and federal government pages in your phone book.

### National Citizen's Coalition for Nursing Home Reform (NCCNHR)

1224 M St., NW, Suite 301
Washington, DC 20015-5183
1-202-393-2018
Contact: Information Clearinghouse

NCCNHR was founded in 1975 by twelve citizen advocacy groups to improve the long-term-care system and the quality of life for nursing home residents. It is now a coalition of over 300 member groups and individuals, all of them concerned in one way or another with nursing homes. As a clearinghouse, NCCNHR provides the public and health professionals with information and analysis, training and consultation, networking opportunities, regulatory monitoring and advocacy, and a number of publications. People interested in becoming a volunteer for the ombudsmen program can obtain information from the Information Clearinghouse of NCCNHR, which includes a state-by-state listing of ombudsmen offices.

## New York State Long Term Care Ombudsman Program (LTCOP)

New York State Office for the Aging
Empire State Plaza, Agency Building #2
Albany, NY 12223-0001
1-518-474-7329, FAX 1-518-474-0608
New York State: 1-800-342-9871
Contact: David R. Murray

There are thirty-nine LTCOPs throughout New York State advocating for residents in nursing homes and adult care facilities. Volunteer ombudsmen receive thirty-six hours of training before being certified to investigate and resolve the concerns and complaints of residents and their families. The training is intensive, and to be certified a person must become familiar with the laws and the systems that regulate long-term-care facilities and patients' rights, benefits, and entitlements, and they must master the skills necessary to communicate with the residents. Ongoing training continues with monthly in-service meetings. Ombudsmen make weekly visits to assigned facilities, where they meet with residents to assist them in adjusting to life in a long-term facility and to resolve a wide range of concerns that might include questions about public benefits, lost or stolen personal belongings, food, resident rights, and quality care. For information, contact the Albany office of the State Ombudsman.

# Sports

## Sports for the Disabled

Sports for people who are physically disabled or mentally retarded have come into their own. More and more disabled athletes are competing in mainstream tournaments and races, a fact that benefits all the athletes who compete, all the volunteers who assist in whatever capacity, and all the sports fans who acknowledge and applaud the power and ability of disabled people.

The Paralympic Games are the International Olympic equivalent for the elite athletes on the United States Disabled Sports Teams (USDST, page 214). The Paralympics are patterned after the regular Olympics: Most of the competitions are for the same sports, and the games are held two weeks after the Olympics in the same country and in the same sports venues. The first Paralympics were held in Rome in 1960, and they have taken place in every Olympic year since then.

Volunteers are at the very heart of sports organizations for people with disabilities. Volunteers coach, train, deliver various kinds of therapy, transport athletes to and from meets, and accompany athletes as they compete. They do fund-raising and organize competitions from the local to the international level; they do office work and public relations; and they donate services and goods in kind. In fact, it's just like volunteering for a lot of other organizations, but better, because everyone really is a winner.

Here are a few of the organizations helping to meet the needs of disabled athletes. (For wheelchair athletics, *Wheelchair Sports and Recreation,* a free brochure published by Paralyzed Veterans of America (PVA, page 212), has a very detailed listing.)

### Achilles Track Club (ATC)

9 E. 89th St.
New York, NY 10128
1-212-967-9300
Contact: Dick Traum

ATC, a running club for people with physical disabilities, is dedicated to the idea that the disabled should run with the general population, competing in all local races, regional meets, and marathons. For that reason, ATC's cooperative relationships are only with regular running groups, such as some of the Road Runners Clubs. There are over 100 ATC chapters worldwide, about 35 of them in the United States, whose athletes' disabilities include blindness, impairment from stroke, cerebral palsy, arthritis, and amputation.

The people who make it safe for disabled runners to participate in races are volunteers. For instance, during a recent New York City Marathon, 200 volunteers assisted 125 disabled runners—holding tethers for the blind, running ahead and alongside those in wheelchairs. Some volunteer runners must be swift enough to enter Olympic trials so that they can keep up with speedy blind runners. Volunteers also attend many training sessions during the year. Although people with training in movement or physical therapy can offer athletes advice on running, their principal job is safety, motivation, and companionship. According to ATC, the main qualification for volunteers is a helpful and cheerful but no-nonsense personality.

Recently, ATC began providing foreign amputee runners with artificial legs, specially developed for running marathons, which are donated at cost by manufacturers. In another overseas program, ATC gives each blind runner an eye exam and, if it is appropriate, arranges for the athlete to have an operation, with all transportation, medical help, and room and board donated by airlines, doctors, hotels, and so on. In each of these programs volunteers make most of the arrangements. Contact the New York headquarters for the location of your nearest ATC chapter, or, if you want to start a chapter of your own, ask for the ATC "Chapter Organizer's Guide."

## Breckenridge Outdoor Education Center (BOEC)

P.O. Box 697
Breckenridge, CO 80424
1-303-453-6422
Contact: Kate McNerny, Administrative Coordinator, or Elise Bowne, Adaptive Ski Director

BOEC is a chapter of National Handicapped Sports (NHS, page 211) and its motto is "Empowering people through wilderness experiences," which the organization does by conducting year-round adventure-based wilderness programs for people with disabilities. Outdoor experiences are individually designed to the abilities and needs of participants so that each person can achieve the full range of his or her capabilities. Programs include snowshoeing, rock climbing, fishing, downhill and cross-country skiing, backpacking, accessible high ropes courses, and orienteering. All programs are directed by professional staff, with the assistance of interns and volunteers. BOEC interns work with instructors to run the wilderness and ski programs. A background in wilderness skills and/or working with people who are physically challenged is helpful, but more important are enthusiasm and willingness to learn new skills. Interns are provided with room, board, and a small monthly stipend. There are five to ten internships available for both summer and winter seasons for administrative and field positions. Contact Kate McNerny about the internship program.

Currently, BOEC's greatest need is for volunteer instructors in the Adaptive Ski Program to teach downhill skiing to people with special needs whose abilities range from beginner to expert. Instruction is given using adaptive ski equipment for wheelchair users, amputees, and those with hearing or visual impairments or developmental disabilities. For information, get in touch with Elise Bowne.

## Disabled Ski Program at Ski Windham (DSP)

Eastern Professional Ski Instructors Association—Educational Foundation
1-A Lincoln Ave.
Albany, NY 12205
1-518-452-6095

DSP, another chapter of National Handicapped Sports (NHS, page 211), is a nonprofit organization located at Ski Windham, a commercial ski area in the Catskill Mountains in upstate New York. Specialized ski instruction is available for the beginner through advanced skier for amputees, the blind and visually impaired, the deaf and hearing impaired, the developmentally disabled, people with cerebral palsy or muscular dystrophy, the spinal cord injured, the neurologically impaired, and others. The ski program begins in November with the training of volunteer ski instructors and ends in late March. Over 300 disabled participants are instructed by over 100 trained volunteers. Volunteers must themselves be intermediate to advanced skiers, interested in teaching people with disabilities to ski, and willing to commit sixteen to eighteen days to teaching participants to ski. Once that commitment is made, volunteers must also complete a twelve-day training program before the commencement of the season at the first of the year. According to DSP, a great diversity of people pledge to give up a month of their lives to do the work—physical therapists, firemen, doctors, computer people—most recruited by word of mouth. Certified adaptive volunteer ski instructors from DSP are active in helping form disabled ski groups at other northeastern sites, giving counseling, on-hill instruction, and adaptive equipment demonstrations. For more information, contact the Albany office.

## Dwarf Athletic Association of America (DAAA)

3725 W. Holmes Rd.
Lansing, MI 48911
1-517-393-3116
Contact: Len Sawisch, President

DAAA, a member of the U.S. Olympic Committee (USOC, page 217), was formed in 1985 to develop, promote, and provide quality amateur athletic opportunities for dwarf athletes (four feet ten inches, or under). DAAA sponsors national competitions in track and field, basketball, boccia, power lifting, swimming, skiing, table tennis, and volleyball, and outstanding athletes are invited to join the United States Disabled Sports Teams (USDST, page 214). Competitions are held all over the country, and volunteers from local colleges are recruited to assist in managing events. Medical professionals are also invited to participate. For information about upcoming competition venues and volunteer opportunities, call the president.

## National Foundation of Wheelchair Tennis (NFWT)

940 Calle Amanecer, Suite B
San Clemente, CA 92672
1-714-361-6811

NFWT was founded in 1980 to meet the increased interest in wheelchair tennis, one of the fastest-growing sports for wheelchair athletes. As the umbrella organization for numerous local and regional wheelchair tennis and other sports programs, NFWT presents instructional clinics, exhibitions, and competitive tournaments, and conducts Junior Wheelchair Sports Camps for disabled youth. Camp participants learn tennis, swimming, basketball, archery, and track from counselors who are also disabled athletes. Volunteers are needed on many levels: to work with kids at sports camps, to help out at regional tennis tournaments, and to do fund-raising. For information about the NFWT-sponsored program nearest you, contact the San Clemente office.

### National Handicapped Sports (NHS)

National Headquarters
451 Hungerford Drive, Suite 100
Rockville, MD 20850
1-301-217-0960, FAX 1-301-217-0968

NHS has eighty-six chapters nationwide whose goal is to make sports available to everyone. Chapters are community-based and offer a range of sports for individuals with disabilities. A number of the chapters are primarily for people who want to ski, others are specifically for children, and some offer a broad spectrum of sports for disabled people of all ages and abilities. Although the national organization and individual chapters have small core staffs, volunteers are what propel NHS: They serve on the board and organize every element of races, competitions, and other sports events; they train and serve as volunteer sports instructors; they transport participants and equipment, provide pro bono legal aid, answer mail, stuff envelopes, and answer telephones. Volunteers come from every part of American life. Although most of the volunteers live in the same area as the chapter they serve, others who work for a particular company might take their vacations together for a week and help out at a one-week competition. For information about the location of the chapter nearest you, contact the national headquarters.

### National Wheelchair Athletic Association (NWAA)

3595 E. Fountain Blvd., Suite L-1
Colorado Springs, CO 80910
1-719-574-1150

NWAA is a member of the U.S. Olympic Committee (USOC, page 217) family and serves as the sanctioning body for wheelchair sports. Since 1957 NWAA has promoted and sponsored wheelchair sports and competitions at the local, national, and international levels. All of these competitions take place at sites across the country and internationally, and all of them require the assistance of volunteers. If you are interested in volunteering for one or more of NWAA's events, call or write for a list of regional wheelchair sports organizations and for a calendar of the year's events, most of which give the name and phone number of the person to contact.

### North American Riding for the Handicapped Association (NARHA)

P.O. Box 33150
Denver, CO 80233
1-800-369-RIDE (1-800-369-7433), 1-303-452-1212

NARHA is an organization of over 450 affiliated therapeutic riding centers across the United States and Canada, serving over 21,000 riders who are physically, mentally, or emotionally challenged. There are many benefits from therapeutic riding: It builds self-confidence, concentration, and self-discipline; it improves physical health; and it gives handicapped people a feeling of freedom and independence. All NARHA centers are accredited, and all instructors are certified. A network of more than 13,000 trained volunteers, many of whom are horse professionals or individuals who work with disabled people, assist the staff at NARHA riding centers. Volunteers help out with riding exercises as leaders and side walkers and assist with NARHA's horse science education program for schoolchildren. NARHA will send a Start-Up Information Packet to anyone who wishes to start a therapeutic riding program. Therapeutic horses can be donated or leased to the organization. According to NARHA's newsletter, such a horse should possess "a quiet, spookproof attitude, smooth gaits, good manners and temperament and physical soundness" and be no younger than five years old. To donate or lease your horse, or for information about NARHA, starting a local program, or becoming a volunteer, call the 800 number.

## Paralyzed Veterans of America (PVA)

801 18th St., NW
Washington, DC 20006
1-800-424-8200, 1-202-872-1300

PVA is a national organization for veterans with spinal cord injury or disease. As an advocate for all persons with disabilities, PVA works to enact and enforce legislation protecting their legal and civil rights and cooperates with other organizations with similar missions. PVA is the nation's largest sponsor of wheelchair sports, annually sponsoring such events as the National Veterans Wheelchair Games (the largest wheelchair sporting event, cosponsored with the Veterans Administration, VA, page 232), the National Wheelchair Basketball Tournament, and the U. S. Open Wheelchair Tennis Championships (page 213). Volunteers are needed to facilitate these three programs as well as PVA's instructional programs introducing newly injured persons to wheelchair sports. For information about volunteering, call the 800 number.

## Special Olympics International, Inc.

1350 New York Ave., NW, Suite 500
Washington, DC 20005
1-202-628-3630

Special Olympics is an international movement that provides year-round sports training and athletic competition in a variety of Olympic-type sports for all individuals with mental retardation. Through these twenty-two sports, the athletes become confident and improve their self-image, and these changes carry over into every other aspect of their lives. Special Olympics would not exist without the more than 500,000 volunteers of all ages and backgrounds worldwide who offer sports training and competition programs to nearly 1 million persons with mental retardation. For instance, it takes 50,000 volunteers to stage International Summer Special Olympics Games. There are volunteers at local, state, national, and international levels, and some of their work encompasses:

- Sports training: coaching, helping to run sports camps, setting up sports clinics or training camps, and obtaining equipment or uniforms for athletes or teams.
- Service at competitions as officials, timers, scorers, drivers, and food service workers.
- Working with schools to include Special Olympics training programs, organize school sports team members as Special Olympics coaches, and provide volunteer support at games.
- Hosting Special Olympics athletes during local competitions.
- Fund-raising, raising public awareness, administrative work, and offering pro bono legal, medical, or other professional services.

For information about becoming a Special Olympics volunteer, check your local phone directory for the chapter nearest you.

## United States Association for Blind Athletes (USABA)

33 N. Institute
Colorado Springs, CO 80903
1-719-630-0422
Contact: Executive Director or Assistant Executive Director

USABA is the official organization that promotes athletic competition among the blind and visually impaired, providing recreational and competitive sports programs for people aged six to over sixty, from beginners to world-class athletes. Sports include goal ball, gymnastics, judo, power lifting, swimming, tandem cycling, track and field, wrestling, alpine skiing, nordic skiing, and speed skating. With forty-nine chapters and over 1,900 members nationwide, USABA athletes participate in local, regional, national, and inter-

## FEATURED PUBLICATION

*Sports 'n Spokes, the Magazine for Wheelchair Athletes and Recreation,* PVA's bimonthly magazine, publishes articles about every sport in which wheelchair athletes participate and compete. Although the magazine's audience is largely wheelchair athletes, volunteers might find *Sports 'n Spokes* useful as well, especially for its calendar of coming events and its list of sports associations for athletes with disabilities. PVA members receive the magazine free; for others, a yearly subscription is $9. Contact Paralyzed Veterans of America, Inc., 5201 N. 19th Ave., Suite 111, Phoenix, AZ 85015, 1-602-246-9426, FAX: 1-602-242-6862.

*Wheelchair Sports & Recreation* is a booklet describing and illustrating the enormous range of possibilities for wheelchair athletes. Potential volunteers (and others) will find useful information about PVA, including the location of its chapters; an extensive listing of resource organizations, equipment, and programs for children; and a list of magazines and books related to sports and people with disabilities. For a free copy, call 1-800-424-8200.

## FEATURED ORGANIZATION: SHAKE-A-LEG, INC. (SAL)

P.O. Box 1002
Newport, RI 02840
1-401-849-8898
Contact: Program and Operations Director

SAL is a nonprofit organization serving people who are physically disabled, with emphasis on spinal cord and related nervous system impairments. SAL's founder, Harry Horgan, was himself paralyzed in an accident, and from his own experiences he knew that once the initial phases of rehabilitation were over, there were very few opportunities for the physically challenged to improve their lives. SAL now offers a number of imaginative programs designed so that participants can build confidence, strengthen their bodies, have fun, and benefit from group support—training and conditioning programs, body awareness training, aquatics, and performing arts. But SAL is most famous for its innovative sports programs, which include sailing, scuba diving, rowing, horseback riding, swimming, and other sports. Some participants become so proficient in their individual sports that they compete in (and win!) national races. All of SAL's programs are structured so that participants develop skills at their own pace. Trained physical therapists, helped by volunteers, administer all the rehabilitation programs. SAL has facilities on land in Miami, Florida, and Portsmouth, Rhode Island, and water facilities in Miami and Newport, Rhode Island. Volunteers are the basis of the organization; they are needed all year long, but especially during the summer when the sports programs are running. Office workers, people with sailing skills, physical therapists who want to donate time, fund-raisers, special events coordinators, and cooks are all welcome. For more information, contact the program and operations director.

national competitions, including winter and summer Paralympics (page 208). Sighted and visually impaired volunteers are a significant factor in USABA's success. They participate in fund-raising, coordinate special events, assist with sports management, act as guides, and contribute public relations time and skills. Volunteer coaches are especially in demand. There are about twenty-five athletic programs located in different regions of the United States with 10 to 250 participants, depending on the sport and the location. Volunteers often are recruited from local schools for the blind, which have access to community volunteers. Lions Clubs (page 115) offer major support, as do Delta Gamma Sororities. For a calendar of events and the location of the nearest USABA chapter, contact the Colorado Springs office.

## United States Cerebral Palsy Athletic Association (USCPAA)

34518 Warren Rd., Suite 264
Westland, MI 48185
1-313-425-8961, FAX 1-313-425-6510
Contact: Volunteer Coordinator

USCPAA (which is no longer a division of United States Cerebral Palsy Association) is the national governing body of sports for individuals with cerebral palsy and those who have had strokes or closed-head injuries. USCPAA's focus is on providing sports programs and program support at the local, regional, national, and international levels, with competitive opportunities for the entire gamut of athletes from beginners through those of international caliber. Membership in USCPAA is individual, and there are seventy-five to eighty programs nationwide affiliated with recreation and parks departments, school districts, and other nonprofit organizations. Sports programs include archery, boccia, bowling, cycling, horseback riding, power lifting, shooting, slalom, soccer, swimming, table tennis, track and field, and wheelchair team handball. USCPAA also hosts national championships and sends teams to international competitions. About 10,000 volunteers perform 90 percent of USCPAA's work every year, including administrative and committee service, coaching, training, various kinds of physical therapy, fund-raising, transportation arrangement and actual transportation, and much more. For information about volunteering, call the Michigan headquarters and ask for the volunteer coordinator, who will be able to direct you to the program or committee that best suits your experience and interests.

## United States Disabled Sports Teams (USDST)

34518 Warren Rd., Suite 264
Westland, MI 48185
1-313-425-8961, FAX 1-313-425-6510
Contact: Michael Mushett, Director

USDST represents all the teams participating in the Paralympic Games (page 208) and is a coalition of five organizations, all members of the U.S. Olympic Committee (USOC, page 217): Dwarf Athletic Association of America (DAAA, page 210), National Wheelchair Athletic Association (NWAA, page 210), United States Association for Blind Athletes (USABA, page 212), United States Cerebral Palsy Athletic Association (USCPAA, page 214), and National Handicapped Sports (NHS, page 211).

Volunteers who work with the U.S. Paralympic Team are similar in many ways to the athletes they assist: They've worked their way up from the local and regional levels, proving their worth along the way as coaches, trainers, medical professionals, people who can deal with the logistics of travel, and general troubleshooters. For information, get in touch with USDST.

## PORTRAIT OF A SPECIAL ADMINISTRATOR VETERANS ADMINISTRATION (VA) NATIONAL VETERANS WINTER SPORTS CLINIC (NVWSC)

Medical Center
Grand Junction, CO 81501
1-303-242-0731
Contact: Sandy Trombetta, ext. 2412

*NVWSC is one of four yearly sports clinics for disabled service veterans run by the VA in cooperation with Disabled American Veterans (DAV, page 232) and similar organizations. The event, which receives support from local businesses and other groups, uses more than fifty certified handicapped ski instructors, including several members of the U.S. Disabled Olympic Ski Team. Sandy Trombetta is the creator and director of NVWSC and other sports events in Grand Junction. He is passionate about his work.*

I'm from Brooklyn, and I grew up in Red Hook, and I experienced some prejudice during my childhood. I was a very athletic kid, and I played on teams that went to other neighborhoods for games or tournaments, and I remember how people would scream at us because we were from Red Hook. Years later when I was around fourteen or fifteen, I was lying on the ground just looking at the sky, wishing that I'd had someone who cared enough to set me straight, and it was right then that I decided that I'd try to help those who needed and wanted help. So many kids I grew up with had lots of potential, and no one cared. It wasn't that families didn't love their children—I had the best family in the world—but they didn't know how to help get their kids educated, help them use whatever talent they had.

I dropped out of college, worked here and there, but I couldn't get a really good job because I hadn't finished school. Eventually I came in contact with disabled athletes, and I began to see that I could help them, that I was needed. So I went back to school and got a degree in human services. Then for four years I worked at Job Corps, and since then I've been with the VA in Colorado.

I'm the director of the National Veterans Winter Sports Clinic. It's a one-week clinic and I put a whole program together every year working with different veterans' groups. Four or five sports are involved. When we started in 1987 there were 87 participants and about 100 volunteers. Right now, we have over 200 disabled veterans and over 300 volunteers, who work at various activities, including ski instruction, transportation, and so on. It's quite intensive. I personally recruit and train the ski instructors—there are quite a few people around here who ski. I used to have to spend a lot of time recruiting; now they're calling me. We also work closely with the local VAC [volunteer action center] in Aspen.

We're eight miles outside of Aspen at the Snowmass ski area; it's for family skiing. This is a really expensive resort area and prices are steep, but we've been offered services, including lift tickets, hotel rooms, and food, at more than 50 percent off—at cost. If these people weren't invested at the gut level, they wouldn't do it.

*Continued*

*Continued*

This program affects the lives of everyone involved with it. The veterans, they're a group of people who've been disabled for life, and modern technology has made it possible for them to do a lot, and they *want* to; they're *ready* to. These people want to participate, and all they need is an open door; all they need is access. And the clinic gives them a way to do it themselves. A guy looks up at a mountain and thinks, "God, I came down that. If I can do that, I can do anything." Their lives have been transformed; they've developed confidence, and it carries over into every other aspect of their lives.

It's an amazing effect, how one little ripple can start a huge wave. Because everyone who's worked with the vets has been changed, too. I've been a recreation therapist for a long time, and I was prepared for the changes in the vets, but I wasn't prepared for the people who work with the athletes, how it affects them and their perception of disabled people as real individuals with personalities and abilities and human worth. I'm still totally amazed by their response. That's why this work is a major part of my life.

*For information about NVWSC, contact Sandy Trombetta. For material about other VA sports clinics, contact the Department of Veterans Affairs (VA, page 232) Recreation and Sports Program.*

# Other Sports

Volunteers are needed by virtually every nonprofit sports organization in the country: they serve as timers, referees, umpires, coaches, trainers; and they provide food, refreshment, transportation, and upkeep for sports areas. Businesses and other groups sponsor competitions, donate sports equipment, and raise scholarship money. Call your local service clubs and sports and parks department to see what opportunities are available and ask about other programs in the area. The *USOC Olympic Fact Book* (page 218) is the source for all the Olympic sports federations and other amateur sports organizations.

## Little League Baseball, Inc. (LL)

International Headquarters
P.O. Box 3485
Williamsport, PA 17701
1-717-326-1921
Contact: Steve Keener

The purpose of Little League Baseball is to provide a wholesome, beneficial community activity for young people. Little League is the largest organized youth sports program in the world, with over 2.5 million participants playing on 169,000 teams in forty-eight countries, assisted by more than 750,000 adult volunteers. So far, most of the Little League programs are located in the United States, which has roughly 6,300 chartered programs, 2 million participants, and about 600,000 dedicated adult volunteers who foster the values of teamwork, fair play, courage, loyalty, and discipline. There are seven baseball and softball divisions for youth of different age ranges, with a new Challenger Division for players six to eighteen years old with mental or physical disabilities. Each Little League unit is started, funded, and run completely by local volunteers, usually parents of participating children and other adults who themselves played when they were young and just enjoy the games. Volunteers serve as managers, coaches, and umpires, and in other positions. For information about volunteering for your local Little League, get in touch with a school administrator, the community chamber of commerce, or your town's parks and recreation department. To find out about starting a Little League in your area, contact the Williamsport office.

**National Federation of State High School Associations, TARGET Program (page 229)**

**Optimist International (page 82)**

## Road Runners Club of America (RRCA)

629 S. Washington St.
Alexandria, VA 22314
1-703-836-0558

RRCA is a national volunteer organization of more than 480 running clubs in most states and in Guam, with a membership of more than 150,000 runners. Thousands of volunteers on the local club level administer and carry out the national programs the club has adopted, and they create new programs of their own. National programs range from a women's distance festival series to personal fitness to state, regional, and national championships to a children's running development program. Some RRCA clubs coordinate with Achilles Track Club (ATC, page 208), which was created by the New York Road Runners Club. For information about the Road Runners Club in your area, or for material on starting a new club, contact the Alexandria office.

## U.S. National Senior Sports Organization (USNSSO)

U.S. National Senior Sports Classic—The Senior Olympics
14323 S. Outer Forty Rd., Suite N300
Chesterfield, MO 63017
1-314-878-4900, 1-314-878-9957

USNSSO is the umbrella organization for local and regional senior games throughout the United States, offering technical assistance and support to its eighty-five member games, which offer a full range of senior sports categories. USNSSO also organizes the U.S. National Senior Sports Classic—The Senior Olympics, a biennial national athletic competition, with over 5,000 participating athletes aged fifty-five and over. None of the senior games would take place without the assistance of volunteers, preferably in a ratio of one athlete to one volunteer. With the exception of a paid event director, trained volunteers do the rest. They register athletes, keep track of the athletes during the games, act as timekeepers, hand out water, write newsletters, and more. Donations of cash or goods in kind from local and/or national businesses are welcome. Call or write USNSSO for a list of member games and a current calendar of events to see if any of the senior games will be held in your area.

## United States Olympic Committee (USOC)

1750 E. Boulder St.
Colorado Springs, CO 80909
1-719-632-5551, FAX 1-719-578-4654
Contact: USOC Public Information/Media Relations or Volunteer Coordinator

USOC is a member of the International Olympic Committee and is the sole agency in the United States responsible for training, entering, and underwriting the full expenses for the U.S. teams in the Olympic and Pan-American Games. USOC uses many kinds of volunteers at its offices and training centers and during all its competitions: Physicians, chiropractors, and certified athletic trainers work with thousands of athletes every year. Other volunteers work in administration and helping at events—selling tickets, ushering, and so on.

*USOC Olympic Fact Book* gives a satisfactory explanation of USOC, which, with its member organizations for various sports, federations, committees, programs, and competitions, is quite a complex structure. For people who want to volunteer time to a particular sport, or who want to know the location of the nearest Olympic sports organization, see the book's very useful directory of organizations for each sport, from archery to yachting. Also listed are other national amateur athletic organizations. For a free copy, contact the Public Information Department. If you live in the Colorado Springs area and want to donate time to the USOC headquarters, call the volunteer coordinator.

### United States Tennis Association (USTA)

707 Alexander Rd.
Princeton, NJ 08540
1-800-223-0456, 1-609-452-2580

As the national governing body for tennis, USTA promotes amateur and recreational tennis, conducts tournaments on all levels, including the U. S. Open, and sets and maintains the rules of play and high standards of sportsmanship. USTA has an extremely broad range of programs that serve a constituency beginning with children and continuing to players over eighty-five: USTA School Programs; USTA National Junior Tennis League; USTA Junior Team Tennis; the USTA Player Development Program; educational workshops; and many yearly tournaments, which include international seniors championships, Davis Cup competitions, and the Olympics.

Thousands of USTA members work in these programs as tour organizers, coaches, fund-raisers, and providers of transportation, media, and publicity. The broad base of USTA volunteer organizations are the more than 1,100 community tennis associations (CTAs), which bring tennis to new audiences and offer programs and activities for all ages and all levels of experience. Volunteer umpires and referees, trained and certified by USTA for on-court and off-court assignments, are needed to work in more than 8,000 tournaments a year. For information about USTA membership and programs, call the 800 number.

# Resources

## SPORTS FOR THE DISABLED

*Sports 'n Spokes, the Magazine for Wheelchair Athletes and Recreation,* a publication of Paralyzed Veterans of America (PVA). (See box, page 213.)

*Wheelchair Sports and Recreation,* a brochure published by Paralyzed Veterans of America (PVA). (See box, page 213).

## OTHER SPORTS

*USOC Olympic Fact Book,* a publication of United States Olympic Committee. (USOC, page 217.)

# Student Volunteers

The principle of youth community service, which is embraced by all the great children's clubs, is that a person who begins volunteering early will become a lifelong volunteer and a full participant in the community. Community service and other forms of student volunteer activity are now part of thousands of programs run for and by students throughout the country. The programs are extremely diverse in focus, structure, and sponsorship, but all of them give students the opportunity to educate themselves, to broaden their scope, and to participate meaningfully in the lives around them.

## School Programs

Service Learning Education (SLE) integrates voluntary community service with school subject matter. The idea is for students to connect what they learn about community needs with classroom course work and in turn bring classroom theory to bear on real-life problems. At the same time students learn that volunteering is part of everyday life, not just a response to disaster or calamity. There are variations on this theme: In some schools SLE for credit is optional; others have a graduation requirement of twelve and a half hours of community service over the course of each school year, although not necessarily connected to schoolwork. There are programs that pay a small stipend to students who would ordinarily work after school instead of volunteering; in others there is no payment at all. SLE schools work closely with nonprofit community agencies servicing the needy, the elderly, at-risk children, and the disabled, among others. SLE in one form or another is being adopted by schools, from elementary through high school, and colleges nationwide, and it is not just the students who volunteer: Teachers, other school faculty, and sometimes parents donate time and skills to some of the projects.

Internships with nonprofit organizations are another way of receiving academic credit for volunteer work. Although interns usually receive a stipend, it usually is barely enough to live on, and some internships are purely volunteer, except for earning school credit. A few are listed here, as well as resources for finding more.

# Service Learning Organizations

## Bentley College

Bentley Service Learning Project (BSLP)
c/o Edward Zlotkowski, Program Director
Morison 324
Bentley College
175 Forest St.
Waltham, MA 02154-4706

Bentley, a business school near Boston, has introduced a comprehensive range of service activities into the curriculum, with an ultimate goal of producing service-literate business professionals, capable of providing community as well as corporate leadership. Students volunteer for field experience in various classes throughout the curriculum. Some serve in shelters and soup kitchens or tutor children; others use their business expertise to help nonprofit organizations—by setting up data bases for groups aiding the needy, helping to make a shelter's financial operations more cost-effective, or implementing projects that bring together the skills of an interdisciplinary business team. Over 800 students a year participate in BSLP, about one-quarter of the undergraduate student body, and 20 percent of the faculty is involved as well. The program director says that it is impossible to go through the four-year program without being offered a strong incentive to do service work. When students are given a choice between library research and hands-on field research, most students choose the hands-on work. For information, contact the program director.

**Burr & Burton Seminary (page 29)**

## Magic Me (MM)

808 N. Charles St.
Baltimore, MD 21201
1-301-837-0900
Contact: Program Director

MM's goal is to motivate and educate at-risk youth by involving them in long-term service to elderly, mentally retarded, and handicapped people. Working with schools and facilities in twenty-five cities across the United States and Europe, MM matches volunteer students (sixth- to eighth-graders) with partners whom they visit every week. Both partners are encouraged to become intimately involved with each other as they spend time together dancing, reading, and keeping fit, and taking short trips. MM's headquarters in Baltimore will provide comprehensive training and technical assistance for those interested in starting MM programs. Contact the program director for the location of an MM project in your area or for information about founding one.

## New York City Department for the Aging (NYCDFTA)

Intergenerational Work/Study Program (IWSP)
2 Lafayette St., 9th Fl.
New York, NY 10007-1392
1-212-577-1247
Contact: Director, Intergenerational Program

IWSP, administered by NYCDFTA and the New York City Public Schools, is a dropout prevention program that brings at-risk students into nursing homes and other senior centers to work with and for the elderly. This arrangement benefits students and seniors, and members of both groups are volunteers. The student volunteers, who have agreed to remain in school, also commit to working a certain number of hours a week at their senior citizen worksites and then keeping journals about the experience. In return, students re-

## FEATURED ORGANIZATION: SERVERMONT

P.O. Box 516
Chester, VT 05143
Contact: Cynthia Parsons, Coordinator

SerVermont has been a Vermont state initiative since 1986, a volunteer service learning program for grades K–12 stimulating participation by 90 percent of Vermont's public schools. SerVermont, a privately funded organization, is the brainchild of Cynthia Parsons, an educator and former education editor of *The Christian Science Monitor*. Parsons believes that if school-based community service is part of every young person's total learning experience, participation in volunteer service is more likely to continue after school is over. Not a structured program in the ordinary sense, SerVermont provides workshops, liaison with local nonprofit agencies, and project ideas, and it offers $200 mini-grants to defray the costs of community service projects integrated with the curriculum. SerVermont is concerned that students provide direct, person-to-person services in projects that the community needs and actively approves. For information about SerVermont and about similar programs in other states, write to Cynthia Parsons.

*Service Learning from A to Z* by Cynthia Parsons is for children, adolescents, teachers, and people who manage volunteers. It's a stimulating, directly written book of ideas about service learning and citizenship, practical recommendations for projects, and suggestions for integrating projects into the curriculum. For a copy, send $5 plus $1.25 postage to the SerVermont address.

ceive academic credits and learn employment skills. Senior volunteers act as mentors, becoming informal grandparents to the kids and taking an interest in their lives and welfare.

The program may be administrated by school systems, social service agencies for the aging, and government departments. IWSP offers technical assistance and training for groups interested in replicating the program, which is described in detail in *Between Friends: Creating Intergenerational Work/Study Programs for Youth at Risk and Older Adults*, a free book that you can order from NYCDFTA.

### The Partnership for Service-Learning (PSL)

815 Second Ave., Suite 315
New York, NY 10017
1-212-986-0989
Contact: Howard A. Berry, Co-Director

PSL is a consortium of colleges, universities, service agencies, and related organizations united in the belief that classroom learning combined with volunteerism is a more powerful experience than just volunteering. As part of its mission to foster service learning in higher education, PSL operates off-campus programs lasting a summer, a semester, a year, or for the January intersession. Programs are currently being offered in Ecuador, England, France, India, Jamaica, Liberia, Mexico, the Philippines, Scotland, and South Dakota, and service opportunities include teaching, health care, and development projects. Students from over 140 American colleges and universities receive academic credit for PSL programs. Write to the New York office for more information.

### Thomas Jefferson Forum (TJF)

131 State St., Suite 628
Boston, MA 02109
1-617-523-6699, FAX 1-617-723-4918
Contact: Assistant Director

TJF is a nonprofit organization that engages youth in high school–based community service. The Forum assists faculty coordinators at participating schools with technical assistance, financial support for a three-year period, and workshops. Much of this help is in recruitment, placement, supervision, and assessment of student volunteers, and in working with students to develop leadership skills through service. Each volunteer program for which the Forum provides assistance is individual to the school and its community. Part of the organization's operating philosophy is that students must be assigned to agencies and tasks in direct service projects that attempt to meet the greatest human needs, such as food, shelter, medicine, a clean environment, and special help for those who are physically and mentally challenged. The Forum also believes that to benefit from community service, students must have the opportunity to reflect on their service experience and to discuss it with others. There are forty-one Forum high schools and more than 2,200 students in Massachusetts working with diverse service organizations within their communities—children's hospitals, Big Brothers/Big Sisters (BB/BSA, page 164), town recreation departments, shelters, soup kitchens, the Museum of Science, Boston (MOS, page 96), public libraries, food banks, day-care centers, and many, many others. Once the volunteer program has been instituted, very often local organizations will come to the school volunteer coordinator asking for help with both long- and short-term projects. Students are not paid for their service, and although the Forum encourages schools to award credit and other incentives, the final decision is up to the school. For information about the Forum, contact the assistant director.

Accuracy in Media, Inc. (AIM, page 194)

Common Cause (CC, page 195)

# Other Student Organizations

Students create their own volunteer programs and operate them from within the schools with faculty advisers, or as part of off-campus activities. The school volunteer office is the place to start, then campus newspapers, bulletin boards, and word of mouth will keep you posted about organizations that spring up over a public issue, political groups, ethnic groups, and chapters of national organizations with strong youth components—such as National Association for the Advancement of Colored People (NAACP, page 165), environmental agencies, and religious groups.

Amigos de las Americas (AMIGOS, page 186)

### Campus Outreach Opportunity League (COOL)

386 McNeal Hall, University of Minnesota
St. Paul, MN 55108-1011
1-612-624-3018, FAX 1-612-624-1296

COOL's objective is to promote community service among college students, and it does so by providing resources, advice, and information that student leaders need to build effective community service programs on their campuses. There are more than 600 campuses in the COOL network working on a variety of community projects including literacy, tutoring and mentoring children, working for and with the needy and the elderly, combating racism, AIDS education, and the environment. COOL's national outreach pro-

*The Coordinator's Handbook of the Thomas Jefferson Forum: A Comprehensive Guide for Developing High School-Based Community Service Programs* is a guide and workbook and an indispensable tool for anyone coordinating the student volunteer services in a school. It's bursting with ideas and commentary that are extremely helpful in setting up programs and then following through on them, with nineteen chapters on getting started, developing plans, setting goals, getting school support, recruiting students, the specifics of program administration, through to assessment of the program and a discussion of a comprehensive model of service learning. Although the book is intended for high school faculty coordinators working with the Thomas Jefferson Forum (page 222), it is a valuable resource for any school volunteer coordinator and would be helpful in developing other volunteer programs. Send $10 to TJF.

gram, Into the Streets, matches thousands of student volunteers with community agencies such as Volunteers in Service to America (VISTA, page 88), Florida's Office for Campus Volunteers, American Red Cross (ARC, page 129), and ASPIRA (page 79), where they work for one day. After consideration of the day's experience, students are invited to make a one-year commitment to the agencies with which they worked. In cooperation with Youth Service America, COOL promotes National Youth Service Day (NYSD), on which a number of youth organizations work together. COOL's programs are run completely by students and recent graduates. If you are interested in working with COOL, contact the national office for the name and address of your regional COOL contact.

**Constitutional Rights Foundation (CRF, page 150)**

## National Student Campaign Against Hunger and Homelessness (NSCAHH)

29 Temple Pl.
Boston, MA 02111
1-617-292-4823
Contact: Directors

NSCAHH, a project of the Public Interest Research Groups (PIRGs, page 197), is a network of college and high school students, educators and community leaders working to fight hunger and homelessness in the United States and worldwide. NSCAHH works with over 450 schools in forty states across the country, providing resources, programming ideas, and advice to students, faculty, and administrators. Major NSCAHH programs are:

- National Hunger and Homelessness Week, a series of coordinated community-wide events held the week before Thanksgiving.
- The Hunger Clean-up, a national one-day workathon in April to complete specific neighborhood projects.
- Food Salvage Program, which, in cooperation with Share Our Strength (SOS, page 175) and other similar organizations, provides students with the tools and resources needed to carry out food salvaging programs in their communities.

Each affiliate also has ongoing projects that help meet local needs. Members receive "Students Making a Difference," a quarterly newsletter with current news and listings for jobs, internships, and volunteer opportunities. For information about volunteering, call your school affiliate. If you'd like to start an affiliate, get in touch with the Boston office.

### Student Community Service Program (SCSP)

ACTION
1100 Vermont Ave., NW
Washington, DC 20525
1-202-606-4845

SCSP is an ACTION (page 35) program that provides grant money for community projects that help educate students as they serve low-income people—the homeless, the illiterate, and others in need of various social services. There are over 24,000 SCSP volunteers participating in Head Start (page 99), juvenile diversion programs, drug abuse prevention and education, shelters, soup kitchens, and many other programs. College students who want to become part of SCSP can contact their school volunteer coordinators to see if there is an ongoing project. Nonprofit agencies interested in working with SCSP can call their regional ACTION offices.

**Accuracy in Media, Inc. (AIM, page 194)**

**Common Cause (CC, page 195)**

**Student Conservation Association (SCA, page 106)**

**Students Against Drunk Driving (SADD, page 230)**

**U.S. Department of Agriculture, Forest Service, Human Resource Programs (page 100)**

# Resources

## SERVICE LEARNING ORGANIZATIONS

*The Coordinator's Handbook of the Thomas Jefferson Forum: A Comprehensive Guide for Developing High School–Based Community Service Programs,* a publication of the Thomas Jefferson Forum. (See box, page 223.)

*Service Learning from A to Z,* by Cynthia Parsons. Chester, VT: Vermont Schoolhouse Press, 1991. (See box, page 221.)

## INTERNSHIPS

*New Careers: A Directory of Jobs and Internships in Technology and Science,* published by Student Pugwash, is a practical and straightforward listing of jobs and internships at nonprofit organizations that specialize in science and technology, including the fields of medicine, the environment, the social sciences, human rights, and the abolition of war. Each organization has been chosen for its ability to provide the intern with "opportunities and experience in the exploration of the ethical and social implications of science and technology," and each organization is evaluated for the percentage of time spent on those two issues and the percentage devoted to the social implications of science. Information includes: mission, programs, staff, interns, atmosphere, stipends, how to apply, and other locations. Applicants' qualifications run the gamut from a good sense of humor, an eagerness to learn, and a willingness to do a variety of tasks and work hard, to computer literacy, good communications skills, maturity, intellectual honesty, self-discipline, and other thought-provoking capabilities. To order a copy, send a check for $20 to Student Pugwash USA, 1638 R St., NW, #32, Washington, DC 20009, 1-202-328-6555, FAX 1-202-797-4664.

*Time Out: Taking a Break from School, to Travel, Work, and Study in the U.S. and Abroad,* by Robert Gilpin with Caroline Fitzgibbons. New York: Fireside Books, 1991. This is a useful and stimulating guide for high school students and college freshmen seeking a pause from their mainstream education to get new perspectives or to learn another language or a new skill. The opening section has questionnaires for students and their parents and practical advice on how to decide on what it is you want to do on your break and then how to follow through. The heart of the book is the description of over 350 organizations, arranged by type of program: academic programs, work opportunities, internships, apprenticeships, travel/study, environmental programs, language study, cultural exchange and community service programs, and work camps. Each listing has information about costs, financial aid, stipends, housing, number of participants, and application procedures. The entries are wide ranging and written to stimulate the imagination; they give a strong feeling for each organization's aims, methods, and requirements. $12.

# Substance Abuse

Despite millions of words, thousands of programs, and innumerable volunteer hours devoted to its prevention, substance abuse is still with us. Education is one of the most effective countermeasures, especially if the education begins early. Some of the organizations discussed here either have strong educational programs or can refer you to agencies that do. Members of the national drug prevention organizations receive newsletters and bulletins, which keep the membership up to date about current research findings and successful programs. Local drug prevention programs are run by Scout organizations, churches, schools, service groups, and others concerned about substance abuse. Support groups and counseling and rehabilitation services for recovering abusers, if not listed in the phone book, can be reached through one of the 800 hotline numbers.

## Al-Anon * Alateen

P.O. Box 862, Midtown Station
New York, NY 10018-0862
1-212-302-7240, FAX 1-212-869-3757
For meeting information: 1-800-245-4656 (New York), 1-800-344-2666 (USA), 1-800-443-4525 (Canada): For free literature: 1-800-356-9996

Al-Anon Family Groups are a fellowship of families and friends of alcoholics and provides information and help for the family whether the alcoholic seeks help or not. There are currently 32,000 groups in 104 different countries where members share their experiences, strength, and hope in order to solve their common problems. Although Al-Anon, which includes Alateen for younger members, is an outgrowth of Alcoholics Anonymous (AA, page 226), it is a completely separate organization. Anyone who feels his or her life has been affected by close contact with a problem drinker is eligible for membership. For information, look for Al-Anon in your telephone directory or call one of the 800 numbers.

## Alcoholics Anonymous, Inc. (AA)

General Service Office
475 Riverside Dr.
New York, NY 10115
1-212-870-3400, FAX 1-212-870-3003

AA is perhaps the most famous support group in the world, with more than 94,000 local groups and activities in 131 countries. AA's program is based on the well-known Twelve Steps, which help members lead lives of total abstinence. The men and women who attend AA meetings describe their experiences with alcoholism and the changes in their lives since coming to AA. By sharing with others, members work at solving their own problems and assist other recovering alcoholics. Some meetings are open to alcoholics and nonalcoholics (open meetings); others are held for alcoholics or prospective members (closed meetings). AA's sole concern is to help each member achieve and maintain sobriety. There are no dues or membership fees, and the only requirement for membership is the desire to stop drinking. For more information about the nearest AA chapters, check your local telephone directory. For a catalog of AA literature, write to Alcoholics Anonymous World Services, Inc., Box 459, Grand Central Station, New York, NY 10163.

## Chemical People Institute (CPI)

1 Allegheny Square, Suite 720
Pittsburgh, PA 15212
1-412-322-0900
Contact: Executive Director

CPI is a nonprofit organization dedicated to increasing community awareness, understanding, and action concerning alcohol and other drug problems. Among its goals are to promote and develop community-based volunteer task forces, which carry out local projects: sponsoring seminars and workshops, publishing community newsletters, reviewing school policies and curricula, and other activities. Task force membership is open to anyone in the community concerned with substance abuse and willing to spend some time educating the public about it. Task forces can have as few as three members, although most have more, and they very often work in cooperation with other community-based organizations with similar goals. CPI's "Community-Based Task Force Description and Training Manual," and "Teen Action Day" are detailed guides, the first to creating and training a task force, and the second to planning and carrying through a single event. Both publications would be useful for fledgling community groups.

## Institute on Black Chemical Abuse (IBCA)

2616 Nicollet Ave.
Minneapolis, MN 55408
1-612-871-7878
Contact: Volunteer Coordinator

IBCA is a local Minneapolis organization with services related to black substance abuse. Services include referral to local organizations, advocacy, community education, family counseling, adult aftercare management, and support groups, among others. IBCA also consults nationwide on program design, offers written materials about alcoholism and drug abuse among blacks, and maintains a Resource Center, which collects and disseminates, at very low cost, information on black chemical abuse. IBCA works with volunteers and student interns in its Minnesota office. For more information, write to IBCA and request "The Undergraduate Internship" and "Volunteer Program" materials.

## Mothers Against Drunk Driving (MADD)

511 E. Carpenter Frwy., Suite 700
Irving, TX 75062-8187
1-214-744-MADD (1-214-744-6233),
FAX 1-214-869-2206/2207
1-800-GET-MADD (1-800-438-6233)
Contact: Volunteer Administrator

MADD is a grassroots organization founded in 1980 by Candy Lightner, whose own daughter was killed by a drunk driver. MADD now has over 400 chapters whose mission is to stop drunk driving and to support its victims by giving them a voice. MADD's programs include:

- Victim Impact Panels (VIPs), at which MADD chapters or other victim groups select a panel of three or four victims to speak to groups of offenders about the drunk driving crashes in which they were injured or in which a loved one was killed. As with certain kinds of face-to-face victim-offender mediation (page 160), the victims are able to some extent to relieve their personal pain and at the same time help effect a change in the offenders. There are presently over 200 VIPs nationwide.

- Educating TV producers to curtail alcoholic beverage ads shown on programs watched by younger viewers.
- Sending Crisis Response Teams to the sites of serious crashes to offer training for immediate and long-term crisis counseling to community care givers helping survivors and victims' families.
- Holding a yearly candlelight vigil for the victims of drunk drivers.
- Advocacy for effective laws governing drunk drivers and for other aspects of effective criminal justice.

MADD is essentially a volunteer organization and offers opportunities for many kinds of work. Call your local chapter or the 800 number for more information.

## OSAP's National Clearinghouse for Alcohol and Drug Information (ONCADI)

P.O. Box 2345
Rockville, MD 20852-2345
FAX 1-301-468-6433
1-800-729-6686, TDD 1-800-487-4889

ONCADI is a service of the Office for Substance Abuse Prevention (OSAP), itself a division of the U. S. Department of Health and Human Services. ONCADI is the largest single source within the federal government for current information about alcohol and other drugs, answering thousands of telephone and mail inquiries each month. ONCADI also supports OSAP's Regional Alcohol and Drug Awareness Resource Network (RADAR), comprised of state agencies and other organizations that serve the special needs of individual communities.

ONCADI distributes more than 200 free educational, prevention, and research materials targeting community groups and volunteers, children, parents, teachers, minority populations, employers, and researchers. Many publications are bilingual (English and Spanish) and include brochures, monographs, posters, resource guides, and videotapes. The Drug-Free Community Series is of special interest to individuals and groups who want to make the best use of their talents and community resources. The series includes these bilingual publications: *Turning Awareness into Action* and *What Your Community Can Do About Drug Use in America* as well as posters and other materials.

ONCADI also publishes *Prevention Pipeline,* a bimonthly publication with current information about the field of drug prevention. For information and a catalog of publications, call either of the 800 numbers.

## National Council on Alcoholism and Drug Dependence, Inc. (NCADD)

12 W. 21st St.
New York, NY 10010
1-800-622-2255, 1-212-206-6770

NCADD is a volunteer organization dedicated to educating Americans to understand that alcoholism and drug abuse are treatable, preventable diseases. This message is delivered by 185 NCADD affiliates in thirty-six states and Washington, DC. Each affiliate responds to its community's particular needs through a variety of programs: instruction about alcohol- and other drug-related birth defects; awareness and information campaigns; conferences and workshops; drinking and driving education; media advocacy; work with special populations—the elderly, offenders, school-age children; treatment programs; and education for young children. NCADD affiliates are heavily staffed with volunteers, who perform a myriad of services, depending on the programs and the populations they serve. NCADD also provides a dependence helpline (the 800 number), which is publicized by public service announcements on television and radio and in newspaper spots. If you are interested in volunteering, contact the 800 number for an affiliate near you.

*Citizen's Alcohol and Other Drug Prevention Directory: Resources for Getting Involved,* published by ONCADI, (see page 228) is the first place to look if you want to get involved with a substance abuse program. It is a directory of over 3,000 federal, national, and state agencies dealing with drug abuse and includes a description of each organization, its audience and services, and ways for people to get involved. The book is an essential resource and can be ordered at no cost by calling one of ONCADI's 800 numbers.

## National Families in Action (NFIA)

2296 Henderson Mill Rd., Suite 300
Atlanta, GA 30345
1-404-934-6364, FAX 1-404-934-7137

NFIA is a national organization dedicated to preventing substance abuse among families and in communities. NFIA groups are composed of local concerned citizens who form committees and task forces to educate the community and to carry out programs that address the problem of drugs. Very often the people who establish an NFIA chapter are parents who have discovered their own children's drug use. NFIA's National Drug Information Center also serves as a clearinghouse for information about drug abuse. *Drug Abuse Update,* NFIA's quarterly digest, contains abstracts of current articles about the issues. Write to NFIA for information about joining a group in your local area or creating a new one.

## National Federation of State High School Associations

TARGET Program (TARGET)
11724 Plaza Circle, P.O. Box 20626
Kansas City, MO 64195
1-800-366-6667, 1-816-464-5400
Contact: Executive Director, TARGET

The National Federation, the service and administrative organization of high school athletics and activities associations, is committed to interscholastic sports and activities. The organization's membership includes 500,000 high school coaches and another 500,000 officials and judges. TARGET is a National Federation program helping schools prevent the use of tobacco, alcohol, and other drugs by young people. Among the services provided to schools free or at very low cost are:

- Target Leadership Training (TLT) workshops for volunteer school and community leaders nationwide. Volunteers receive a four-and-a-half-day training session, which prepares them to return to their communities and establish and implement local school programs.
- TARGET's National Resource Center (the 800 number), a national clearinghouse for educational and prevention materials related to substance abuse.

For more information about TARGET services, contact the Kansas City office.

## Partnership for a Drug-Free America

666 Third Ave.
New York, NY 10017
1-212-922-1560, FAX 1-212-922-1750
Contact: External Affairs Director

Partnership is a nonprofit, private-sector coalition of volunteers from the advertising, public relations, production, research, media, and entertainment industries. Their mission, accomplished almost entirely by volunteers, is to research, develop, create, and distribute antidrug messages targeted at specific segments of the population. The media—the three major networks, cable TV networks, newspapers, radio, magazines—and many other participants contribute air time or space for Partnership's messages. For information about Partnership and what you or your business can volunteer to do, get in touch with the external affairs director.

## Remove Intoxicated Drivers (RID)

P.O. Box 520
Schenectady, NY 12301
1-518-372-0034
Contact: Doris Aiken, Founder

RID is a national organization working to prevent drunk driving through the group activities of concerned citizens working at the local level with the criminal justice system and officials and with all groups that share its goals. RID, which accepts no funds from the alcohol industry, is deterrence-oriented and supports programs that will prevent even the first occurrence of drunk driving. There are over 150 autonomous RID chapters and coordinators in forty states, all completely operated by volunteers who work in these areas: victim support, court monitoring and research, publicity, writing, office work, speakers bureau, legislative policies, fund-raising, and more. For information about volunteering or starting a RID chapter in your own community, write to the Schenectady office.

## Students Against Drunk Driving (SADD)

P.O. Box 800
Marlboro, MA 01752
1-508-481-3568, FAX 1-508-481-5759
Contact: Executive Director

SADD began as a high school organization in 1981, and now has programs for middle schools, high schools, and colleges. Among SADD's goals are to prevent underage drinking and drunk driving, to save lives, and to eliminate the illegal use of drugs. SADD chapters also organize peer counseling programs and conduct community awareness projects. If you are interested in starting a chapter in your school, write to the executive director and ask for SADD's literature, including "How to Start Your SADD Chapter and New Ideas for Existing SADD Chapters," a useful manual.

# Resource

*Citizen's Alcohol and Other Drug Prevention Directory: Resources for Getting Involved,* a publication of National Clearinghouse for Alcohol and Drug Information (ONCADI). (See box, page 229.)

# Veterans' Groups

Veterans' groups are exceptionally active around the country, assisting not only their own members, but working on behalf of the entire community, often in cooperation with other local groups and charities. Although each group's membership generally consists of military veterans and their spouses, many organizations, particularly the Department of Veterans Affairs (VA, page 232) and disabled veterans' groups, rely on individuals and group volunteers to fill a wide range of positions. Check the telephone directory for these and other veterans' agencies.

## American Legion

National Headquarters
P.O. Box 1055, 700 N. Pennsylvania St.
Indianapolis, IN 46206
1-317-635-8411

There are about 16,000 American Legion posts nationwide and in some foreign countries, with a membership of over 3.1 million veterans. Among the Legion's national programs are: working with the Department of Veterans Affairs (VA, page 232) for the benefit of disabled veterans and their families; the National Americanism Commission, which sponsors youth programs and baseball teams, provides educational scholarships, and donates millions of hours of community service yearly; and money contributions to other nonprofit organizations. The Legion's community service involves cooperating with other local agencies for the welfare of the entire community. For more information about Legion activities in your area, check the phone directory for the nearest post.

## Blinded Veterans Association (BVA)

477 H St., NW
Washington, DC 20001-2964
1-202-371-8880
Contact: R.G. Fazakerley, National Director of Field Service Programs

BVA, through its thirty-five regional groups and Field Service Program, is determined to provide all visually impaired veterans with information they need to take charge of and improve their lives. BVA's Field Service Representatives, themselves blinded veterans, search out and target blinded veterans and their families who need services. Field Service Representatives make referrals to various services—rehabilitation, training and job opportunities, and benefits from the Department of Veterans Affairs (VA, page 232)—and state and local agencies. There are eight BVA volunteer offices nationwide assisting regional groups. For information about volunteering, or if you know of any blinded veterans who are not receiving services, write to the Washington office for information. BVA also has a volunteer program for blind BVA members, who can be trained and certified as Volunteer Regional Group Service Officers.

## Department of Veterans Affairs (VA)

Voluntary Service
810 Vermont Ave. (161A)
Washington, DC 20420
1-202-535-7377
Contact: Director of Volunteers

Nearly 88,000 volunteers help support the VA's medical care system, performing over 250 different types of tasks, including home visits to discharged outpatients, reading to and writing for patients, office administration, and organizing and running recreational committees. VA Voluntary Service sets policy with the help of a National Advisory Committee composed of fifty-eight groups representing the broad spectrum of the community, from civic agencies to the American Red Cross (ARC, page 129) to Disabled American Veterans (DAV, page 232) and many others. The chief of voluntary service at each facility recruits, orients, and trains volunteers from the community, coordinating VA activities with those of other local groups. For instance, preschoolers from a day-care center may "adopt grandparents" at VA nursing-home care units, teenagers learn while they work at various jobs at VA medical centers, Scouts place American flags at grave sites for special observances, and garden club members plant flower beds and shrubs at national cemeteries. For information about volunteering, call your local VA medical facility and ask for the volunteer office. If you are a member of a local health or service organization, find out if your group is already working with the VA and what you can do to help. The VA has four sports clinics for disabled veterans (see the VA's National Winter Sports Clinic, page 215); for information about the clinics and other VA national sports and recreation events, contact the sports and recreation director at the VA.

## Disabled American Veterans (DAV)

807 Maine Ave., SW
Washington, DC 20024
1-202-554-3501

DAV is a nonprofit organization whose more than 1 million members are veterans disabled in wartime or under conditions similar to war. More than 95 percent of DAV's professional and management staff is made up of disabled Vietnam veterans. Among DAV services (to members and nonmember veterans) are counseling to help vets get all their entitlements, disaster relief funds for disabled vets, advocacy, and member service projects, which are carried out by member volunteers. Some of these projects include:

- Assisting the professional counselors in DAV's sixty-seven offices across the country.
- Active involvement in local communities, helping care for patients in VA hospitals, state veterans' homes, and other veterans' medical facilities.
- Working as volunteer drivers, transporting veterans to hospitals and clinics nationwide.
- An Older Veterans Assistance Program, helping older vets with everyday problems.
- A Sports for the Disabled program run in cooperation with the Department of Veterans Affairs (VA, page 232).

If you are interested in becoming a member of DAV, call or write to the Washington office.

## Navy–Marine Corps Relief Society (NMCRS)

801 N. Randolph St., Room 1228
Arlington, VA 22203-1978
1-703-696-4904

NMCRS is a private nonprofit organization, which nevertheless maintains close ties with the U.S. Navy and Marine Corps. NMCRS field activities are located on over 260 navy and marine installations ashore and afloat throughout the world. An average of 3,600 volunteers annually

—many of them families of servicemen and -women, and some of them retired naval personnel—operate NMCRS programs. These include financial assistance for service persons and their families, budget counseling, a visiting nurse program, layettes for newborn babies, thrift shops, helping out in children's waiting rooms, and an educational program. Volunteers are needed for office work, including computer data base input; as interviewers, publicists, thrift shop workers, counselors; and to put together layettes. For information, check your local phone book for the nearest naval base, or write to the Arlington office for the activity nearest you.

### Paralyzed Veterans of America (PVA, page 212)

## Veterans of Foreign Wars of the United States (VFW)

Broadway at 34th St.
Kansas City, MO 64111
1-816-756-3390

VFW was founded in 1899 by veterans of the Spanish-American War. There are now over 10,600 VFW posts and a membership of over 2 million that encompasses veterans from WWI through Operation Desert Storm in 1991. VFW works for the rights of America's 27 million veterans and their families by providing them with assistance in getting their entitlements, lobbying for legislation beneficial to veterans, and monitoring laws involving veteran employment. Youth and community activities are among VFW's major priorities, and many programs are specially designed to benefit a particular area or town. All of the programs are carried out by volunteers from both VFW and its Ladies Auxiliary, which presently numbers more than 765,000. For more information about the VFW's many volunteer opportunities, call your local VFW post.

## Vietnam Veterans of America, Inc. (VVA)

1224 M St., NW
Washington, DC 20005-5183
1-202-628-2700, FAX 1-202-628-5880

VVA is the only congressionally chartered veterans service organization devoted exclusively to improving the lives of those who served in the Vietnam War. Among its national initiatives, VVA serves as an advocate for the rights of all veterans to quality health care service; promotes legislation for continuing VA counseling services, treatment of post-traumatic stress disorder, and services for veterans exposed to Agent Orange and other toxic substances. At the local community level, each of VVA's 500 chapters and thirty-seven state councils has initiated its own volunteer service programs to assist veterans and other needy members of their communities, including support for homeless shelters, substance abuse education projects, crime prevention campaigns, sponsorship of youth sports, Scout troops, and Big Brothers/Big Sisters (BB/BSA, page 164). VVA members are primarily Vietnam veterans. Check your phone directory for the chapter nearest you, or write to the Washington office.

PART THREE

# Starting A Volunteer Organization

Who wants it? Who needs it? Who's going to do it when you leave? Those are the first questions asked and answered before any project is undertaken at Dwight Hall, the Yale University student-run volunteer office, and they're exactly what you should ask yourself before you start a volunteer group. If the answers you get reinforce your intention to form a group, and you don't know how to go about it, self-help is on the way.

Neighborhood associations are often a direct response to unmet local needs for housing, health care, food, physical security, day care, and education. Depending on a group's purposes and resources, there are advantages to becoming a chapter or an affiliate of an existing organization, one that has already worked out successful programs to meet basic needs and also provides technical assistance in setting up, staffing, and running the chapter.

But if your group is small, local in scope, singular in focus, activist, or idiosyncratic in any way, you might want to keep its structure loose. Even so, guidelines are useful. The National Volunteer Center (NVC, page 37) publications catalog offers a range of books on every phase of starting and running an organization: programs, volunteer recruitment, volunteer management, workshops, meetings, editing newsletters, grassroots fund-raising, and board membership. Volunteer centers and United Way (UWA, page 38) chapters provide advice and some technical assistance for groups that intend to provide social services.

The publications below offer suggestions and instructions for setting up organizations and programs in specialized fields, but the advice they give covers basic procedures to follow for any nascent group. Check the reference section at libraries and bookstores for other titles.

*Becoming an Activist: PETA's Guide to Animal Rights Organizing,* by Sue Brebner and Debbi Baer (page 48), is required reading for anyone thinking about organizing a group. Even though some of the examples are specific to animal rights, most of the book is practical advice and detailed instructions, which include choosing an issue, starting a group, speaking in public, lobbying, researching, campaigning, fund-raising, and incorporating and applying for tax-exempt status. $5.

## EDUCATION

New York City Department of Aging, Intergenerational Work/Study Program (NYCDAIWSP, page 220). *Between Friends: Creating Intergenerational Work/Study Programs for Youth at Risk and Older Adults* is meant primarily for volunteer professionals who set up such programs.

## THE ENVIRONMENT

American Free Tree Program (AFTP, page 109). "How to Plan a Free Tree-Planting Program in Your Area" is a short but excellent guide to organizing a local group with a single purpose.

*Call to Action: Handbook for Ecology, Peace and Justice,* edited by Brad Erickson. San Francisco: Sierra Club Books, 1990. This is a practical resource for committed activists and concerned individuals—anyone interested in working to preserve and improve the earth. Activism and the changes most effectively created by group action are the common threads running through the book, which appropriately begins with a primer on grassroots organizing that can be used by any small group. The atmosphere, human oppression, the colonial legacy, economic justice, healing the earth, making war obsolete, media and education, poison, and power are Erickson's concerns. Each section features articles by naturalists, civil libertarians, and scientists; ideas for individual and group activities that can impact the problem; and lists of organizations and publications. A glossary of tools, terms, and tactics related to activism make the book even more useful.

## GARDENING

Minnesota State Horticultural Society, Minnesota Green (MSHS/MG, page 122). "Creating Community Gardens" has applications for creating other local action groups.

## LEGAL/DISASTER

State Bar of California, Office of Legal Services (SBC, page 94). "Disaster Legal Services: A Guide for the Private Bar," a guide to developing legal disaster services, written after the 1989 San Francisco earthquake, can be used by other areas vulnerable to natural disasters.

## STUDENTS

Thomas Jefferson Forum (TJF, page 222). *The Coordinator's Handbook of the Thomas Jefferson Forum: A Comprehensive Guide for Developing High School–Based Community Service Programs* is exactly what it says, and very useful, too, for anyone working with groups of high school–aged kids. Lots of good ideas.

## SUPPORT

National Self-Help Clearinghouse (NSHC, page 38). "How to Organize a Self-Help Group" is a practical guide to setting up support groups. American Self-Help Clearinghouse (ASHC, page 38). *The Self-Help Sourcebook* is another useful guide.

# Funding

Fund-raising is the ability to persuade individuals, businesses, foundations, other charitable agencies, and the government to give away money. It is an art and a skill practiced by paid development directors in nonprofit organizations and by hundreds of thousands of volunteers, from board members who contribute money themselves to individuals who are happy to donate time and energy to raising funds for their favorite causes and organizations.

There's no question that fund-raisers are people of the most varied personalities, talents, and experience (including no prior experience). Fund-raising can be as straightforward as a bake sale for the volunteer fire department or as elaborate as a major campaign that involves long-term planning and coordination of special events, direct mail, writing grant proposals, and other money-raising strategies. However basic or complex the method, anyone soliciting money directly or indirectly for a nonprofit organization must be well informed about the group, its philosophy, its programs, and its achievements.

An affiliate of a large organization generally raises money locally using professional and/or volunteer fund-raisers who follow procedures that have been established by the parent organization and adapted to community circumstances.

If your group is unaffiliated and you need ideas and scenarios for raising money, ask the United Way (UWA, page 38) for suggestions and literature, or see the National Volunteer Center (NVC, page 37) catalog, which lists almost ten titles related to raising money, beginning with *101 Ways to Raise Resources,* by Steve McCurley and Sue Vineyard, $8, and "How to Ask for Money without Fainting!" by Susan M. Scribner, $10. For serious fund-raising, contact the Foundation Center (below).

## FEATURED ORGANIZATION: FOUNDATION CENTER

79 Fifth Ave.
New York, NY 10003
1-212-620-4230

For an individual or group seeking information about any aspect of foundation or corporate philanthropy, the Foundation Center (TFC) is Mecca. An indepenent national service organization, the Center has reference collections in New York, Washington, DC, Cleveland, and San Francisco, each offering the public a wide variety of free services and comprehensive information on foundations and grants. About 100 Foundation Center cooperating affiliates nationwide also provide free public access to a core collection of Foundation Center directories and other reference publications, and they provide funding-research guidance or other fund-related technical assistance in their communities or regions. Two data bases with extensively detailed information about corporate and community foundations and the grants they have awarded are accessible by computer. A booklet written for novice grant seekers, "The Foundation Center's User-Friendly Guide," $9.95, answers the most commonly asked questions about fund-raising. Call or write to the Center for information and ask for a list of the cooperating collections network and the publications catalog.

# Regional ACTION Offices/ Index of Directories

## REGIONAL ACTION OFFICES

**REGION I**
(CT,ME,MA,NH,RI,VT)
ACTION
10 Causeway St., Room 473
Boston, MA 02222-1039
1-617-565-7000

**REGION II**
(NJ,NY,PR,VI)
ACTION
6 World Trade Center, Room 758
New York, NY 10048-0206
1-212-466-3481

**REGION III**
(DE,DC,KY,MD,OH,PA,VA,WV)
ACTION
U.S. Customs House, Room 108
2nd and Chestnut Sts.
Philadelphia, PA 19106-2912
1-215-597-9972

**REGION IV**
(AL,FL,GA,MS,NC,SC,TN)
ACTION
101 Marietta St., N.W., Room 1003
Atlanta, GA 30323-2301
1-404-841-2860

**REGION V**
(IL,IN,IA,MI,MN,WI)
ACTION
175 West Jackson Blvd., Suite 1207
Chicago, IL 60604-2702
1-312-353-5107

**REGION VI**
(AR,KS,LA,MO,NM,OK,TX)
ACTION
Federal Building, Room 6B11
1100 Commerce St.
Dallas, TX 75242-0696
1-214-767-9494

**REGION VIII**
(CO,MT,NE,ND,SD,UT,WY)
ACTION
Executive Tower Building, Suite 2930
1405 Curtis St.
Denver, CO 80202-2349
1-303-844-2671

**REGION IX**
(AZ,CA,HI,NV)
ACTION
211 Main St., Room 530
San Francisco, CA 94105
1-415-744-3013

**REGION X**
(AK,ID,OR,WA)
ACTION
Federal Office Building
Suite 3190
915 Second Ave.
Seattle, WA 98174-1103
1-206-553-4520

## INDEX OF DIRECTORIES

### Clearinghouses and Umbrella Groups



### Volunteering for the Arts



### Working with and for Children



### The Environment



### Disaster Relief



### Health



### Pro Bono Legal Services



### Working with and for Minorities



### Working with Offenders



### Overseas Service



### Public Affairs

## Religious Organizations



## Sports



## Student Volunteers



## Substance Abuse

# National Volunteer Centers

## ALABAMA

United Way Volunteer Center
407 Noble Street, Suite 504
P.O. Box 1122
Anniston, AL 36202
1-205-236-8229
Contact: Administrative Coordinator

United Way Volunteer Center
3600 8th Avenue South, Suite 504
Birmingham, AL 35222
1-205-251-5131, FAX: 1-205-323-8730
Contact: Volunteer Coordinator

The Volunteer Center of Morgan County
303 Cain Street N.E., Suite D
P.O. Box 986
Decatur, AL 35602-0986
1-205-355-8628, 1-205-351-2501
Contact: Executive Director

Volunteer Action of the Eastern Shore
150 South Greeno Road, Suite P
P.O. Box 61
Fairhope, AL 36533
1-205-928-0509
Contact: Executive Director

Volunteer Center of Huntsville/Madison Counties
1101 Washington St.
Huntsville, AL 35801
1-205-539-7797
Contact: Executive Director

Volunteer Mobile, Inc.
2504 Dauphin Street, Suite K
Mobile, AL 36606
1-205-479-0631
Contact: Executive Director

VAC/Information & Referral, Inc.
2125 East South Blvd.
P.O. Box 11044
Montgomery, AL 36111-0044
1-205-284-0006, FAX: 1-205-281-9814
Contact: Executive Director

## ALASKA

UW of Anchorage/Volunteer Center
341 West Tudor Road, Suite 106
Anchorage, AK 99503-6638
1-907-562-4483, FAX: 1-907-563-0020
Contact: Director of Community Relations

Voluntary Action Center of UW
P.O. Box 74396
Fairbanks, AK 99707
1-907-452-7000, FAX: 1-907-452-7270
Contact: Director

## ARIZONA

Volunteer Center of Maricopa County
1515 E. Osborn
Phoenix, AZ 85014
1-602-263-9736
Contact: Executive Director

Volunteer Center of Yavapai County
107 N. Cortez, Room 208
Prescott, AZ 86301
1-602-776-9908
Contact: Executive Director

Volunteer Center
877 S. Alvernon Way
Tucson, AZ 85711
1-602-327-6207
Contact: Executive Director

## ARKANSAS

Voluntary Action Center
222 Van Buren
Camden, AR 71701
1-501-836-8166
Contact: Coordinator

Beautification Commission
P.O. Box 700
Hot Springs, AR 71902
1-501-321-6870, FAX: 1-501-321-6832
Contact: Director

United Way VAC
P.O. Box 3257
Little Rock, AR 72203
1-501-376-4567
Contact: Vice President, Volunteer Services

## CALIFORNIA

Volunteer Center of Kern County
601 Chester Avenue
Bakersfield, CA 93301
1-805-327-9346
Contact: Interim Director

Community Action Volunteers in Education
W. 2nd & Cherry Streets
Chico, CA 95929-0750
1-916-898-5817
Contact: Executive Director

Volunteer Center of Contra Costa County
1070 Concord Avenue, Suite 100
Concord, CA 94520
1-415-246-1050, FAX: 1-415-246-1064
Contact: Executive Director

The Volunteer Bureau of Fresno County, Inc.
2140 Merced Street, Suite 102
Fresno, CA 93721
1-209-237-3101
Contact: Executive Director

VAC of Nevada County
10139 Joerschke Drive
Grass Valley, CA 95945
1-916-272-5041
Contact: Executive Director

Volunteer Center Orange County West
16168 Beach Blvd., Suite 121
Huntington Beach, CA 92647
1-714-375-7751, FAX: 1-714-375-7757
Contact: Executive Director

La Mirada Volunteer Center
12900 Bluefield Avenue
La Mirada, CA 90638
1-213-943-0131
Contact: Executive Director

Volunteer Center of Los Angeles
2117 W. Temple Street, 3rd Floor
Los Angeles, CA 90026
1-213-484-2849, FAX: 1-213-484-8011
Contact: Executive Director

Volunteer Center Stanislaus
2125 Wylie Drive, #4
Modesto, CA 95355
1-209-524-1307
Contact: Executive Director

Monrovia Volunteer Center
119 W. Palm Avenue
Monrovia, CA 91016-2888
1-818-357-3797
Contact: Director

VC of the Monterey Peninsula
801 Lighthouse Avenue
Monterey, CA 93940
1-408-655-9234
Contact: Executive Director

VC of Napa County
1820 Jefferson St.
Napa, CA 94559
1-707-252-6222, FAX: 1-707-226-5179
Contact: Executive Director

VC of Alameda County
1212 Broadway, Suite 622
Oakland, CA 94612
1-415-893-6239, FAX: 1-415-893-5017
Contact: Executive Director

Volunteer Center of San Fernando Valley
8134 Van Nuys Blvd., #200
Panorama City, CA 91402
1-818-908-5066, FAX: 1-818-908-5147
Contact: Director

Volunteer Center of San Gabriel Valley
3301 Thorndale Road
Pasadena, CA 91107
1-818-792-6118
Contact: Executive Director

Volunteers Involved for Pasadena
234 Colorado Blvd., Suite 508
Pasadena, CA 91101
1-818-405-4073
Contact: Volunteer Coordinator

Valley Volunteer Center
333 Division Street
Pleasanton, CA 94566
1-415-462-3570, FAX: 1-415-462-0596
Contact: Director

VC of the Greater Pomona Valley
436 W. Fourth Street, Suite 201
Pomona, CA 91766
1-714-623-1284
Contact: Executive Director

VC of Riverside
2060 University Ave., #206
Riverside, CA 92507
1-714-686-4402
Contact: Executive Director

VC of Sacramento/Yolo Counties
8912 Volunteer Lane, #140
Sacramento, CA 95826-3221
1-916-368-3110, FAX: 1-916-368-3190
Contact: Executive Director

Volunteer Center of the Inland Empire
1669 N. "E" St.
San Bernardino, CA 92405
1-714-886-6737
Contact: President/CEO

VC-United Way of San Diego County
4699 Murphy Canyon Road
P.O. Box 23543
San Diego, CA 92123
1-619-492-2090, FAX: 1-619-492-2059
Contact: Vice President

VC of San Francisco
1160 Battery Street #400
San Francisco, CA 94111
1-415-982-8999, FAX: 1-415-399-9214
Contact: Executive Director

The Volunteer Exchange of Santa Clara County
1310 S. Bascom Ave., Suite B
San Jose, CA 95128-4502
1-408-286-1126, FAX: 1-408-286-1186
Contact: Executive Director

VC of San Mateo County
436 Peninsula Avenue
San Mateo, CA 94401
1-415-342-0801, FAX: 1-415-342-1399
Contact: Executive Director

VC of Marin County
70 Skyview Terrace
San Rafael, CA 94903
1-415-479-5660, FAX: 1-415-479-9722
Contact: Executive Director

VC of Greater Orange County
1000 E. Santa Ana Blvd., Suite 200
Santa Ana, CA 92701
1-714-953-5757, FAX: 1-714-834-0585
Contact: President/CEO

VC of Santa Cruz County
1110 Emeline Avenue
Santa Cruz, CA 95060
1-408-423-0554, FAX: 1-408-423-6267
Contact: Executive Director

VC of Sonoma County
1041 Fourth Street
Santa Rosa, CA 95404
1-707-573-3399
Contact: Executive Director

VAC of South Lake Tahoe
P.O. Box 878
South Lake Tahoe, CA 95705
1-916-541-2611
Contact: Executive Director

The VC of United Way
12 E. Park Street
P.O. Box 1585
Stockton, CA 95201
1-209-943-0870, FAX: 1-209-943-7312
Contact: Director

VC South Bay Harbor–Long Beach
1230 Cravens Avenue
Torrance, CA 90501
1-213-212-5009, FAX: 1-213-212-7201
Contact: Executive Director

Tulare Volunteer Bureau
115 South "M" Street
P.O. Box 1704
Tulare, CA 93274
1-209-688-0539
Contact: Director

Volunteer Center of Victor Valley
15561 Seventh Street
Victorville, CA 92392
1-619-245-8592
Contact: Coordinator

City of Visalia Volunteer Services Program
417 N. Locust
Visalia, CA 93291
1-209-738-3483, FAX: 1-209-627-9155
Contact: Director of Voluntary Services

### CANADA

The Vancouver Volunteer Centre
#301-3102 Main Street
Vancouver, BC, CAN V5T 3G7
1-604-875-9144, FAX: 1-604-875-0710
Contact: Executive Director

Moncton Volunteer Centre Du Benevolat
236 St. George Street, Suite 406
Moncton, NB, CAN E1C 1W1
1-506-857-8005
Contact: Executive Director

Saint John Volunteer Centre
P.O. Box 7091, Station A
Saint John, NB, CAN E2L 4S5
1-506-658-1555, FAX: 1-506-633-7724
Contact: Director

Volunteer Ontario
2 Dunbloor Road, Suite 203
Etibicoke, Ontario, CAN M9A 2E4
1-416-236-0588, FAX: 1-416-487-6150
Contact: Executive Director

Kingston Community Volunteer Bureau
23 Carlisle Street
Kingston, Ontario, CAN K7K 3X1
1-613-542-8512
Contact: Director

### COLORADO

Center for Information & Volunteer Action
400 E. Main Street
Aspen, CO 81611
1-303-925-7887, FAX: 1-303-925-3979
Contact: Executive Director

Volunteer Boulder County
3305 N. Broadway, Suite 1
Boulder, CO 80304
1-303-444-4904
Contact: Executive Director

Volunteer Center of Mile High United Way
2505 18th Street
Denver, CO 80211-3907
1-303-433-6060, FAX: 1-303-455-6462
Contact: Program Director, Community Services Division

Volunteer Resource Bureau of UW of Weld County
1001 9th Avenue
P.O. Box 1944
Greeley, CO 80631-1944
1-303-353-4300
Contact: Director

## CONNECTICUT

UW Volunteer Center of Eastern Fairfield
Bridgeport, CT 06604
1-203-334-5106
Contact: Director, Volunteer Development

The Volunteer Bureau of Greater Danbury
337 Main Street
Danbury, CT 06810
1-203-797-1154
Contact: Executive Director

VAC/United Way
United Way Building
99 Woodland Street
Hartford, CT 06105
1-203-247-2580, FAX: 1-203-247-7949
Contact: Vice President, Volunteer Services Div.

VAC of Greater New Haven, Inc.
70 Audubon Street
New Haven, CT 06510
1-203-785-1997, FAX: 1-203-498-0331
Contact: Executive Director

VAC of Mid-Fairfield
83 East Avenue
Norwalk, CT 06851
1-203-852-0850, FAX: 1-203-852-9357
Contact: Director

VAC of SE Connecticut
12 Case Street, Suite 302
Norwich, CT 06355
1-203-887-2519
Contact: Executive Director

The VC of SW Fairfield County
62 Palmer's Hill Road
Stamford, CT 06902
1-203-348-7714, FAX: 1-203-967-9507

## DISTRICT OF COLUMBIA

Washington Clearinghouse of the District of Columbia
1313 New York Avenue, NW #303
Washington, DC 20005
1-202-638-2664
Contact: Chief Executive Officer

## FLORIDA

Manatee County Volunteer Services, Inc.
1701 14th St., West #2, Suite 350
Bradenton, FL 34205
1-813-746-7117
Contact: Director

The VC of Volusia/Flagler Counties
3747 Volusia Avenue
Daytona Beach, FL 32124
1-904-253-0563 x254
Contact: Director, Volunteer Center

Volunteer Broward
1300 South Andrews Avenue
P.O. Box 22877
Fort Lauderdale, FL 33335
1-305-522-6761, FAX: 1-305-462-4877
Contact: Executive Director

VAC of Lee County, Inc.
P.O. Box 061039
Fort Myers, FL 33906-1039
1-813-433-5301
Contact: Executive Director

The VC of Alachua County
220 N. Main Street
P.O. Box 14561
Gainesville, FL 32604
1-904-378-2552
Contact: Executive Director

Volunteer Jacksonville, Inc.
1600 Prudential Drive
Jacksonville, FL 32207
1-904-378-7777
Contact: Executive Director

UW of Central Florida Volunteer Center
1825 North Gilmore Avenue
P.O. Box 51
Lakeland, FL 33802
1-813-686-6171, FAX: 1-813-688-9298
Contact: Director of Agency Relations & Volunteer Services

Dade County's Center for Voluntarism
600 Brickell Avenue
Miami, FL 33131
1-305-579-2300, FAX: 1-305-579-2212
Contact: Director

VC of Collier County
955 Creech Road
Naples, FL 33940
1-813-649-4747
Contact: Director

Volunteer Service Bureau of Marion County, Inc.
520 S.E. Fort King, Suite C-1
Ocala, FL 32671
1-904-732-4771
Contact: Executive Director

VC of Central Fla.
1900 N. Mills Avenue, Suite 1
Orlando, FL 32083
1-407-896-0945, FAX: 1-407-895-4749
Contact: Executive Director

Volunteer Pensacola/VAC, Inc.
7 North Coyle Street
Pensacola, FL 32501
1-904-438-5649
Contact: Executive Director

The Volunteer Bureau of Palm Beach County
3700 N. Broadway
Southeast Bank-2nd Floor
Riviera Beach, FL 33404
1-407-881-9503
Contact: Executive Director

Volunteer Center of Sarasota
1750 17th Street, #C-3
Sarasota, FL 34234
1-813-366-0013
Contact: Executive Director

Alternative Human Services' Volunteer Action Center
5200 16th Street, N.
P.O. Box 13087
St. Petersburg, FL 33733
1-813-526-1100, FAX: 1-813-527-1646
Contact: Director of Community Services

United Way Volunteer Center
P.O. Box 362
Stuart, FL 34995
1-407-220-1717, FAX: 1-407-220-7771
Contact: Volunteer Center Director

Volunteer Tallahassee, Inc.
307 East Seventh Avenue
Tallahassee, FL 32303
1-904-222-6263
Contact: Executive Director

Volunteer Center of Hillsborough County, Inc.
4023 N. Armenia Avenue, Suite 300
Tampa, FL 33607
1-813-878-2500, FAX: 1-813-872-6517
Contact: Executive Director

Volunteer Center South
101 W. Venice Avenue, Suite 25
Venice, FL 34285
1-813-484-4305
Contact: Executive Director

## GEORGIA

Volunteer Albany
P.O. Box 7
Albany, GA 31702
1-912-883-6700
Contact: Director of Community Resources UW

UW of Metropolitan Atlanta's Volunteer Resource Center
100 Edgewood Avenue, NE, 3rd Floor
P.O. Box 2692
Atlanta, GA 30303
1-404-527-7336, FAX: 1-404-527-7444
Contact: Director, Volunteer Resource Center

Help Line
630 Ellis Street
P.O. Box 1724
Augusta, GA 30909
1-404-826-4460, FAX: 1-404-826-4462
Contact: Director

Voluntary Action Center-Hand-Up, Inc.
206 Pine Street, S.W.
P.O. Box 631
Calhoun, GA 30720
1-404-629-7283
Contact: Executive Director

The Volunteer Center
1425 3rd Avenue
P.O. Box 1157
Columbus, GA 31902
1-404-596-8657, FAX: 1-404-571-2271
Contact: Director

VAC of NW Georgia
305 S. Thornton Avenue, Suite 2
Dalton, GA 30705
1-404-226-4357
Contact: Executive Director

Volunteer Gainesville
P.O. Box 1193
Gainesville, GA 30503
1-404-535-5445
Contact: Executive Director

Volunteer Macon
2484 Ingleside Avenue, A103
Macon, GA 31204
1-912-742-6677
Contact: Executive Director

VAC of United Way
P.O. Box 9119
Savannah, GA 31412
1-912-234-1636, FAX: 1-912-238-0281
Contact: Vice President, Comm. Services

Volunteer Thomasville
144 E. Jackson Street
P.O. Box 1540
Thomasville, GA 31799
1-912-228-3190
Contact: Director

Volunteer Houston County
P.O. Box 266
Warner Robins, GA 31099
1-912-922-4486
Contact: Vice-Chairman

## HAWAII

VAC of Oahu
680 Iwilei, Suite 430
Honolulu, HI 96817
1-808-536-7234
Contact: Director

## IDAHO

United Way Volunteer Connection
1975 Broadway, Suite B
Boise, ID 83706
1-208-345-4357
Contact: Director

## ILLINOIS

The Volunteer Center of NW Suburban Chicago
306 W. Park Street
Arlington Heights, IL 60005
1-708-398-1320
Contact: Executive Director

UW/Crusade of Mercy County
560 W. Lake Street
Chicago, IL 60606-1499
1-312-906-2425, FAX: 1-312-876-0721
Contact: The Volunteer Center

Volunteer Center of Knox County
140 E. Main Street
Galesburg, IL 61401
1-309-343-4434
Contact: Director

The Volunteer Center for Lake County
United Way of Lake County
2020 O'Plaine Road
Green Oaks, IL 60048
1-708-816-0063, FAX: 1-708-816-0093
Contact: Director of Volunteer Leadership Development

Volunteer Center of the Greater Quad Cities
1417 6th Avenue
Moline, IL 61265
1-309-764-6804
Contact: Executive Director

Volunteer Center of UW (of Champaign County)
1802 Woodfield Drive-Box 44
Savoy, IL 61874
1-217-352-5151, FAX: 1-217-352-6494
Contact: Director

Community Volunteer Center
Lincoln Land Community College
Shepherd Road
Springfield, IL 62794-9256
1-217-786-2289, FAX: 1-217-786-2251
Contact: Director, Community Services

Voluntary Action Center
1606 Bethany Road
Sycamore, IL 60178
1-815-758-3932
Contact: Coordinator of Vol. Services

DuPage County Division of Human Services
Office of Volunteer Development
Wheaton, IL 60187
1-708-682-7505, FAX: 1-708-682-7382
Contact: Volunteer Service Coordinator

**INDIANA**

First Call for Help/Volunteer Services
646 Franklin
P.O. Box 827
Columbus, IN 47202
1-812-376-0011
Contact: Executive Director

United Way-VAC
101 NW First Street, Suite 215
P.O. Box 18
Evansville, IN 47701
1-812-421-2801, FAX: 1-812-421-7474
Contact: Director of Volunteer & Outreach Services

Volunteer Connection
227 East Washington Blvd., Suite 202B
Fort Wayne, IN 46802
1-219-420-4263
Contact: Executive Director

The Window Community Volunteer Center
302 Mt. Vernon Drive
Goshen, IN 46526
1-219-533-9680
Contact: Executive Director

The Human Resources Department of United Way
221 West Ridge Road
Griffith, IN 46319
1-219-923-2302, FAX: 1-219-923-8601
Contact: Director

Volunteer Action Center
United Way of Central Indiana
1828 N. Meridian Street

Indianapolis, IN 46202
1-317-921-1233, FAX: 1-317-921-1355
Contact: Director

Volunteer Action Center
210 W. Walnut Street
Kokomo, IN 46901-4512
1-317-457-4481
Contact: VAC Coordinator

Greater Lafayette Volunteer Bureau
301½ Columbia Street
Lafayette, IN 47901
1-317-742-8241
Contact: Executive Director

Community Resource Center of St. Joseph
914 Lincolnway West
South Bend, IN 46616
1-219-232-2522
Contact: Executive Director

Volunteer Action Center
721 Wabash Avenue, Suite 502
Terre Haute, IN 48707
1-812-232-8822
Contact: Executive Director

## IOWA

Voluntary Bureau of Story County
510 5th Street
Ames, IA 50010
1-515-232-2736
Contact: Director

The Volunteer Bureau of Council Bluffs
523 6th Ave.
Council Bluffs, IA 51503
1-712-322-6431
Contact: Executive Director

UW of Central Iowa Volunteer Center
1111 Ninth Street, Suite 300
Des Moines, IA 50314
1-515-246-6545, FAX: 1-515-246-6546
Contact: Sr. Director Community Services Division

Johnson County VAC
c/o United Way
20 E. Market
Iowa City, IA 52245
1-319-338-7823
Contact: Volunteer Coordinator

The Voluntary Action Center of Muscatine
113 Iowa Avenue
Muscatine, IA 52761
1-319-263-0959
Contact: Director

VAC of the Iowa Great Lakes, Inc.
1713 Hill Avenue
Spirit Lake, IA 51360
1-712-336-4444
Contact: Executive Director

The Volunteer Bureau
Cedar Valley United Way
3420 University Avenue, Suite C
Waterloo, IA 50701
1-319-235-6211, FAX: 1-319-235-6963
Contact: Community Resources Coordinator

## KANSAS

Wyandotte County Volunteer Center
710 Minnesota Avenue
P.O. Box 17-1042
Kansas City, KS 66117-0242
1-913-371-3674, FAX: 1-913-371-2718
Contact: Director

Roger Hill Volunteer Center
211 E. 8th, Suite G
P.O. Box 116
Lawrence, KS 66044
1-913-865-5030
Contact: Coordinator

Volunteer Center of Johnson County
5311 Johnson Drive
Mission, KS 66205
1-913-432-0766
Contact: Director

Volunteer Center of Topeka
4125 Gage Center Drive, Suite 214
Topeka, KS 66604
1-913-272-8890
Contact: Executive Director

United Way Volunteer Center
212 N. Market Street, Suite 200
Wichita, KS 67202
1-316-267-1321, FAX: 1-316-262-0937
Contact: Volunteer Director

## KENTUCKY

Bowling Green-Warren County Community Education Board
200 High St.
Bowling Green, KY 42101
1-502-842-4281
Contact: Executive Director

Volunteer and Information Center, Inc.
236 N. Elm Street
P.O. Box 2009
Henderson, KY 42420
1-502-831-2273, FAX: 1-502-826-2111
Contact: Executive Director

Volunteer Center of the Bluegrass
2029 Bellefonte Drive
Lexington, KY 40503
1-606-278-6258, 1-606-276-3388
Contact: Executive Director

The Volunteer Connection
334 East Broadway
P.O. Box 4488
Louisville, KY 40204-0488
1-502-583-2821, FAX: 1-502-583-0330
Contact: Manager

The Volunteer Center
920 Frederica Street, Suite 404
P.O. Box 123
Owensboro, KY 42302-0123
1-502-683-9161
Contact: Executive Director

## LOUISIANA

Volunteer Baton Rouge!
8776 Bluebonnet Blvd.
Baton Rouge, LA 70810
1-504-767-1698, FAX: 1-504-767-1897
Contact: Executive Director

Volunteer Center of Lafayette
P.O. Box 52074
Lafayette, LA 70505
1-318-233-1006
Contact: Executive Director

Volunteer Center of SW Louisiana, Inc.
809 Kirby St.
Lake Charles, LA 70601
1-318-439-6109
Contact: Executive Director

United Way of NE Louisiana, Inc.
1300 Hudson Lane, Suite 7
Monroe, LA 71201
1-318-325-3869
Contact: Community Services Director

Volunteer & Information Agency, Inc.
4747 Earhart Blvd., Suite 111
New Orleans, LA 70125
1-504-488-4636, FAX: 1-504-482-6511
Contact: Volunteer Center Director

## MAINE

Volunteer! York County
36 Water Street, Unit C
Kennebunk, ME 04043
1-207-985-6869
Contact: Director

United Way's Center for Voluntary Action
233 Oxford Street
Portland, ME 04102
1-207-874-1015, FAX: 1-207-874-1007
Contact: Volunteer Development Director

## MARYLAND

Volunteer Center of Frederick County
22 S. Market St.
Frederick, MD 21701
1-301-663-9096
Contact: Coordinator

Anne Arundel County/Community Services
Anne Arundel Center North
101 Crain Highway, Suite 505
Glen Burnie, MD 21061
1-301-222-6880, FAX: 1-301-787-0338
Contact: Volunteer Coordinator

Prince Georges Voluntary Action Center
6309 Baltimore Avenue, Suite 305
Riverdale, MD 20737
1-301-779-9444
Contact: Executive Director

Montgomery County Volunteer Center
50 Monroe Street, #400
Rockville, MD 20850
1-301-217-9100
Contact: Director

## MASSACHUSETTS

VAC/United Way of Mass. Bay
2 Liberty Square
Boston, MA 02109
1-617-482-8370, FAX: 1-617-482-6021
Contact: VAC Operations Manager

VAC/United Way of Pioneer Valley
184 Mill Street
P.O. Box 3040
Springfield, MA 01102-3040
1-413-737-2691, FAX: 1-413-788-4130
Contact: Director

Volunteer Bureau of the UW of Greater Taunton, Inc.
4 Court Street
P.O. Box 416
Taunton, MA 02780
1-508-824-3985

Volunteer Resources Division
United Way of Central Mass.
484 Main Street, Suite 300
Worcester, MA 01608
1-508-757-5631
Contact: Director, VAC

## MICHIGAN

Alpena Volunteer Center
Alpena Community College
666 Johnson Street
Alpena, MI 49707
1-517-356-9021 x271
Contact: Director

Washenaw United Way Volunteer Action Center
2301 Platt Road
P.O. Box 3813
Ann Arbor, MI 48104
1-313-971-5852, FAX: 1-313-971-6230
Contact: Director

Volunteer Bureau of Battle Creek, Inc.
182 W. Van Buren Street
Battle Creek, MI 49017
1-616-965-0555
Contact: Executive Director

Volunteer Action Center of Bay County
1308 Columbus Avenue, Room 105
Bay City, MI 48708
1-517-893-6060
Contact: Executive Director

The Center for Volunteerism/UCS
1212 Griswold at State
Detroit, MI 48226-1899
1-313-226-9429, FAX: 1-313-226-9397
Contact: Senior Manager

United Way of Genesee & Lapeer Counties
202 E. Boulevard Drive, Rm. 110
Flint, MI 48503
1-313-232-8121
Contact: Director, Community Resources Division

Volunteer Connection
500 Commerce Building
Grand Rapids, MI 49503-3165
1-616-459-6281, FAX: 1-616-459-8460
Contact: Volunteer Associate

VAC of Greater Kalamazoo
709-A Westnedge
Kalamazoo, MI 49007
1-616-382-6382, FAX: 1-616-344-7250
Contact: Executive Director

Voluntary Action Center of Greater Lansing
6035 Executive Drive, Suite 105
Lansing, MI 48911
1-517-887-8004
Contact: Executive Director

Voluntary Action Center of Midland County, Inc.
220 W. Main Street
Midland, MI 48640-5137
1-517-631-7660
Contact: Executive Director

Southwestern Michigan Volunteer Center
1213 Oak Street
Niles, MI 49120
1-616-683-5464
Contact: Executive Director

Voluntary Action Center of Saginaw County
118 E. Genesee
Saginaw, MI 48607
1-517-755-2822
Contact: President/CEO

SW Michigan Volunteer Center–St. Joseph
508 Pleasant Street
St. Joseph, MI 49085
1-616-983-0912

## MINNESOTA

Bemidji Area Volunteer Center
300 Bemidji Avenue
Bemidji, MN 56616
1-218-759-2802
Contact: Executive Director

Voluntary Action Center of United Way
402 Ordean Building
424 W. Superior Street
Duluth, MN 55802
1-218-726-4776
Contact: VAC Director

United Way's Voluntary Center
404 South 8th Street
Minneapolis, MN 55404
1-612-340-7537, FAX: 1-612-340-7675
Contact: Executive Director

The Volunteer Connection, Inc.
903 W. Center, Suite 200
Rochester, MN 55902
1-507-287-2244, FAX: 1-507-287-2063
Contact: Executive Director

Voluntary Action Center of the St. Paul Area, Inc.
251 Starkey Street, Suite 127
Bolander Building
St. Paul, MN 55107-1821
1-612-296-4731
Contact: Executive Director

Community Voluntary Service of the St. Croix Valley
1965 S. Greeley Street
Stillwater, MN 55082-6012
1-612-439-7434
Contact: Executive Director

## MISSISSIPPI

Volunteer Center of United Way
843 N. President Street
P.O. Box 23169
Jackson, MS 39225-3169
1-601-354-1765, FAX: 1-601-968-8596
Contact: Director

Volunteer Jackson County
3510 Magnolia Street
P.O. Box 97
Pascagoula, MS 39567
1-601-762-8557
Contact: Community Resources Specialist

### MISSOURI

Voluntary Action Center
111 South Ninth
200 Strollway Centre
Columbia, MO 65201
1-314-874-2273
Contact: Executive Director

Voluntary Action Center of Eastern Jackson County
10901 Winner Road, Suite 102
Independence, MO 64052
1-816-252-2636
Contact: Director

Volunteer Center–Heart of America United Way
1080 Washington Street
Kansas City, MO 64112
1-816-474-5112, FAX: 1-816-931-8725 x203
Contact: Director

Voluntary Action Center
401 N. 12th Street
P.O. Box 188
St. Joseph, MO 64502-0188
1-816-364-2381
Contact: Director

United Way of Greater St. Louis VAC
1111 Olive
St. Louis, MO 63101
1-314-421-0700, FAX: 1-314-539-4154
Contact: Vice President

### MONTANA

Community Help Line, Inc.
113 6th Street North
Great Falls, MT 59401
1-406-761-6010
Contact: Executive Director

### NEBRASKA

United Way of the Midlands Volunteer Bureau/VAC
1805 Harney St.
Omaha, NE 68102-1972
1-402-342-8232 x531, FAX: 1-402-342-7402
Contact: Director of Volunteer Services

Scotts Bluff County Volunteer Bureau
1721 Broadway, Room 409
Scottsbluff, NE 69361
1-308-632-3736
Contact: Executive Director

### NEVADA

United Way Services, Inc.
1055 E. Tropicana, #300
Las Vegas, NV 89119
1-702-798-4636, FAX: 1-702-798-9415
Contact: Vice President, Community Resources

VAC/United Way of No. Nevada
500 Ryland Street
P.O. Box 2730
Reno, NV 89505-2730
1-702-329-4638, FAX: 1-702-322-8721
Contact: Director of VAC

### NEW HAMPSHIRE

Monadnock Volunteer Center
331 Main Street
Keene, NH 03431
1-603-352-2088
Contact: Director

The Voluntary Action Center
102 N. Main Street
Manchester, NH 03431
1-603-668-8601
Contact: Program Manager

## NEW JERSEY

The Volunteer Center of Camden County
CPAC/HSC
North Gate 1
7th & Linden Streets
Camden, NJ 08102
1-609-541-3939
Contact: Senior Manager

Volunteer Center of Bergen County, Inc.
64 Passaic Street
Hackensack, NJ 07601
1-201-489-9454, FAX: 1-201-489-1995
Contact: Executive Director

Volunteer Center of Mercer County
3131 Princeton Pike, Bldg. #4
P.O. Box 29
Lawrenceville, NJ 08648
1-609-896-1912, FAX: 1-609-895-1245
Contact: Director of Comm. Services

Volunteer Services Center
32 Ford Avenue
P.O. Box 210
Milltown, NJ 08850
1-201-247-3727
Contact: Director

Voluntary Action Center of Morris County
36 South Street
Morristown, NJ 07960
1-201-538-7200
Contact: Executive Director

Volunteer Center of Greater Essex County, Inc.
303-9 Washington Street, 5th Floor
Newark, NJ 07039
1-201-622-3737
Contact: Executive Director

Volunteer Center of Atlantic County
P.O. Box 648
Northfield, NJ 08225
1-609-646-5528
Contact: Executive Director

Volunteer Action Center of Passaic County
c/o United Way of Passaic Valley
2 Market Street, 4th Floor
Paterson, NJ 07501
1-201-279-6526, FAX: 1-201-279-0059
Contact: Director

Volunteer Center of Monmouth County
227 East Bergen Place
Red Bank, NJ 07701
1-201-741-3330
Contact: Executive Director

Volunteer Center of Somerset County
United Way of Somerset County
205 W. Main Street, 4th Floor
P.O. Box 308
Somerville, NJ 08876-0308
1-908-725-6640, FAX: 1-908-725-5598
Contact: Manager

## NEW MEXICO

The Volunteer Center of Albuquerque
302 Eighth Street, NW
P.O. Box 1767
Albuquerque, NM 87103
1-505-247-3671, FAX: 1-505-242-3576
Contact: Director

Volunteer Involvement Service
LaSalle B-108
College of Santa Fe
Santa Fe, NM 87501
1-505-473-1000
Contact: Executive Director

## NEW YORK

The Volunteer Center of Albany, Inc.
340 First Street
Albany, NY 12206
1-518-434-2061
Contact: Executive Director

Voluntary Action Center of Broome County
Vestal Parkway E. at Jensen Road

P.O. Box 550
Binghamton, NY 13902
1-607-729-2592, FAX: 1-607-729-2597
Contact: Director of Community Programs

Volunteer Center of the UW of Buffalo/Erie Counties
742 Delaware Avenue
Buffalo, NY 14209
1-716-887-2632, FAX: 1-716-882-0071
Contact: Director of Agency Services

The Volunteer Connection
22 W. 3rd Street
Corning, NY 14830
1-607-936-3753, FAX: 1-607-936-0537
Contact: Director

Nassau County Office of Volunteer Services
320 Old Country Road
Garden City, NY 11530
1-516-535-3897, FAX: 1-516-535-4229
Contact: Administrator

VAC of Greater Glens Falls, Inc.
65 Ridge St.
Glens Falls, NY 12801
1-516-793-3817
Contact: Executive Director

Volunteer Service Bureau
c/o United Way of S. Chautauqua County
413 North Main Street
P.O. Box 1012
Jamestown, NY 14701
1-716-483-1562
Contact: Coordinator

Volunteer Center of Orange County
691 E. Main
Milltown, NY 10940
1-914-342-3393
Contact: Director

Mayor's Voluntary Action Center
61 Chambers Street
New York, NY 10007
1-212-566-5950, FAX: 1-212-406-3587
Contact: Executive Director

Volunteer Resources Division
55 St. Paul Street
Rochester, NY 14604
1-716-454-2770, FAX: 1-716-454-6568
Contact: Vice-President for Community Resources

Rome Voluntary Action Center
City Hall on the Mall
Rome, NY 13440
1-315-336-5638
Contact: Executive Director

VAC of the Human Services Planning Council
152 Barrett Street
Schenectady, NY 12305
1-518-372-3395
Contact: Director

Volunteer Center, Inc. of Syracuse & Onondaga County
115 E. Jefferson Street, Suite 400
Syracuse, NY 13202
1-315-474-7011, FAX: 1-315-479-6772
Contact: Executive Director

Volunteer Center of Rensselaer County
502 Broadway
Troy, NY 12180
1-518-272-1000
Contact: Volunteer Center Coordinator

Voluntary Action Center of Greater Utica, Inc.
1644 Genesee Street
Utica, NY 13502
1-315-735-4463
Contact: Executive Director

Jefferson County Volunteer Center
37 Empsall Plaza
Watertown, NY 13601
1-315-788-5631
Contact: CPO

Volunteer Center of United Way
470 Mamaroneck Avenue, Room 204
White Plains, NY 10605
1-914-948-4452, FAX: 1-914-948-3032
Contact: Executive Director

**NORTH CAROLINA**

The Volunteer Center
c/o United Way of Asheville & Buncombe County
50 S. French Broad Avenue
Asheville, NC 28801
1-704-255-0696
Contact: Director

Moore County Volunteer Center
P.O. Box 905
Carthage, NC 28327
1-919-947-6395, FAX: 1-919-947-1874
Contact: Director

The Volunteer Center
P.O. Box 845
Chapel Hill, NC 27515
1-919-929-7273
Contact: Executive Director

The Volunteer Center
301 South Brevard Street
Charlotte, NC 28202
1-704-372-7170, FAX: 1-704-342-4482
Contact: Director

Volunteer Center of Greater Durham, Inc.
119 Orange Street
Durham, NC 27701
1-919-688-8977, FAX: 1-919-688-7445
Contact: Executive Director

The Cumberland County VAC, Inc.
P.O. Box 20001
Fayetteville, NC 28302
1-919-323-8643
Contact: Executive Director

Voluntary Action Center of Greensboro, Inc.
1301 N. Elm Street
Greensboro, NC 27401
1-919-373-1633
Contact: Executive Director

Volunteer Center of Vance County, Inc.
414 S. Garnett Street
P.O. Box 334
Henderson, NC 27536
1-919-492-1540
Contact: Executive Director

United Way Volunteer Center
475 South Church Street
P.O. Box 487
Hendersonville, NC 28793
1-704-692-8700
Contact: Director

Volunteer Center of Greater High Point
Holt McPherson Center
305 N. Main Street
High Point, NC 27260
1-919-883-6171, FAX: 1-919-883-6928
Contact: Acting Director

Dare Voluntary Action Center, Inc.
P.O. Box 293
Manteo, NC 27954-0293
1-919-473-2400
Contact: Executive Director

United Way of Wake County Voluntary Action Center
1100 Wake Forest Road
P.O. Box 11426
Raleigh, NC 27511
1-919-833-5739
Contact: Director

United Way of Cleveland County, Inc.
132 Graham Street
P.O. Box 2242
Shelby, NC 28150
1-704-482-7344
Contact: Community Planner

Volunteer & Information Center
P.O. Box 334

Supply, NC 28462
1-919-754-4766
Contact: Executive Director

Volunteer Center–United Way
311 W. 4th Street
Winston-Salem, NC 27101
1-919-723-3601, FAX: 1-919-724-1045
Contact: Director

## NORTH DAKOTA

Missouri Slope Areawide United Way
P.O. Box 2111
Bismarck, ND 58502
1-701-255-3601
Contact: Volunteer Development Coordinator

United Way of Cass-Clay
315 N. Eighth Street
P.O. Box 1609
Fargo, ND 58107-1609
1-701-237-5050, FAX: 1-701-237-0982
Contact: Vice President

United Way Volunteer Center
321 De Mers Avenue
P.O. Box 207
Grand Forks, ND 58206-0207
1-701-775-0671
Contact: Director

## OHIO

The Volunteer Center
425 West Market Street
Akron, OH 44302
1-216-762-8991
Contact: Executive Director

Voluntary Action Center/A Service of United Way
618 Second Street, NW
Canton, OH 44703
1-216-453-9172, FAX: 1-216-455-8909
Contact: Executive Director

Info-Line/Volunteer Bureau
107 Water Street
Chardon, OH 44024
1-216-729-7931, FAX: 1-216-286-3442
Contact: Volunteer Bureau Associate

VAC/United Appeal & Community Chest
2400 Reading Road
Cincinnati, OH 45202
1-513-762-7192, FAX: 1-513-762-7138
Contact: Manager

The Volunteer Center/United Way Services
3100 Euclid Avenue
Cleveland, OH 44115-2577
1-216-361-1010, FAX: 1-216-432-4863
Contact: Director

CALLVAC Service, Inc.
370 South Fifth Avenue
Columbus, OH 43215
1-614-221-6766
Contact: Director, Volunteer Center

Voluntary Action Center of United Way/Greater Dayton Area
184 Salem Avenue
Dayton, OH 45406-5877
1-513-225-3066, FAX: 1-513-225-3074
Contact: Director

United Way Voluntary Action Center/Warren County
20 N. Mechanic
Lebanon, OH 45036
1-513-923-3987, FAX: 1-513-932-0214 (Red Cross)
Contact: Director

The Volunteer Center of Richland County
35 N. Park Street
Mansfield, OH 44902-1711
1-419-525-2816, FAX: 1-419-524-3467
Contact: Director

Medina County United Way Volunteer Center
113 E. Homestead Street
Medina, OH 44256

1-216-725-3926, FAX: 1-216-725-3000
Contact: Executive Director

The Volunteer Center in Huron County
Shady Lane Complex #4
258 Benedict Avenue
Norwalk, OH 44857
1-419-663-1179
Contact: Executive Director

Voluntary Action Center of Erie County, Inc.
108 West Shoreline Drive
Sandusky, OH 44870
1-419-627-0074
Contact: Executive Director

Volunteer Service Bureau
616 N. Limestone St.
Springfield, OH 45503
1-513-322-4262
Contact: Director

United Way/Voluntary Action Center
1 Stranahan Square, Suite 141
Toledo, OH 43604
1-419-244-3063, FAX: 1-419-246-4614
Contact: Director

United Way/W.H.I.R.E.
215 S. Walnut Street
Wooster, OH 44691
1-216-264-9473, 1-800-247-9473, FAX: 1-216-264-7879

**OKLAHOMA**

Tulsa Volunteer Center
1430 S. Boulder
Tulsa, OK 74119
1-918-585-5551, FAX: 1-918-582-5588

**OREGON**

Voluntary Action Center/YMCA
2055 Patterson
Eugene, OR 97405
1-503-686-9622
Contact: Director

Volunteer Bureau of Greater Portland
718 West Burnside, Room 404
Portland, OR 97209
1-503-222-1355
Contact: Executive Director

**PENNSYLVANIA**

Voluntary Action Center of the United Way
520 E Broad Street
P.O. Box 6478
Bethlehem, PA 18018
1-215-691-6670, FAX: 1-215-865-5871
Contact: Co-Directors

Volunteer Center of Clearfield County
103 N. Front Street
P.O. Box 550
Clearfield, PA 16830
1-814-765-1398, FAX: 1-814-765-2760
Contact: Community Services Supervisor

COVE
1110 West 10th Street
Erie, PA 16501-1466
1-814-456-6248
Contact: Director

The Volunteer Center
546 Maclay Street
Harrisburg, PA 17110
1-717-238-6678
Contact: Executive Director

Volunteer Center of Lancaster County
630 Janet Avenue
Lancaster, PA 17601
1-717-299-3743, FAX: 1-717-394-6118
Contact: Director

Volunteer Action Council, Inc.
Seven Benjamin Franklin Parkway
Philadelphia, PA 19103
1-215-665-2474, FAX: 1-215-665-2531
Contact: Director, Community Services

Volunteer Action Center
United Way of Allegheny County
200 Ross Street
P.O. Box 735
Pittsburgh, PA 15230
1-412-261-6010, FAX: 1-412-394-5376
Contact: Director

Voluntary Action Center of NE Pennsylvania
225 N. Washington Avenue
Scranton, PA 18510
1-717-347-5616, FAX: 1-717-341-5816
Contact: Executive Director

Voluntary Action Center of Centre County, Inc.
1524 W. College Avenue, #8
State College, PA 16801-2715
1-814-234-8222
Contact: Executive Director

Clyde J. Tracanna Volunteer Resource Center
c/o United Way of Washington County
58 East Cherry Avenue
Washington, PA 15301
1-412-225-3322, FAX: 1-412-222-8459
Contact: Associate Director

VAC of Wyoming Valley
United Way of Wyoming Valley
9 E. Market Street
Wilkes-Barre, PA 18711-0351
1-717-822-3020, FAX: 1-717-822-0522
Contact: Director

The Volunteer Center of York County
800 E. King Street
United Way Building
York, PA 17403
1-717-846-4477, FAX: 1-717-843-4082
Contact: Director

## RHODE ISLAND

Volunteers in Action, Inc.
160 Broad Street
Providence, RI 02903
1-401-421-6547
Contact: Executive Director

## SOUTH CAROLINA

Western Foothills United Way Volunteer Center
114 W. Greenville Street
P.O. Box 2067
Anderson, SC 29622-2067
1-803-226-1078
Contact: Director

Volunteer & Info Center of Beaufort
706 Bay Street (upstairs)
P.O. Box 202
Beaufort, SC 29901-0202
1-803-524-4357, FAX: 1-803-524-1915
Contact: Director

VAC-Trident United Way
P.O. Box 20696
Charleston, SC 29413-0696
1-803-745-1710
Contact: Director, VAC

United Way of the Midlands
1800 Main Street
P.O. Box 152
Columbia, SC 29202
1-803-733-5400, FAX: 1-803-779-7803
Contact: Director of Volunteer Services

Volunteer Greenville—A Volunteer Center
301 University Ridge, Suite 5300
Greenville, SC 29601-3672
1-803-232-6444, FAX: 1-803-240-8535
Contact: Director

Voluntary Action Center
P.O. Box 4759
Hilton Head Island, SC 29938
1-803-785-6646
Contact: Director

Oconee Volunteer & Information Services
409 E. North First Street
P.O. Box 1828
Seneca, SC 29679-1828
1-803-882-8899
Contact: Executive Director

United Way of the Piedmont Volunteer Center
101 East St. John Street, Suite 307
P.O. Box 5624
Spartanburg, SC 29304-0624
1-803-582-7556, FAX: 1-803-582-9826
Contact: Director Community Resources

Volunteer Sumter, Inc.
P.O. Box 957
Sumter, SC 29151-0957
1-803-775-9424
Contact: Director

**SOUTH DAKOTA**

Volunteer & Information Center
304 S. Phillips, Suite 310
Sioux Falls, SD 57102
1-605-339-4357
Contact: Executive Director

Yankton Volunteer Center and Information
P.O. Box 851
Yankton, SD 57078-0851
1-605-665-6067
Contact: Executive Director

**TENNESSEE**

The Volunteer Center of Chattanooga & the Tri-state Area
451 River Street
P.O. Box 4029
Chattanooga, TN 37405-4029
1-615-265-0514, FAX: 1-615-752-0350
Contact: Executive Director

Volunteer-Johnson City, Inc.
200 E. Main
P.O. Box 1443
Johnson City, TN 37605-1443
1-615-926-8010
Contact: Executive Director

Volunteer ETSU
Student Activities Center, East Tennessee State
P.O. Box 21040A
Johnson City, TN 37614
1-615-929-4254
Contact: Director

Volunteer Kingsport, Inc.
1701 Virginia Avenue, Suite 17
Kingsport, TN 37664
1-615-247-4511
Contact: Executive Director

Volunteer Center of Greater Knoxville
1514 East Fifth Avenue
P.O. Box 326
Knoxville, TN 37901-0326
1-615-521-0890, FAX: 1-615-522-7312
Contact: Director

Volunteer Center of Memphis
263 S. McLean Boulevard
Memphis, TN 38104
1-901-276-8655, FAX: 1-901-276-5700
Contact: Executive Director

Volunteer Center-United Way of Middle Nashville
P.O. Box 24667
Nashville, TN 37202-4667
1-615-256-8272, FAX: 1-615-780-2426
Contact: Volunteer Center Director

**TEXAS**

Volunteer Center of Abilene, Inc.
P.O. Box 3953
Abilene, TX 79604-3953
1-915-676-5683
Contact: Executive Director

The United Way Volunteer Action Center
2207 Line Avenue
P.O. Box 3069
Amarillo, TX 79116-3069
1-806-376-6714
Contact: Executive Director

Volunteer Resource Center of Brazoria County
P.O. Box 1959

Angelton, TX 77516-1959
1-409-849-4404, FAX: 1-409-848-0259
Contact: Director

Capital Area Volunteer Center
5828 Balcones, Suite 205
Austin, TX 78731
1-512-451-6651, FAX: 1-512-454-2565
Contact: Executive Director

Volunteer Action Center of Southeast Texas
P.O. Box 2945
Beaumont, TX 77704-2945
1-409-898-2273, FAX: 1-409-832-5964
Contact: Executive Director

Volunteer Resource Center
1301 Los Ebanos, Suite B-3
Brownsville, TX 78520
1-512-544-0321
Contact: Director

Volunteer Center of the Coastal Bend
1721 S. Brownlee Boulevard
Corpus Christi, TX 78404
1-512-887-4545
Contact: Executive Director

Volunteer Center of Dallas County
1215 Skiles
Dallas, TX 75204
1-214-826-6767, FAX: 1-214-821-8716
Contact: Executive Director

Volunteer Bureau of the UW of El Paso County
1918 Texas Street
P.O. Box 2388
El Paso, TX 79923-2388
1-915-532-4919
Contact: Director of Service Programs

Volunteer Center of Metropolitan Tarrant County
210 East Ninth Street
Ft. Worth, TX 76102-6494
1-817-878-0099, FAX: 1-817-878-0005
Contact: Director

The Volunteer Center of the Texas Gulf Coast
3100 Timmons Lane, Suite 100
Houston, TX 77027
1-713-965-0031, FAX: 1-713-965-9601
Contact: Executive Director

The Volunteer Center of Longview
500 E. Whaley Street
P.O. Box 3443
Longview, TX 75606-3443
1-214-758-2374
Contact: Executive Director

Volunteer Center of Lubbock
1706-23rd Street, Suite 101
Lubbock, TX 79411
1-806-747-0551
Contact: Executive Director

Volunteer Resource Center, Inc.
2213 Primrose
McAllen, TX 78504
1-512-630-3003
Contact: Director

The Volunteer Center of Midland Texas
1030 Andrews Highway, Suite 207
P.O. Box 2145
Midland, TX 79702-2145
1-905-697-8781
Contact: Executive Director

Volunteer Center of Plano
301 W. Parker Road, Suite 213
Plano, TX 75023
1-214-422-1050
Contact: Executive Director

Volunteer Center, UW of San Antonio & Bexar County
700 South Alamo
P.O. Box 898
San Antonio, TX 78293-0898
1-512-224-5000, FAX: 1-512-224-4245
Contact: Director

Texarkana Volunteer Center
3000 Texas Boulevard

Texarkana, TX 75503
1-903-793-4903
Contact: Director

Volunteer Center of Tyler
113 E. Houston
Tyler, TX 75702
1-903-592-6342
Contact: Program Director

Volunteer Center of Waco
201 West Waco Drive
P.O. Box 2027
Waco, TX 76703-2027
1-817-753-LOVE
Contact: Director

## UTAH

Volunteer Center of Cache Valley
236 North, 100 East
P.O. Box 567
Logan, UT 84321-0567
1-801-752-3103
Contact: Director

Weber County Volunteer Services
2650 Lincoln Avenue, Room 268
Ogden, UT 84401
1-801-625-3782
Contact: Director

United Way Volunteer Center
60 E. 100 St.
P.O. Box 135
Provo, UT 84604
1-801-374-8108, FAX: 1-801-374-2591
Contact: Director

The Volunteer Center
212 West 1300 South
Salt Lake City, UT 84115
1-801-486-2136
Contact: Director

## VERMONT

Volunteer Connection
United Way of Chittenden County
One Burlington Square
Burlington, VT 05401
1-802-864-7498, FAX: 1-802-864-7401
Contact: Director, Community Services

## VIRGINIA

Alexandria Volunteer Bureau
801 N. Pitt Street, #102
Alexandria, VA 22314
1-703-836-2176
Contact: Executive Director

The Arlington Volunteer Office
2100 Clarendon Boulevard
#1 Court House Plaza, Suite 314
Arlington, VA 22201
1-703-358-3222
Contact: Director

Volunteer Action Center of Montgomery County
Corner of W. Roanoke and Otey Streets
P.O. Box 565
Blacksburg, VA 24063-0565
1-703-552-4909
Contact: Executive Director

Volunteer-Bristol
600 Cumberland Street
Second Floor
Bristol, VA 24201
1-703-669-1555
Contact: Executive Director

Appalachian Agency Senior
Citizens SW Virginia
P.O. Box 765
Cedar Bluff, VA 24609-0765
1-703-964-4915
Contact: VAC Director

United Way Volunteer Center
413 E. Market, Suite 101

P.O. Box 139
Charlottesville, VA 22902-0139
1-804-972-1705, FAX: 1-804-972-1719
Contact: Director

VAC of Fairfax County Area, Inc.
10530 Page Avenue
Fairfax, VA 22030
1-703-246-3460
Contact: Executive Director

Voluntary Action Center of the United Way
1520 Aberdeen Road, Suite 109
Hampton, VA 23666
1-804-838-9770, FAX: 1-804-838-5930
Contact: Director

Volunteer Services of Hanover County
P.O. Box 470
Hanover, VA 23069-0470
1-804-537-6074, FAX: 1-804-752-6860
Contact: Volunteer Services Coordinator

VAC of United Way of Central Virginia
1010 Miller Park Square
P.O. Box 2434
Lynchburg, VA 24501
1-804-847-8657, FAX: 1-804-847-8335
Contact: Director of United Way Community Services

VAC of the Prince William Area, Inc.
9300 Peabody Street, Suite 104
Manassas, VA 22110
1-703-369-5292
Contact: Director

VAC of S. Hampton Roads
253 West Freemason Street
Norfolk, VA 23510
1-804-624-2403
Contact: Executive Director

Volunteer Center/United Way Services
233 S. Adam Street
P.O. Box 227
Petersburg, VA 23804
1-804-861-9330
Contact: Director

Volunteer Center
224 East Broad Street
P.O. Box 12209
Richmond, VA 23241-2209
1-804-771-5855, FAX: 1-804-225-7344
Contact: Director

Voluntary Action Center
920 South Jefferson Street
P.O. Box 496
Roanoke, VA 24003
1-703-985-0131
Contact: Director

## WASHINGTON

Volunteer Center of American Red Cross
2111 King Street
Bellingham, WA 98225
1-206-733-3290
Contact: Executive Director

United Way of Shohomish County's Volunteer Center
917-134th Street SW, A-6
Everett, WA 98204
1-206-742-5911, FAX: 1-206-743-1440
Contact: Director, United Way Services

Benton-Franklin Volunteer Center
205 N. Dennis
Kennewick, WA 99336
1-509-783-0631
Contact: Executive Director

Voluntary Action Center
613 South Second
P.O. Box 1507
Mt. Vernon, WA 98273-1507
1-206-336-6627, FAX: 1-206-336-9771
Contact: Program Specialist

United Way Volunteer Center of King County
107 Cherry Street, 9th Floor

Seattle, WA 98104
1-206-461-4539, FAX: 1-206-461-4872
Contact: Director, Volunteer Center

United Way's Volunteer Center
P.O. Box 326
Spokane, WA 99210-0326
1-509-624-2279
Contact: Coordinator

UW of Pierce County
734 Broadway
P.O. Box 2215
Tacoma, WA 98401
1-206-272-4267, FAX: 1-206-597-7481
Contact: Director of Volunteer Center

Volunteer Bureau of Clark County
1703 Main Street
P.O. Box 425
Vancouver, WA 98666
1-206-694-6577
Contact: Director

Greater Yakima Volunteer Bureau
302 Lincoln
Yakima, WA 98902
1-509-248-4460
Contact: Director

**WISCONSIN**

Information and Referral Center
120 N. Morrision Street
P.O. Box 1091
Appleton, WI 54911
1-414-739-5126
Contact: Director

Volunteer Service Bureau/VAC
431 Olympian Boulevard
Beloit, WI 53511
1-608-365-1278
Contact: Director

Volunteer Center
338 S. Chestnut
Green Bay, WI 54303
1-414-435-1101
Contact: Director

Kenosha Voluntary Action Center of Kenosha, Inc.
716-58th Street
Kenosha, WI 53140
1-414-657-4554
Contact: Executive Director

VAC/United Way of Dane County
2059 Atwood Avenue
P.O. Box 7548
Madison, WI 53704
1-608-246-4380, FAX: 1-608-246-4349
Contact: Director-Agency Services

Volunteer Center of Ozaukee
14135 N. Cedarburg Rd.
Mequon, WI 53092
1-414-377-1616
Contact: Executive Director

Volunteer Center of Greater Milwaukee, Inc.
600 E. Mason Street, Suite 100
Milwaukee, WI 53202
1-414-273-7887, FAX: 1-414-273-0637
Contact: Executive Director

Volunteer Center of Waukesha County, Inc.
2220 Silvernail Road
Pewaukee, WI 53072
1-414-544-0150
Contact: Executive Director

The United Way Volunteer Center
1045 Clark Street, #204
Stevens Point, WI 54481
1-715-341-6740
Contact: Director of Planning and Allocations

The Volunteer Center of Marathon County
407 Grant Street
Wausau, WI 54401
1-715-843-1220
Contact: Executive Director

Volunteer Center of Washington County
120 N. Main Street, #340
West Bend, WI 54095
1-414-338-8256, FAX: 1-414-334-5402
Contact: Executive Director

United Way of S. Wood County Volunteer Center
1120 Lincoln Street, Suite 2
Wisconsin Rapids, WI 54494
1-715-421-0390
Contact: Volunteer Coordinator

**WYOMING**

Volunteer Information Center
900 Central
P.O. Box 404
Cheyenne, WY 82003
1-307-632-4132
Contact: Director

# State Offices of Volunteerism

### ALABAMA

State of Alabama
Governor's Office on Volunteerism
560 S. McDonough Street
Montgomery, AL 36130
1-205-242-3020, FAX: 1-205-242-4407
Contact: Director

### ARKANSAS

State of Arkansas
Arkansas Division of Volunteerism
P.O. Box 1437—Slot #1300
Little Rock, AR 72203-1437
1-501-682-7540, FAX: 1-501-682-6571
Contact: Director

### CONNECTICUT

Governor's Council on Voluntary Action
80 Washington Street
Hartford, CT 06106
1-203-566-8320
Contact: Executive Director

### DELAWARE

State of Delaware
Division of Volunteer Services
156 S. State Street
P.O. Box 1401
Dover, DE 19901
1-302-736-4456, FAX: 1-302-735-6281
Contact: Director

### FLORIDA

Volunteer Services
Dept. of Health and Rehabilitation Services
1323 Winewood Boulevard
Building 1, Room 217
Tallahassee, FL 32399-0700
1-904-488-2761, FAX: 1-904-488-4227
Contact: Associate Director

### GEORGIA

Georgia Office of Volunteer Services
Department of Comm. Affairs
1200 Equitable Building
1000 Peachtree Street, NW
Atlanta, GA 30303
1-404-656-9790, FAX: 1-404-656-9792
Contact: Coordinator

### HAWAII

Statewide Volunteer Services
Office of the Governor
State Capitol, Room 444
Honolulu, HI 96813
1-808-548-8539
Contact: Program Coordinator

### ILLINOIS

Lt. Governor's Office of Voluntary Action
100 West Randolph, Suite 15-200
Chicago, IL 60601
1-312-814-5225, FAX: 1-312-814-4862
Contact: Director

### INDIANA

Governor's Voluntary Action Program
1 North Capitol, Room B-2
Indianapolis, IN 46204
1-317-232-2504
Contact: Director

### IOWA

Governor's Office for Volunteers
State Capitol
Des Moines, IA 50319
1-515-281-8304
Contact: Director

### KENTUCKY

Kentucky Office of Volunteer Services
275 East Main Street
Frankfort, KY 40601-0001
1-502-564-HELP, FAX: 1-502-564-2096
Contact: Executive Director

### MAINE

Maine State Office of Volunteerism
State House Station #73
Augusta, ME 04333
1-207-289-3771
Contact: Director

### MARYLAND

Governor's Office on Volunteerism
301 West Preston Street, Suite 1501
Baltimore, MD 21201
1-301-225-4496, FAX: 1-301-333-7124
Contact: Director

### MINNESOTA

Minnesota Office on Volunteer Services
Dept. of Administration
500 Rice Street
St. Paul, MN 55155
1-612-296-4731, FAX: 1-612-296-2265
Contact: Director

### MISSOURI

Missouri Volunteers
c/o Missouri Division of Family Services
615 East 13th Street
Kansas City, MO 64106
1-816-472-2293
Contact: President

### NEVADA

Nevada Office of Volunteerism
Capitol Complex
Carson City, NV 89710
1-702-885-4990
Contact: Program Administrator

### NEW HAMPSHIRE

Governor's Office on Volunteerism
The State House Annex, Room 410E
Concord, NE 03301
1-603-271-3771, FAX: 1-603-271-2131
Contact: Executive Director

### NEW JERSEY

New Jersey Office of Volunteerism
The State House
West State Street, CN001
Trenton, NJ 08625
1-609-777-1289
Contact: Director

### NEW YORK

Governor's Office for Voluntary Service
2 World Trade Center
57th Floor
New York, NY 10047
1-212-587-2255, FAX: 1-212-587-4709
Contact: Director, Deputy Director

### NORTH CAROLINA

Governor's Office of Citizen Affairs
116 West Jones Street
Raleigh, NC 27603-8001
1-919-733-5017, FAX: 1-919-733-5166
Contact: Executive Director

### NORTH DAKOTA

North Dakota Office of Volunteer Services
Capitol Building
Bismarck, ND 58505
1-701-224-4777

### OHIO

Ohio Office of Volunteerism
State Office Tower
30 East Broad Street, Room 3920
Columbus, OH 43266-0401
1-614-466-5087, FAX: 1-614-644-9152
Contact: Volunteer Program Manager

### PENNSYLVANIA

PennSERVE
The Governor's Office of Citizen Service
Dept. of Labor & Industry
1304 Labor & Industry Building
Harrisburg, PA 17120
1-717-787-1971, FAX: 1-717-783-5225
Contact: Director

### RHODE ISLAND

Volunteers in ACTION
229 Waterman Street
Providence, RI 02906
1-401-421-6547
Contact: Assistant Director

### SOUTH CAROLINA

Office of the Governor
1205 Pendleton Street
Columbia, SC 29201
1-803-737-6570
Contact: Volunteer Services Liaison

### SOUTH DAKOTA

Governor's Office
500 East Capitol Avenue
Pierre, SD 57501-5070
1-605-773-3661
Contact: Special Assistant to the Governor for Volunteerism

### TENNESSEE

Tennessee Dept. of Human Services
400 Deadrich Street
Nashville, TN 37219
1-615-741-4614

### TEXAS

Governor's Office of Community Leadership/Volunteer Services
P.O. Box 12428
Austin, TX 78711
1-512-463-1782, FAX: 1-512-463-1849
Contact: Director

### VIRGINIA

Virginia Dept. of Volunteerism
6th Floor, 8th Street Office Bldg.
223 Governor Street
Richmond, VA 23219
1-804-786-1431
Contact: Director

### WASHINGTON

Washington State Center for Voluntary Action
9th and Columbia Building
MS-GH-51
Olympia, WA 98504-4151
1-206-753-9684, FAX: 1-206-586-5880
Contact: Coordinator

### WYOMING

Wyoming Volunteer Assistance Corporation
Box 3963, University Station
Laramie, WY 82071
1-307-766-6310
Contact: Executive Director

# INDEX